Doing Social Network Research

⑤SAGE | 50 YEARS

SAGE was founded in 1965 by Sara Miller McCune to support the dissemination of usable knowledge by publishing innovative and high-quality research and teaching content. Today, we publish more than 750 journals, including those of more than 300 learned societies, more than 800 new books per year, and a growing range of library products including archives, data, case studies, reports, conference highlights, and video. SAGE remains majority-owned by our founder, and after Sara's lifetime will become owned by a charitable trust that secures our continued independence.

Los Angeles | London | Washington DC | New Delhi | Singapore

Doing Social Network Research

Network-based Research Design for Social Scientists

Garry Robins

Los Angeles | London | New Delhi
Singapore | Washington DC

Los Angeles | London | New Delhi
Singapore | Washington DC

SAGE Publications Ltd
1 Oliver's Yard
55 City Road
London EC1Y 1SP

SAGE Publications Inc.
2455 Teller Road
Thousand Oaks, California 91320

SAGE Publications India Pvt Ltd
B 1/I 1 Mohan Cooperative Industrial Area
Mathura Road
New Delhi 110 044

SAGE Publications Asia-Pacific Pte Ltd
3 Church Street
#10-04 Samsung Hub
Singapore 049483

Editor: Katie Metzler
Assistant editor: Lily Mehrbod
Production editor: Ian Antcliff
Copyeditor: Richard Leigh
Proofreader: Kate Campbell
Marketing manager: Sally Ransom
Cover design: Shaun Mercier
Typeset by: C&M Digitals (P) Ltd, Chennai, India
Printed in Great Britain by Henry Ling Limited at
The Dorset Press, Dorchester, DT1 1HD

Library of Congress Control Number: 2014942697

British Library Cataloguing in Publication data

A catalogue record for this book is available from
the British Library

MIX
Paper from
responsible sources
FSC
www.fsc.org   FSC™ C013985

ISBN 978-1-4462-7612-9
ISBN 978-1-4462-7613-6 (pbk)

At SAGE we take sustainability seriously. Most of our products are printed in the UK using FSC papers and boards.
When we print overseas we ensure sustainable papers are used as measured by the Egmont grading system.
We undertake an annual audit to monitor our sustainability.

Table of contents

List of boxes   vii
List of figures   ix
About the author   xi
Preface   xiii

1 The difference with social network research   1
2 Fundamental network concepts and ideas   17
3 Thinking about networks: Research questions and study design   39
4 Social systems and data structures: Relational ties and actor attributes   63
5 Network observation and measurement   89
6 The empirical context of network data collection   123
7 Ethical issues for social network research   149
8 Network visualization: What it can and cannot do   161
9 A review of social network analytic methods   175
10 Drawing conclusions: Inference, generalization, causality and other
     weighty matters   211

References   231
Index   255

List of boxes

1.1 Some good reasons to incorporate networks into social science research   1
1.2 You need more to incorporate networks into social science research   2
1.3 Pulling back the curtain: What goes on in real network studies   14

2.1 Some important terminology for graphs and networks   20
2.2 The bottom line in this section   22
2.3 Key social network theoretical ideas   28
2.4 Pulling back the curtain: What goes on in real network studies   37

3.1 Binary, valued and ranked ties   46
3.2 Pulling back the curtain: What goes on in real network studies   60

4.1 Some network notation   64
4.2 Creating an adjacency matrix from an edge list   69
4.3 Common types of individual constructs   79
4.4 Pulling back the curtain: What goes on in real network studies   86

5.1 Simple methods for sampling within networks   94
5.2 The wording of name generators   98
5.3 Egonet name generators from the 2005 US General Social Survey   104
5.4 Illustrative instructions for alter–alter data collection   106
5.5 An example of network measurement using position and
resource generators   108
5.6 Egonet measurement in the field   109
5.7 The BKS results   110
5.8 Pulling back the curtain: What goes on in real network studies   119

6.1 Some sources for existing network datasets   123
6.2 Some network datasets relating to schools   135
6.3 Pulling back the curtain: What goes on in real network studies   146

7.1   Ethics review boards and statistical power   151
7.2   Good practices in reporting social network results   155
7.3   Pulling back the curtain: What goes on in real network studies   159

8.1   Some visualization programs used in social network research   163
8.2   Pulling back the curtain: What goes on in real network studies   172

9.1   Selected social network analysis software   176
9.2   Different types of centrality   183
9.3   Bipartite network analysis   201
9.4   Pulling back the curtain: What goes on in real network studies   206

List of figures

1.1 The network of collaboration among 40 organizations   6
1.2 The sporting team   8

2.1 Graphs and subgraphs   21
2.2 Degree distribution for the collaboration network   24
2.3 Out- and in-degree distributions for the sporting team network 24
2.4 Some network patterns   24
2.5 Connectivity   25
2.6 Centrality   26

3.1 Unipartite, bipartite, and multilevel networks   44

4.1 Undirected binary network data structure   67
4.2 Undirected valued network data structure   67
4.3 Directed network data structure   68
4.4 Snowball sample design   71
4.5 Regions of an adjacency matrix for a snowball sample design 72
4.6 Bipartite network data structure   73
4.7 Multilevel network data structure   74
4.8 Panel longitudinal network data structure   75
4.9 Panel network data with changing node set   76
4.10 Attribute variables   80
4.11 Matrix multiplication of binary adjacency matrix and attribute vector 81
4.12 Dyadic covariate matrices   82
4.13 Data structure for an egonet study   83
4.14 Egonet   84
4.15 Expanded ego file   85

5.1 Alter–alter ties   105

8.1 Four different visualizations of the one network   165
8.2 Directed and weighted visualizations   166

8.3	Unrevealing visualizations	168
8.4	Visualizations with attributes	169
8.5	A visualization with multiple attributes	169
8.6	Visualization of a multiplex network	170
8.7	Visualization of a multiplex network with three structural equivalence classes	171

9.1	Mutual, asymmetric and null dyads	178
9.2	Undirected triads	179
9.3	Directed triads	180
9.4	Important directed triads	180
9.5	Blockmodelling	188
9.6	ERGM configurations	193

About the author

Garry Robins is a Professor in the School of Psychological Sciences at the University of Melbourne. He has won research awards from the Psychometric Society and the American Psychological Association, and is a past winner of the Freeman Award for the scientific study of social structure. He is co-editor of the journal *Network Science,* a member of the Board of the International Network for Social Network Analysis, and former editor of the *Journal of Social Structure*. His research has been centred on the development of exponential random graph models for social networks, as well as a wide range of empirical and applied social network studies from cattle herding to criminal networks, from drug-sharing to environmental management, from little data to Big Data.

Preface

This book is principally intended for social scientists wanting to undertake social network research. It assumes the reader already knows a thing or two (perhaps even a lot) about social science research, but perhaps not much about social networks. But the book also has material, especially in later chapters, of interest to experienced social network researchers more generally.

I will explain why and how social network research is different, how it can give particular insights into your research question, and how it can be integrated with existing social science. But social network research is not just a methodological 'add-on': I hope to convince you that it requires a different way of thinking. I will show you how to conceptualize your network research, how to design empirical network studies, taking into account ethical concerns, and how to get good data from your specific research context. I will give you some directions on analysis of your data and guidance about drawing conclusions. I will point you to some of the big issues in network research, issues that will be to the fore in future years.

In a relatively short book, I cannot do justice to all types of social network research. In Chapter 6, I try to give a flavor of the wide sweep of research that is currently being conducted across many different social science areas; and in Chapter 9, the broad range of methods that are available for social network analysis. Yet, there are so many developments that necessarily I have had to pick and choose. Let me apologize in advance if my choices do not reflect others' preferred studies or methods. Many of the examples I use are from research in which I personally have been involved. That is a deliberate decision – not intended to privilege such research but rather to provide illustrations that I best know and from which I can provide practical advice. This is particularly the case with the two empirical examples that run through the book, discussed in the 'Pulling back the curtain' boxes at the end of most chapters. Chapter 10 discusses some difficult debates at the forefront of network research, including network causality, interventions and Big Data. Because these debates are not resolved, that chapter necessarily includes some of my own opinions. Elsewhere, I have tried to give advice that is borne out by solid research and experience, although my own slant on doing social network research will still be apparent.

I want to thank the many collaborators with whom I have worked over the years on social network studies. I particularly want to thank the past and present members of the Social Networks laboratory (Melnet) in the School of Psychological Sciences at the University of Melbourne, especially my long-term colleague and mentor, Pip Pattison. I want to thank people who have directly helped with advice, comments or other contributions for this book, especially Rob Ackland, Anuska Ferligoj, Bernie Hogan, Betina Holstein, Kayla de la Haye, Yuval Kalish, Emi Kashima, Susan Kinnear, Dean Lusher, David Rolls, Giovanni Sadewo, and Tom Snijders. A special thanks to Diane and David who gave me a Room with a View in which to write. And most importantly, to Jane and Olivia for supporting me unflinchingly through the whole process.

Garry Robins

ONE

The difference with social network research

Why have you decided to do social network research?

You are a social science researcher and you decide that your next empirical research project will include social networks. Ask yourself, very carefully, why. In ways that will be explained in this book, the precise answer to this question will drive the theory, the empirical measures and the analytic methods for your project.

You study social networks because your research requires you to examine a social system, a social environment, or a social context in quite specific ways. Perhaps your theoretical arguments are akin to those in Box 1.1.

BOX 1.1

Some good reasons to incorporate networks into social science research

- You want to study *whether the social environment affects individual outcomes*. Social partners might affect individuals, through contagion or influence or other social processes. Perhaps some property (disease, money, health, opinions, information) 'flows' across the network from one individual to another.

(Continued)

(Continued)

- You want to study *whether individuals in certain social positions have different individual outcomes*. Popular individuals may have different outcomes from isolates or peripheral individuals; or network entrepreneurs might reap benefits from bridging between distinct groups.
- You want to study *how individuals affect social structure*. Are there individual factors that affect why individuals choose their social partners, or why they seek certain positions in the social system?
- You want to study *the social processes that underpin and sustain the social system*. How best can you describe and understand the social structure?
- You want to study *how individual outcomes and the social system are intertwined*. What causal processes might be present: are individual or social factors (or both) the best explanation of the issue you are studying?
- You want to study the *global outcomes of the social system*. Is the system effective or responsive for some purpose? Is it possible to intervene to improve either individual or system outcomes?

Over the years, I have heard many other reasons why a researcher might want to take up a social network study. Here are a few.

- 'I need to get into this networks thing: it is a hot research area.'
- 'My theory and data are already good, but I need to explain more variance and networks might just do it.'
- 'I want to produce a fancy network diagram that will show the network patterns in my data.'
- 'I want to employ sophisticated, cutting edge analytic methods in my research.'
- 'Once I include networks in my research, I won't need to bother with other effects.'
- 'I've got access to a big dataset that may be suitable for network analysis.'
- 'I know a good networks researcher who can help out.'

These reasons are all fine motivators to start social network research. But unless you also have a theoretical imperative, they are not sufficient. In Box 1.2, I explain why I do not think these reasons are quite good enough by themselves.

BOX 1.2

You need more to incorporate networks into social science research

1   **It is a hot research area.** Hot or cold, networks will contribute to a research project only when the theorization matches a network conceptualization.

2 *Explaining more variance.* Sadly – and disappointingly for social science researchers coming to networks for the first time – network methods do not usually explain more variance, because variance explained is a concept *contradictory* to most network conceptualizations. Your new network perspective is not just an add-on: it may fundamentally reshape how you construe the research.

3 *Fancy pictures.* Good network visualization can provide insight, but is seldom enough to produce confident conclusions. If you only plan to draw a picture, think again.

4 *Fancy analysis.* Your new network data may indeed require different methods, but – of course – complex analysis may be difficult to report and interpret. Sometimes, simple network methods might be better. Irrespective of the sophistication of the analysis, you can never be sure beforehand how your results will turn out. With bad data, the results will still be meaningless.

5 *Networks explain everything.* Despite claims to the contrary, network topology alone is hardly ever sufficient for good social science research. Social science involves social entities (or *actors* as I will call them from now on) involved in social action. These entities have a range of individual characteristics that may be crucial. And the range of other possible factors in a networked social system is potentially very wide: geographical space, time, social settings and so on. Do not be fooled into thinking that network structure alone is sufficient, or kid yourself that the messy empirical business of researching real people may be downplayed.

6 *Big Data.* Big datasets can be very helpful, are increasingly common and are often collected digitally (and so perhaps relatively easily). But a big dataset amenable to a network analysis is not going to answer a research question if the data does not match the imperatives of existing knowledge or current theory.

7 *Network experts.* It is not enough to have a collaborator with network skills. Your reason for working with this fine person has to be clear beforehand. You need to explain to your collaborator why you think networks are important to this particular research. Then your collaborator can indeed help with, but not run, your networks research project.

In short, you do networks research because you *must* and because you *will*. Your theoretical understanding of the research question suggests that social processes or structure may be crucial elements in explanation. Even though a network approach may present a new learning curve, you cannot ignore possible network explanations. Either you eliminate networks as an explanation, or you produce evidence for their importance. In either case, you must and you will do network research.

In this book, I describe how and why social networks can add to theory and interpretation, and how to design and conduct research that tests network conceptualizations. In this first chapter, I want to explain why social network research is distinctive within the social sciences.

What is network science?

Network science is the term popularized by burgeoning interest in network research across many disciplines (not just social network research). In part, a new focus on networks from physicists, computer scientists and others this century has encouraged the usage. Some have also recently coined the term 'social physics', perhaps without realizing that Comte used this in the 1830s before deciding that he preferred *sociology* as the title for his new discipline. If we claim a new science, we had best make sure we have not simply reinvented someone else's wheel.

So when a new journal entitled *Network Science* appeared in 2013, some of the co-editors set out to define what this new science could be (Brandes et al., 2013b). They pointed out that network research crossed many disciplinary boundaries, so network science was not the domain of one discipline; they noted various long historical antecedents, so it was not the creature of a particular time and place.

They concluded that network science was unified through a common conceptualization: an assumption of complex structure among the entities being studied. For social networks, these entities are most often people, although they may be other social actors such as organizations. Complex structure among the objects of study is in striking contrast to other research that assumes independent observations. So network science, as it applies to social network research, rests on the theoretical claim that outcomes are affected by a structure of relations among people: dependence among individuals. Once we adopt a network perspective, we suppose that individuals are connected and individual outcomes are related. This makes perfect sense in some domains (e.g., transmission of contagious diseases), but less so in others (e.g., intelligence is hardly contagious). So network science is not the right science for all research. But it may be right for some or much of social science research.

Brandes et al. went on to argue that dependence is not just between individuals: the social relationships themselves may depend on one another. What does this mean? Simply, for instance, that your friendship with one person can depend on your friendships with others. In this way, social network connections can organize themselves into certain patterns. Before we know it, we are in the world of self-organizing, complex systems.

No, we do not need to be physicists, understanding complexity theory, to do social network research. Yet we do need to realize the implications of the seemingly simple step to include a network approach. A network perspective is not just a methodological decision; it carries quite explicit theoretical commitments about structure and dependence.

There are myths about networks. Not all networks are the same. The unity in network science arises from a conceptualization, not because of common empirical results about universal theories. Be cautious about claims for a Grand Unified Network Theory intended to traverse the whole of network science. After you read through the range of social network research in Chapter 6, you can ask yourself: how could there be one theory that generalizes to all these different social science domains?

Within network science itself, *social* networks are importantly distinctive in one major regard: the actors in the network have intentionality. Researchers who ignore that obvious fact will not be doing *social* science. So, a social network ontology includes both network relationships and social actors. We need to observe *both* in as much detail as necessary to understand the social processes we study. In that way, many of the measurement and observation techniques commonly used in social science still apply; many of theories about individuals remain relevant even in a networked world.

Thinking about networks

Let us contemplate some actual network data. Consider Figure 1.1, which depicts a network of collaboration among 40 organizations involved in management of a water resource. Later, I will describe how this data was collected and show how such a figure can be produced. (The figure actually depicts what is known as a *graph* – more in Chapter 2). The circles in the figure (the *nodes*) represent the actors in this study, the organizations. A line between a pair of nodes represents a collaboration between two actors. In social network terminology, a social relationship such as collaboration is generally referred to as a *network tie*. Do not read anything into the position of the nodes in the figure: they are simply laid out in a way that hopefully enables the figure to be clearer.

What can we say by inspecting this visualization? You will see readily that there is one organization – one node – with many collaboration partners; one node with no ties (an *isolate*); and most other nodes have a small number of partners (mainly, 2 to 5). In network parlance, the number of network partners is the *degree* of the node, and each of the lines in the figure is termed an *edge*. (My apologies here for the mixed terminology: e*dge* and *node* are from graph theory; *tie* and *actor* are social network terms. You will need to be familiar with both usages, and I will use them interchangeably. More in Chapter 2.)

So the degree of a node is simply the number of edges adjacent to it. The *degree distribution* is a count of the numbers of nodes with each possible degree: so, for instance, in the degree distribution for this network, the number of nodes with degree 0 is one. We could draw the degree distribution as a histogram (Chapter 2), but even without that step we can say that at least one node has high and most of the others low degrees – in other words, there is variation among the nodes in terms of network popularity and activity (hardly surprising!).

The network in Figure 1.1 seems quite *centralized*. The high-degree node is said to be *central* in this network. It is interesting to think about why this particular organization became so popular. (Is it a case that *the rich get richer*, where popular actors become more popular, or is it some other factor?) Presumably, through its high degree, that organization has a much greater chance to influence how this system works. The organization occupies a prominent *network position*. It is in the *core* of the network, whereas some organizations are more *peripheral* (e.g., the isolated node).

What can we say about how well this networked system of organizations manages the water resource? *Very little*, from the figure. Sometimes researchers new to networks think they will be able to draw conclusions about the performance of the system simply by inspection of a network diagram. They anticipate spotting bottlenecks or gaps or other features that might be thought of as structural weaknesses. Sometimes you might be lucky and such may be apparent. But is the high-degree node in Figure 1.1 effective in influencing this system towards good outcomes, whatever they might be; or is that organization rather a problem for the system, accumulating resources at the expense of others? It is impossible to say just from Figure 1.1.

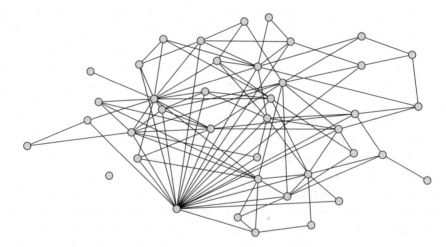

Figure 1.1   The network of collaboration among 40 organizations

Outcomes can be complicated. Different types of outcomes, both individual and network-wide, may not be consistent: what could be good for individual organizations may militate against system effectiveness. If the central organization is grabbing resources for itself, the whole system may not work well.

So networks automatically bring with them multiple levels of analysis (individuals, ties, the whole system). Some of these levels may be *emergent* rather than pre-established. For instance, do the patterns of network ties in Figure 1.1 suggest *cohesive subgroups* of organizations in the system (i.e. groups of organizations collaborating more closely within their own group)? It does not seem apparent from the figure, but further analysis might reveal that to be the case. Apart from the one highly central node, there may be other *network positions* that can be identified. By investigating such patterns in the network, we begin to understand the *network structure*. Perhaps the network structure has implications for the operation of the system as a whole, or for the individual organizations that collaborate in the network. Perhaps individual responses are in part determined by the position occupied in the network, or the type of network partners an organization has.

These are typical network research questions. And they can be different – sometimes subtly, sometimes dramatically so – from other more standard social science hypotheses.

Figure 1.1 depicts a network of organizations. But of course we can also have a network of individual people. Figure 1.2(a) shows a network of an elite sporting team of professional athletes. Here each node represents a player in the team and the network tie is one of *socializing after hours*. (I describe these two datasets in more detail in Box 1.3.) In Figure 1.1, the edges were collaborations between two organizations, and hence *undirected*. Here they are *directed* from one athlete to another, indicated by arrows. A directed edge is termed an *arc*. So, if an athlete nominated a team-mate as someone with whom they spent time after hours, there is an *arc* present from the athlete to the team-mate. Notice there is no requirement for the athletes to agree with whom they socialize, although many do, represented here by arrows at both ends of the line (*reciprocation*). Strictly speaking, there are two possible arcs between two team-mates – from the first to the second and from the second to the first. But notice that the athlete at the extreme right of the diagram nominates one other person but in turn is not nominated by anyone else. It is an interesting question whether in this network there are high levels of reciprocation (*you scratch my back and I'll scratch yours*) and what that means for the team culture.

The athletes do seem to socialize together in smaller groups. In general, the smallest group with a majority and a minority has three actors (a *triad*), and if they are all connected they form a *triangle*. In Figure 1.2(a) we see plenty of triangles, often stacked together in larger collections, suggesting larger groups. The presence of many triangles is often an indication of what is termed *network closure*, where the paths in the network turn back on themselves to create these triangular and cyclic sub-structures (*the friends of your friends become your friends*). These triangles and denser regions of the network may be indications of group-like cooperation and collaboration.

In Figure 1.2(b) the nodes have different sizes. The size of a node here indicates the playing experience of an individual in terms of number of games played at elite level. One of the goals of the research was to study whether athletes socialized with team-mates of similar experience. Experience was only one of several *actor attributes* that were investigated, with the ultimate aim of understanding whether individual demographics and opinions combined with social structure to determine aspects of team culture.

So in this example we have both an individual-level attribute, *experience*, together with a network, *socializes with*. Notice that the network structure as depicted in Figure 1.2(a) is not very revealing. But the addition of the nodal information in Figure 1.2(b) enables us to spot a grouping at the top of the figure, suggesting a tendency for experienced athletes to socialize together (*birds of a feather flock together*). Of course, we might want to do

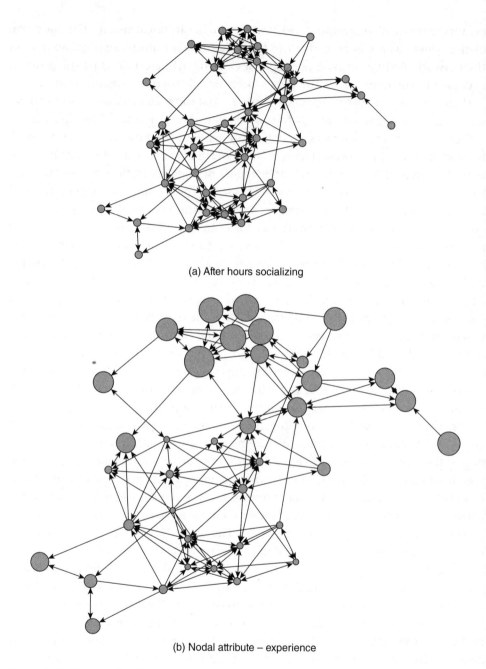

(a) After hours socializing

(b) Nodal attribute – experience

Figure 1.2 The sporting team

further detailed analysis to confirm this. We can also see from the figure that there are a small number of medium-experienced athletes who appear to link the group at the top to the generally less-experienced players at the bottom. It is conceivable that they play an important role in team cohesion in this way: they *bridge* or *broker* between two other groups of athletes.

This brief review of Figures 1.1 and 1.2 has introduced some basic network ideas that may become theoretical elements for your social network research question. Many of these are quite intuitive. In discussing these two quick examples we have met:

- Social activity and popularity (degrees, centrality of individuals)
- Structural position (e.g., being on the periphery of the network, or in the core)
- Subgroups of actors
- Global network structure (e.g., centralization)
- Reciprocation
- Triangulation (network closure)
- Network brokerage
- Outcomes for the system as a whole, as against outcomes for individuals
- The interplay of ties and attributes.

Of course, these are not the only network features, nor do they have to be present in all network studies. But this list gives a flavor of network theorizing, even though the way each element plays out in a particular research study depends on the specific context. Some elements may be indicative of different types of social processes, so the details of the network structure can provide information about the processes that underpin and sustain it.

In Chapter 2, I provide more precise terminology that will enable us to review these and other network ideas. In Chapter 3, I discuss how we can bring such network thinking into designing social science research. This will lead naturally on to chapters on how to collect and analyze data for these network research designs.

At this point I want to focus on the association between network ties and individual attributes, illustrated in Figure 1.2, often powerful in understanding process and structure in networked social systems. A network analysis in the social sciences usually cannot afford to leave out the characteristics of the individual actors that constitute the system (hence my earlier comment about intentionality of the actors in *social* network research). So it is worthwhile reflecting on this interplay between networks and individuals by considering how individuals are researched in classic social science studies.

Individual-based social science research

There are many ways in which good social science research can be designed. Let me describe what I call an *individualized* or *individual-based* research design. In this research design, the research question typically relates to individual outcomes. Perhaps we want to investigate the factors that contribute to unemployment, or the variables that explain student performance in school or job satisfaction in workplaces, or examine the prevalence of a disease in a community. One standard way to proceed is to define the population of interest (e.g., school students, workers, community members); decide on a sampling frame that will determine where the sample comes from; select the actual sample, ideally drawn randomly but in practice often with some constraints; collect data from the sample by measuring relevant variables; perform an analysis, typically using a method derived from the General Linear Model (e.g., a regression); and make an inference from the sample to the population to permit general conclusions about the research question.

Social science experimentation is a variation. We bring our sample into the laboratory and perform manipulations on some but not other groups to investigate the outcomes on the participants under different conditions. Randomized control studies in medicine are often held up as a gold standard for this type of research, where participants are randomly assigned to treatment or control groups, with the treatment group given an intervention, for instance, a new drug. We look for differences between the groups to understand the effect of the drug. Again, we often rely on the General Linear Model and null hypothesis significance testing for our analysis, perhaps in this case an Analysis of Variance. Sometimes we might conduct experiments in the field, giving one intervention to certain individuals in the community (e.g., a weight loss program) and compare with a non-intervention community-based control group. Or we may study change over time, performing a before-and-after analysis of our weight loss program.

These are all different research designs, and it is important to understand their differences to conduct such research well. But each reflects major themes in individualized research: samples, inferences to populations through randomization, use of the General Linear Model for analyses, and, importantly, research questions that pertain primarily to individuals one at a time. For instance, the outcome of the weight loss program occurs for an individual who undertakes it, not for anyone else. The implied causal process is at the individual level: 'If an individual undertakes this weight loss program, the individual is likely to experience effect X.' Here the crucial process happens *within* the individual, irrespective of others: 'my weight loss behavior affects my weight loss'. This may be the case even when a social environment is implicated, such as in some studies of social cognition: 'I perceive person i as a member of group j, so I respond with action k.' The causal process still occurs within the individual. My perception of person i may be a complete misperception (perhaps person i does not even exist, or is not a member of group j at all), but the cognitive process still occurs within me and that is what is studied.

Of course, although the individualized research paradigm is common, not all social science research is exactly like this. There are some particularly important differences, for instance, with qualitative research, which emphasizes understanding of phenomena through a rich detail of individual perceptions and descriptions. Inference arises from supposition based on good interview data, not on quantitative analyses using the statistical apparatus of the central limit theorem and the like. Nevertheless, there is still often a sample from a relevant population, there is still often intent to infer to a population, and a focus on individual outcomes one at a time.

I am not for one minute suggesting that there is anything wrong with these various research designs. Each is telling and powerful in its own way, with its own advantages and disadvantages.

Network-based social systems

But what are we to make of the networks in Figures 1.1 and 1.2? Let us suppose that for the organizations in Figure 1.1, the collaborations matter in important ways, so that we cannot ignore the network ties between them. Begin by asking some very basic questions. What is the population here? For this particular water system, these are the 40 key actors, so do they constitute the population? Or is it, rather, all organizations involved in all water management systems, in which case these 40 constitute a sample (but then it is not a random sample, because they all come from the one system)? Or is the system itself the sample, from a population of all such water management systems? Or are the network ties the topic of investigation if we are studying collaboration? But then what counts as the 'population' of network ties?

If we cannot make the notion of population coherent here, how can we make sense of the idea of sample? Moreover, the thought that we want a random sample of organizations from this system is silly. If we took a random sample of 10 out of 40 organizations, there is a 75% chance that our sample would not contain the prominent node, and that would surely distort inferences about network structure.

We have additional considerations as well, once we shift to a network perspective. We have to consider the *network boundary* for our study. This is essentially the definition that determines the actors that are to be included in our network. In Figure 1.1 we have a boundary that is defined rather loosely as *major organizations involved in management of this water resource*. So 'minor' organizations are excluded; but this is not to say they do not exist and do not collaborate. We focus on major organizations believing that this strategy will capture the most important effects. In Figure 1.2, the boundary is quite natural: being a contracted athlete in this professional sporting team. However, this is not to say that the team is an isolated entity. Doubtless, the athlete at the right of the figure has many social ties outside the club; but only one nomination within the club. So we expect there will be network ties that cross the boundary. Our natural assumption here – and it is one that we must accept could be wrong – is that to investigate team structure and club culture it is the ties within the team that count.

There is a further complication arising from a network approach. We cannot suppose that the observations here are independent, because obviously they are not; otherwise, the network would be irrelevant, contrary to what we have supposed. But once we take our observations to be dependent, we have just ditched the General Linear Model, regressions and analyses of variance, all of which assume independent observations. Those of us social scientists well trained in standard statistics may be somewhat at a loss.

Of course, we can always calculate an average for our actor attribute variables, just as we would do with a normal sample. But it is not clear what sense to give to a mean value when the observations depend on one another. The average mark in an exam is meaningless when all the students are cheating by exchanging answers. So we are rather stripped of the usual means and hence standard deviations. If we do not have sensible standard deviations, we do not have meaningful variance, so we do not have variance explained. Our *R*-squared values, or equivalents in this context, may be quite ambiguous.

This is not dire, just different. Networks are based on connectivity, not atomization. Networks are structured and patterned, not summed and averaged. Yet, this is more than a methodological nuisance denying us the comfort of standard statistics and classic research designs. It is the heart of a network theorization and we need to adapt to its demands, rather than try to contort network research back into a more familiar shape.

Individuals and systems

The contrast between individualized and system-based research in the social sciences goes back at least to the famous Hawthorne studies (Roethlisberger and Dickson, 1939). They were at the very beginnings of organizational studies and of organizational psychology. The research team examined lighting in the Hawthorne Electric Works in Chicago in the 1920s. The goal was to determine an optimal lighting level to enable workers to best connect the wiring in the electrical machinery they were producing. Using classical experimental design, the research team increased and decreased lighting levels to examine how productivity was affected. This turned out to be a small preliminary study but is often given the most attention in organizational psychology texts (sometimes to the point where the description suggests that this was the only study in the Hawthorne research, rather than just the first).

In fact, due to equivocal results the research team won an additional contract to study productivity, using five selected women workers who were separated from the rest of the workforce and placed in the Relay Assembly Test Room where they performed their regular assembly tasks. Over the next two years (1927–1929), the research team conducted a large number of studies and experiments to investigate whether and how productivity increased: from examining standard measures of intelligence and digital dexterity to changing methods of payment and other incentives. They also conducted qualitative interviews with the women to investigate personality factors and to get a sense of their social environments outside the workplace. The bottom line was simple: whatever the research team did, productivity for the women continued to increase across the two years.

The researchers were forced to conclude that placing the women in the study was the principal factor that led to the increase. The women were responding to being studied and observed: the so-called 'Hawthorne effect', much discussed and warned against in undergraduate textbooks on research design.

What these texts often ignore, however, are the further studies in the series, culminating in the Bank Wiring Room study (1931–1932) involving a small group of male workers undertaking normal working activities in their regular workplace. This time there were no experimental interventions, simply observations of the social system as the workers went about their daily tasks. The research conclusion was that the informal social structure of the workers enforced norms of performance, particularly so that workers who tried to work too hard were punished socially (and sometimes even physically, albeit mildly). Consequently, individual productivity hardly varied across workers, sustained at a very similar level week after week. Of course, the Depression was in full play, so the workers may have sought not to over-achieve with the goal of preserving jobs.

The Bank Wiring Room was one of the very first empirical social network studies where multiple types of network tie (friendships, antagonisms and others) were explicitly observed. Social network analysts and sociologists often focus on the Bank Wiring Room studies without mentioning the Hawthorne effect; and organizational psychologists often refer to the Hawthorne effect without noticing the Bank Wiring Room. From nearly a decade of studies, each discipline takes that small portion that suits its purpose.

To my mind, the overall message from the Hawthorne studies rests on the contrast between individualized and social systemic research, a tension that can be observed across the entire spectrum of studies. There is a clear shift from experimental design and intervention to network-based observation over the decade. This shift was forced on the researchers as they realized their early studies were insufficient to capture the processes at work, that an individualized conceptualization was inadequate in this case. But before network analysts feel too smug, the series of studies also point to the many individual factors that could be important. In particular, even in the Bank Wiring Room, the network topology is not enough in itself for a proper understanding. The interesting conclusions are about the motivations of the workers – individual characteristics, even if possibly shared – and their individual behaviors to achieve these aims, even if those behaviors were similar and coordinated. Certainly, individual variables may be affected by the social environment, often substantially: in the Bank Wiring Room, the social system sustained norms that could reinforce individual motivations and so influence individual actions. But the explanation needs simultaneously to reach down to the individual and up to the network-based social system.

In short, the best of network research in social sciences captures this fine balance between the individual and the system: it is a strength, not a tension. It conceptualizes social relationships as central to both individual and systemic outcomes, and measures (observes) those social relationships systematically. It construes the structure of the system as built up of these social relationships. It takes into account the individual factors and outcomes that relate to this system. It is ready to cross multiple levels of explanation simultaneously: individual, dyadic, local social environments, global network structures. And it has a theoretical argument for why this conceptualization is necessary to explain the phenomenon of interest.

If your research is of this nature, then this is a good reason to do social network research. Much better than the reasons in Box 1.2!

BOX 1.3

Pulling back the curtain: What goes on in real network studies

Social science research is never easy. The descriptions of empirical studies in journals often make it seem that they were deeply conceived and expertly implemented. As we all know, this is seldom so. There is always choice in research, and the rationale for particular decisions (and sometimes for compromises) is often glossed over. A bland statement in a journal – 'We decided to do X to handle aspect Y of the research' – may mask weeks of uncertainty and several false starts. At various points in this book, I will describe decision points in two studies in which I have been involved, and how we decided to proceed. The data and descriptions about the two studies, however, are based only on parts of the real empirical research, and are adapted and changed so as to ensure anonymity requirements. Nevertheless, there is enough veracity remaining to describe issues, decisions and difficulties in a real research project.

In short, do not take the data in Figures 1.1 and 1.2 as the gospel truth. Nevertheless, Figure 1.1 comes from a study of 40 organizations involved in the management of water resources. In Figure 1.1, the network relationship is collaboration between organizations. As described in later chapters, a number of different types of network ties were measured on the organizations. There is a growing interest in the study of such systems of organizations managing a collective resource. Such networked organizational systems are often referred to as *network governance*. I will say a little about that field in Chapter 6.

Figure 1.2 comes from a study of elite professional sporting teams. A number of different teams/clubs were studied, but the example in this book relates to only one team. Several types of network tie were examined. The goal was to study whether important aspects of club culture could be inferred from network structures and athlete attitudes (and other attributes).

At the end of most of the following chapters, I will show how the content of the chapter played out in decisions relating to these two studies.

In conclusion: The key point

A network perspective is not just a methodological extension to standard social science research, but carries quite explicit theoretical commitments. At the heart of a network perspective lies dependence and connectivity, for which standard theories and methods may not be well equipped. Good social network research will balance between the individual and the social system, conceptualizing the system as the structure of social relationships among the individuals. Ultimately you adopt such a perspective because it is theoretically compelling for your research, not because it is popular or appealing.

Hot topics and further reading

What is network science? This chapter provides my perspective. Read the Brandes et al. editorial and decide whether you agree with it.

Brandes, U., Robins, G., McCranie, A. and Wasserman, S. (2013b) What is network science? *Network Science*, 1, 1–15.

Reductionism is expired and complexity is tired – now it is all networks. Read the manifesto by the well-known network physicist, Albert-László Barabási. How do we find a balance between parsimony and complexity in social science?

Barabási, A. (2012) The network takeover. *Nature Physics*, 8, 14–16.

How do we balance individual-level and system-level effects in social science? Read Robins and Kashima (2008) about the tensions between social psychological and social network research traditions.

Robins, G. and Kashima, Y. (2008) Social psychology and social networks: Individuals and social systems. *Asian Journal of Social Psychology*, 11, 1–12.

Further reading

Throughout this book, I will give plenty of examples for further reading. Often network research design and data collection are given individual chapters in more general texts that cover network methods and analysis. My intent in this book is to focus on design and data, and give less attention to analysis. There are not that many books of similar ilk; but let me suggest Henning et al. (2012).

Henning, M., Brandes, U., Pfeffer, J. and Mergel, I. (2012) *Studying Social Networks: A Guide to Empirical Research.* Frankfurt am Main: Campus Verlag.

TWO

Fundamental network concepts and ideas

This chapter is about ideas central to social network research and theory. It includes fundamental concepts and common theoretical argument. These ideas will inform the network-based research questions that you are going to formulate for your own research (Chapter 3). They will then affect the way you collect data (Chapters 4–6) and analyze it (Chapters 8 and 9).

In Chapter 1, we met a selection of social network elements, introduced in an intuitive manner:

- Social activity and popularity (degrees, centrality of actors)
- Structural position (e.g., being on the periphery of the network or in the core)
- Subgroups of actors
- Global network structure (e.g., centralization)
- Reciprocation
- Triangulation (network closure)
- Network brokerage
- Outcomes for the system as a whole, as against outcomes for individuals
- And the interplay of ties and attributes.

In this chapter, I want to return to these and other network features in a more precise way. To do so, I need to introduce the terminology and vocabulary that network researchers use. I present enough terminology so that I can then describe basic network elements more exactly. With these fundamental concepts in place, I can discuss important social network theoretical ideas, ideas about how *social* networks function and about the social processes that are implicated.

Then, in the next chapter, I will write about how to build from social network research questions, based on a specific theorization of a social system or of social structural processes, to your own network research design.

What is a social network?

A social network comprises (at least) a set of *social actors* and a relationship among them in the form of dyadic *relational ties*. A network can be represented as a mathematical object known as a *graph* with nodes and edges. The nodes represent social actors and the edges the ties between them. Network and graph terminology are often used interchangeably – as I did in Chapter 1 when introducing the collaboration network of Figure 1.1.

But it is important not to conflate social networks and graphs conceptually. Figure 1.1 visualizes a graph: it has nodes and edges. A graph is a way of presenting and using data: it is a mathematical object. For the purposes of Figure 1.1, the graph *represents* a collaboration network among a number of organizations, but it is not those collaborations. A social network is more than a graph.

It is also important not to conflate a network *visualization* (such as Figure 1.1) with the graph or the network itself. The same graph can be laid out in many different ways, so there are many possible visualizations of the one network or the one graph, just as there may be many different photographs of the one person. We will see this in Chapter 8.

So what distinguishes a social network from a graph? Importantly, a *social* network has social *actors*: they are involved in action in some way, often with motivations and strategies (whether we investigate these or not), and that action may be socially directed, not just individual responses. A graph, on the other hand, simply has nodes and edges. A relational tie in a social network may have many different qualities, positive or negative, with a past and presumably a future (whether we investigate these or not). A graph simply has edges between nodes. And of course a graph can represent many other types of networks – from electricity grids to subway systems to protein–protein interactions, none of which are *social* networks. It is possible that the same graph could represent both a social network and a subway system if it just so happened that they had exactly the same structure (not very likely!)

So the convenience in using a graph to represent a social network is the abstraction that simplifies the reality – but it is not the thing itself, any more than an IQ score used in a study of intelligence is a person. Our choice of a graphical abstraction – and there is more than one choice – is related to our network theory of the actual phenomenon.

That is the point: we have choices about how we represent our social system as a network and as a graph. This is not just pedantry. We need to give careful thought to how we will study social processes within a social system. As we will see later (Chapter 4), there is no 'automatic' graph representation to apply, no standard graphical pro-forma. Rather, we need to think about how best to abstract the observed social system in network form and on that basis represent it as a graph. That means we have to theorize carefully about the major elements of the system, related to the demands of the research question (Chapter 3).

Of course we should never ignore the possibility that networks may not yield good explanations for the phenomenon under study. This will always be an empirical question. In that case, the abstraction to graphical form will have proven of little value. So, just as we might ask other researchers to consider possible network effects, we need to be ready to test our network conceptualization against other explanations, including more individualized arguments.

All that said, we will indeed represent our social system using various graphical forms. So we had best answer our next question precisely:

What is a graph?

Many people, recalling secondary school mathematics classes, think of a graph as a two-dimensional chart with points plotted on x- and y-axes. In fact, that is only one type of graph. At its most general, dispense with the axes and think of a graph as simply a set of points (*nodes* or *vertices*) with *edges* between some of them. For those who like formal mathematical notation, a *graph G(N, E)* has a *node set N* = {1,2,..., n} and an *edge set E* comprising edges between some (not necessarily all) pairs of nodes. Look again at Figure 1.1: you will see that this is exactly what is depicted in the visualization.

So an edge may occur between a pair of nodes (i, j). In the social network literature, the letters i and j are quite popular to describe an arbitrary pair of actors. With your own network data, each actor will be identified by a distinct number, so that (1, 2) will then describe the pair of nodes 1 and 2. Depending on the data, there may or may not be an edge on this pair. The pair (i, j) can be taken to represent any pair of nodes, including (1, 2) in the graph.

Just because I have slipped into mathematical notation here does not mean that I intend to privilege quantitative research to the point of neglecting qualitative studies in this book. If you do qualitative network studies, you will still have pairs of actors (necessarily) and i and j may be a useful short-hand for you. And you cannot ignore the basic concepts that follow.

Most social network studies presuppose that people do not have social ties with themselves, so usually an edge on (i, i) is treated as impossible. In graph theory, when this restriction is not imposed, an edge on (i, i) is termed a *loop*.

As noted in Chapter 1, Figures 1.1 (the collaboration network) and 1.2 (the sporting team network) differ in that the edges are *undirected* for the collaboration network but *directed* for the sporting network (in which case they are called *arcs*). So, for an undirected network, an edge on (*i*, *j*) is the same as an edge on (*j*, *i*). In other words, the ordering of *i* and *j* in the pair does not matter. (If Tom is married to Mary, Mary is married to Tom.)

For a directed network, however, the ordering is important, and an arc on (*i*, *j*) is directed from the *sender* node *i* to the *receiver* node *j*. The direction is usually represented by an arrow on the arc, as in Figure 1.2. The presence of an arc from *i* to *j* does not imply that there need be an arc from *j* to *i*. (If Tom seeks advice from Mary, May need not seek advice from Tom.) Sometimes a directed graph is referred to as a *digraph*.

In Box 2.1, I present some basic terminology about graphs and networks. I know that lists of definitions can be tedious, but this terminology runs through this book and through social network analysis more generally. Do not neglect it.

BOX 2.1

Some important terminology for graphs and networks

- A graph can also be represented as an *n* × *n adjacency matrix* with a cell representing the presence or absence of an edge by 1 or 0, respectively. This can be the case even in qualitative research. I explain adjacency matrices further in Chapter 4.
- A *complete* graph has all possible ties present; an *empty* graph has no ties present.
- A *dyad* is a pair of actors and the state of the network tie between them (which may be the absence of a tie). Dyads, not single actors, are the fundamental unit for networks.
- A *triad*, on the other hand, is a triple of actors and the states of the network ties among them (which may include no ties – an *empty* triad).
- Often ties are assumed simply to present or absent (hence, 1 or 0), in which case the network is said to be *binary*. Sometimes network ties are weighted so that a tie has a *strength*. This can be represented in a graph with valued edges, usually termed a *weighted graph*, and visualized with edges of different thickness to depict the values. A *signed graph* has positive and negative signs attached to the edges, to represent positive and negative ties.
- A *whole network* study, sometimes called a *full network* study, examines a given set of actors and the ties among them.
- An *egocentric* network (*egonet*), or *personal network*, only includes the ties that a focal actor (called *ego*) has to network partners (called *alters*) as well as the ties among alters. An egonet study may include many egos, thereby examining the social environment of a sample of participants. There are important differences between whole and egocentric network studies that will become apparent in later chapters.

- A *two-mode network* has two different types of nodes, for instance, people and their organizations, sometimes called an *affiliation network* or *bipartite network*. Ties occur between different types of node (e.g., people are members of an organization) but not between the same type of node (in other words, a two-mode network only tracks the affiliations or memberships). I use the term *bipartite network* in this book and, where necessary, describe the usual one-mode network as *unipartite*.

- A *multilevel network* extends bipartite networks by also permitting ties between nodes of the same type.

- A *multiplex* or *multivariate* network has more than one type of relational tie possible between nodes. For instance, an organizational network study might include both advice and friendship. A multiplex network can be represented by a graph with two distinct edge sets. These are often visualized by edges of different colors.

- Social actors, of course, have many individual-level properties treated as variables in social science studies. These are termed *actor attributes*. Depending on the measurement of the attribute variables, these can be visualized as nodes of different sizes (for continuous attributes) or nodes of different colors (for binary or categorical variables).

- A *subgraph* is exactly what you expect it to be: a subset of nodes and a subset of the edges among those nodes. An *induced subgraph* includes all the edges from the original graph among the subset of nodes. See Figure 2.1.

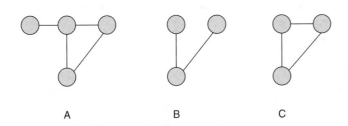

A   B   C

Figure 2.1 Graphs and subgraphs. Graph B is a subgraph (a subset of nodes and of edges between them) from graph A; graph C is an induced subgraph (including all edges in A among the subset of nodes)

Important graph and network concepts

Now, with basic terminology in place, let us turn to fundamental graph and network concepts, some of which you met in Chapter 1. These ideas describe some important features of graphs and networks, and as a network researcher, you need to understand them and the associated vocabulary. But this is a research design text, not a book of analysis, so I have deliberately provided only short descriptions. Robins (2013) provides more formal definitions, and there is greater detail in introductory texts such as Borgatti et al. (2013), Prell (2012), Scott (2013) and the now classic text by Wasserman and Faust (1994).

Once these fundamental features are described, we will have the vocabulary to talk about networks. Then we can turn to important social network theoretical ideas in the following section.

Box 2.2 distils some main points, with a little more detail in the ensuing text.

BOX 2.2

The bottom line in this section

- Network activity and degrees: *Density* and *degree distributions* are basic descriptive statistics of the network. You should examine these as a matter of course in your empirical studies.
- Network patterns: *Reciprocation* and *triangulation* invoke fundamental human social processes. They may prove to be important features of your empirical social network data.
- Connectivity: The essence of a network is that the actors are connected – hence are interdependent – and resources, information, disease or ideas (depending on your research topic) may flow through the *paths* in the network. The shortest path between two nodes is a *geodesic*.
- Centrality: Researchers often wish to understand which actors are most important in the network, but there are several different measures of *centrality*, each serving a different purpose. You need to choose centrality measures to suit your specific research questions.
- Cohesive subsets of nodes: The notion of a *clique* is important in both graph and social network theory, but nowadays there are fewer empirical social network studies using a clique analysis. The idea of a clique has been extended in different ways but without consensus on the best approach for empirical studies.
- Community structure: A more recent idea is to partition the network into regions of greater density. Although several algorithms exist to find community structure, empirically the method has mainly been used in large-scale social networks to simplify network description.
- Structural equivalence: An older idea, often used in smaller-scale network studies, is to partition the nodes into classes based on similar structural positions. Again, this approach can be used to simplify the network structure.

Network activity and degrees

The *density* of a network is a simple measure of the proportion of ties that are present, a description of how much social activity is occurring in the social system. The degree of a node is how much of that activity or popularity is due to the particular actor.

- *Density* is the most basic network measure. It is simply the number of ties in the network as a proportion of the total number of possible ties. A *complete* graph has all possible edges present (density = 1), and an *empty* graph has no edges (density = 0).

For a binary unipartite directed network with n nodes, each node may select any of $n - 1$ network partners, so the total possible ties is $n(n - 1)$. This assumes that loops (self-ties) are not permitted, the usual social network practice. With L arcs present, the density is then $L/n(n–1)$. For an undirected network, there are half as many possible ties because there is no difference between (i, j) and (j, i). With L edges, the density is then $2L/n(n–1)$. For a bipartite graph with two node sets of size n and m, the number of possible edges is nm so the density is L/nm.

- *Degrees:* I introduced the concept of degrees in Chapter 1. For an undirected graph, the degree of a node is the number of edges emanating from it. For a directed graph, the out-degree is the number of ties directed away from a node, and the in-degree the number of ties directed towards it. The out-degree and in-degree of a node are sometimes termed the *activity* (or *expansiveness*) and the *popularity* of the actor, respectively.
- The *degree distribution* is the number of nodes with each given degree, often depicted as a histogram. Figure 2.2 presents the degree distribution for the collaboration network of Figure 1.1. We can see that most nodes have degrees less than 10, but a couple have much higher degrees. Directed graphs have out-degree and in-degree distributions. The out- and in-degree distributions for the sporting team network of Figure 1.2 are presented in Figure 2.3.
- *Average degree*: is the average degree per node.

For a binary undirected network, the average degree is $2L/n$. Given the formula for the density above, average degree is given by $(n - 1) \times$ density. So, for constant average degree, the density must decrease as n increases. In other words, average degree and density do not *scale up* in the same way with the number of nodes. As a consequence, because humans often have only a limited number of network partners (except when it is cost-free to maintain 'friends' such as in Facebook), we often find that larger social networks have lower density.

Network patterns

The presence of small network patterns may reflect the underlying structural processes that are present in the network: for instance, how much reciprocation, how much cooperation in small groups (such as triangles).

- For a dyad (i, j) in a directed graph, if there is an arc from i to j and also from j to i, then the two arcs *reciprocate* each other. Sometimes, the dyad is referred to as *mutual*; with only one arc in the dyad, it is said to be *asymmetric*; and with no arcs, the dyad is *null*. See Figure 2.4(a).
- A *k-star* is a network subgraph centred on one node, with edges to k other nodes. Figure 2.4(b) depicts a 3-star. In a directed network, there can be *in-* and *out-stars*.

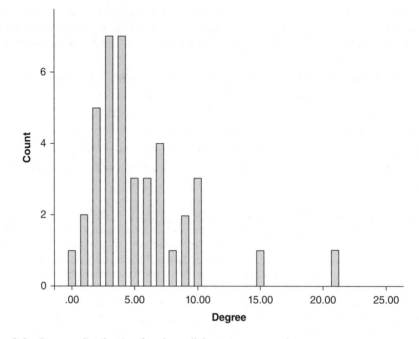

Figure 2.2 Degree distribution for the collaboration network

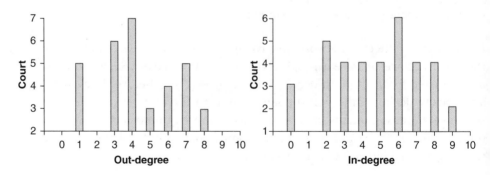

Figure 2.3 Out- and in-degree distributions for the sporting team network

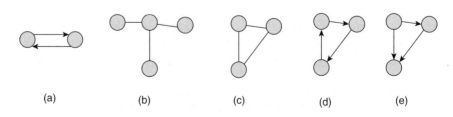

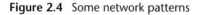

Figure 2.4 Some network patterns

(a) reciprocated arcs (mutual dyad); (b) undirected 3-star; (c) undirected triangle; (d) cyclic triad; (e) transitive triad.

- In an undirected graph, a *triangle* is a complete subgraph of three nodes (Figure 2.4(c)). In a directed graph, a *cyclic triad* is a cycle of length 3 where the arcs follow the same direction (Figure 2.4(d)). A *transitive triad*, however, is a subgraph of three arcs on three nodes where the arcs do not all follow the same direction, as in Figure 2.4(e).

Network connectivity

Network connectivity is at the heart of a network conceptualization. Paths are the network avenues through which information is passed and diseases spread.

- A *path* is a connected sequence of edges from nodes *i* to *j* to *k* and so on. The number of edges is the *length* of the path: if there are *k* edges, it is referred to as a *k*-path. For a directed network, a path requires consistent direction of the arcs; otherwise it is a *semipath*. Figure 2.5 depicts 3-paths and 3-semipaths.
- A *cycle* is a path of length greater than 2 for which the first and last nodes are the same and all other nodes are distinct. So the undirected triangle in Figure 2.4(c) is a 3-cycle, as is the cycle in Figure 2.4(d).
- If there is a path between two nodes, they are said to be *reachable*. A *geodesic* is the shortest length path between two nodes, and the *geodesic distance* is its length. If two nodes are not reachable, the geodesic distance is said to be infinite.
- A graph *component* is a maximal subgraph with paths between all nodes. Here, *maximal* means that adding another node will not make the component larger (i.e., there are no other nodes that are reachable from the nodes in the component). In other words, components divide up the graph into separated regions with no ties between them. For instance, the graph in Figure 2.5(d) has three components (an isolated node is formally a separate component, albeit a trivial one).

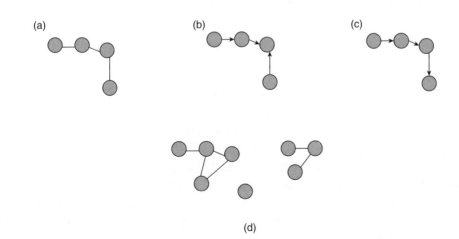

Figure 2.5 Connectivity

(a) undirected 3-path; (b) directed 3-semipath; (c) directed 3-path; (d) a graph with three components.

Centrality

The *centrality* of a node reflects its prominence or importance to the network structure, but there are several different ways to construe importance (Freeman, 1979). The most commonly used measure is *degree centrality*, simply measured by the degree of each node.

However, degree centrality focuses on the activity of a node, rather than its effect on the connectivity of the network. *Betweenness* centrality measures the presence of the node on geodesics, and so how important it is to short paths in the network. Such a node may or may not have high degree centrality. For instance, in Figure 2.6, node *i* has lower degree than other nodes, but if it were not present, the graph would collapse into two separate components, substantially decreasing connectivity.

In addition to degree and betweenness, a number of other centrality measures may be useful depending on the research question. I present some of these in Chapter 9.

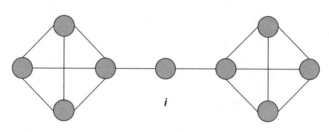

Figure 2.6 Centrality

Node *i* has the highest betweenness centrality, even though all other nodes have higher degree centrality.

Cohesive subsets of nodes

Actors can operate within small cohesive parts of the network with lots of ties, reflective of group or community processes.

A cohesive subset of nodes has an induced subgraph with substantially greater density than the graph as a whole. A *clique*, for instance, is a complete subgraph: a subset of nodes with all possible ties present. For instance, in Figure 2.6 the group of four nodes at the left (and indeed the right) of the visualization constitute a 4-clique, with ties between each pair of the four nodes. Many researchers, however, have seen the definition of a clique as too restrictive, so several extensions based on density and also on connectivity have been proposed. These are discussed in Chapter 7 of Wasserman and Faust (1994), Chapter 7 of Prell (2012) and Chapter 6 of Scott (2013). I note some of these extensions in Chapter 9.

The notion of a clique is an important idea in graph and social network theory. However, in empirical studies it may not be straightforward to use a clique analysis when there is a lot of overlap among cliques.

Community structure

In social networks there are often regions of the network, sometimes with many nodes, that have higher densities than the rest of the network (Girvan and Newman, 2002). These regions can be thought of as *communities*, and once these are identified (there are many current algorithms to do this) the description of the network can be simplified in terms of its *community structure*. One advantage of a community structure is that the nodes are partitioned into distinct sets, which aids the simplification.

Structural equivalence and positions

A social system can have a variety of different structural positions. Actors in the same position may face similar pressures or opportunities arising from that position. Structural equivalence is an approach to partitioning nodes into distinct sets, this time based on position in the network rather than community.

Two nodes are *structurally equivalent* if they occupy identical structural positions in the network. Lorrain and White (1971) defined *structural equivalent* nodes as a pair or subset of nodes connected to the same other nodes. A *position* is a set of structurally equivalent actors. Think of an army and the relationship 'commanded by'. Then all of the soldiers in one unit are structurally equivalent, because they are all commanded by the exact same officers.

Structural equivalence has been generalized in various ways, especially to *regular equivalence*. Nodes that are regularly equivalent do not have to be connected to the same other nodes but rather to other nodes that are regularly equivalent. In the army, all privates are commanded by a sergeant. Privates and sergeants then constitute two regular equivalence classes: every private is not tied to the same sergeant, but to one of a class of sergeants. If you are a private, you will have a sergeant.

Structural equivalence is useful empirically where the actors can be allocated to a smaller number of positions, so that the network can be simplified into a description or analysis of the relations within and between positions. This simplified description is known as a *blockmodel*, which I present in Chapter 9. In practice, depending on the data, equivalence classes may or may not differ from community structure. An important difference is that equivalent nodes do not have to be directly tied to each other, whereas the ties amongst nodes within communities are always relatively dense. In other words, it is an empirical question whether nodes in the same structural position are tied or not.

Some social network theoretical ideas

I now turn to some important social network theoretical arguments. The vocabulary from the previous sections is used to describe possible social network processes.

I want to emphasize that there is no one Grand Unified Network Theory that explains everything about networks (Brandes et al., 2013b). Just because a network idea is prominent (e.g., preferential attachment described below), this does not mean that it will necessarily apply in the particular social context that you are studying. The context counts; do not presume to know the empirical outcomes beforehand.

Box 2.3 summarizes key ideas. There are more extended descriptions in the following text, together with selected research examples. The goal here is not to review the entire corpus fully but to demonstrate social network theoretical thinking, including with illustrative empirical research examples. There is a wealth of work on any of these topics, so if an idea strikes a chord, check the current research literature.

BOX 2.3

Key social network theoretical ideas

- *Reciprocity*: Humans tend to reciprocate relationships, especially those involving positive affect.
- *Preferential attachment*: Popular actors often tend to become more popular because they have high visibility to begin with. In other words, the rich get richer. So degree distributions are often positively skewed, with a small number of actors with very high degree, and many actors with lower degrees.
- *Closure*: Network closure refers to triangulation in networks, reflecting human propensities to operate in small groups.
- *Small worlds*: Human social networks often exhibit short average path lengths (geodesics), at the same time as they exhibit closure. There is a balance here between security and efficiency.
- *Strong and weak ties*: Strong ties tend to exhibit network closure, closing into triangles, whereas weak ties do not, so that weak ties provide connectivity across the network.
- *Network brokerage*: Actors occupying *structural holes* – where they *bridge* (or broker between) different parts of the network – are in special positions. Often network brokers or *entrepreneurs* accrue advantages from their position. These actors do not need to be actors with high degree *status*.
- *Positive and negative ties* close in particular ways in triangles. These reflect old adages, such as 'The enemy of my enemy is my friend'. It can be important to understand the structure of negative ties among social network actors.

- *Actor attributes 1: Social selection*: Actors may select network partners based on attributes. One commonly observed possibility is *homophily*, where a tie is formed between actors with the same attribute.

- *Actor attributes 2: Social influence/diffusion*: Actors may be influenced by network partners, changing certain attributes (opinions, behaviors) to accord with those of their partners. Certain individual-level qualities (e.g., disease, innovation) may diffuse through the network.

- *Network self-organization*: Ties may come into being because of the presence of other ties. Reciprocity, preferential attachment, and closure are examples of network self-organization processes.

- *Dynamic network processes: Co-evolution of structure and attributes*: Networks are not static entities but are involved in dynamic processes as ties change. For a given set of actors, network structure (ties) and actor attributes may co-evolve in ways whereby influence, selection and network self-organization occur simultaneously.

- *Social capital*: The network can be viewed as a form of *capital* for the actors within it. In closed structures actors may benefit from strong, consistent support (bonding capital) but in structural holes, actors may gain brokerage advantages (bridging capital). Social capital may also be present when actors know others in a wide variety of social positions, or have access to a variety of social resources.

- *Embeddedness*: Social action (including markets) takes place within social network structures. The more embedded an actor is within a network, the more opportunities may be available at the same time that more constraints may operate.

- *Multiplexity*: Human relationships are not generic or of only one type. Social action invokes different types of relational ties, for different goals or purposes. *Multiplex relationships*, where dyadic partnerships have multiple types of relational ties, may have qualitatively different properties from uniplex dyadic partnerships. Social network studies often need to consider multiple types of tie, simultaneously.

- *Autocatalysis*: A radical new idea about how social innovation emerges from cycles of multiplex exchanges, where old network structures are adapted to new social goals.

Reciprocity

In directed networks, reciprocation of ties is often common, because reciprocation and exchange are fundamental human social processes. Reciprocation is especially likely to be present when the relationship involves positive emotions such as friendship. But do not expect that every tie will be reciprocated, even in such positive affect networks. Social networks are not deterministic, so there will usually be some unreciprocated ties. Furthermore, there are some types of relationships, often hierarchical, where reciprocity is less likely (e.g., leadership networks).

Research examples: Go way back to the start of social network analysis and look at Moreno and Jennings (1938) in the first issue of the journal *Sociometry*. Studying partner choice in a girls' school, they showed that the probability of reciprocated ties was 213% higher than expected by chance. (They also produced what they termed *sociograms*, one of the earliest examples of network visualizations.)

For more modern work on reciprocity, Lusher et al. (2012) showed that in the top management team of an organization, managers did not express much reciprocity in trust, but nevertheless believed that their own trust was reciprocated. Gaudeul and Giannetti (2013) studied reciprocation in social media, showing that reciprocity among bloggers was important to understand mentions between blogs. For a study of unreciprocated ties, see Ball and Newman (2013).

Preferential attachment

It is common for empirical social networks to have positively skewed degree distributions, with some actors having especially high degree (also shown by Moreno and Jennings back in 1938). Barabási and Albert (1999) proposed a particular degree distribution (*inverse power law* or *scale-free*) to describe these highly skewed degree distributions, especially for networks with a few very high-degree nodes (*hubs*). Albert and Barabási (2002) showed that a scale-free degree distribution could be achieved by a preferential attachment process: a 'new' actor in the network is more likely to connect to an existing actor, depending on that actor's current popularity. In other words, the highly popular are most likely to attract new fans (or 'the rich get richer'). The idea is in fact an old one, going back to Simon (1955), but has become an important element in modern network theory.

Obviously, whether a network can be fully scale-free depends on the type of relationship. If people cannot have a large number of network partners, then the network cannot be extremely skewed with hubs (e.g., ties based on immediate kinship). So, for instance, it may be possible for Facebook friends to exhibit a scale-free degree distribution, but perhaps not face-to-face friends. This does not mean that degree distributions will not be skewed, nor does it mean that the idea of preferential attachment is not useful in understanding network activity and popularity.

Research examples: Liljeros et al. (2001) argued that human sexual contacts exhibited scale-free degree distributions (presumably with hubs arising from prostitution), with important implications for the spread of sexually transmitted disease. In contrast, Jones and Handcock (2003) argued that when these degree distributions were fitted carefully with the best statistical approaches, evidence for scale-free distributions was not universal in sexual or other networks.

Closure

Many human social networks exhibit tendencies toward triangulation (Cartwright and Harary, 1956; Davis, 1970), often termed *network closure* as a 2-path *closes* with an extra edge to form a triangle. Other terms include network *clustering* and *transitivity*.

In some contexts, triangles can be thought of as archetypal small groups. Simmel (1908) observed that triads of individuals were more than just their constituent dyads – that, for instance, they were the smallest structure with a possible majority and a minority. Triangulated structures are often argued to assist in the establishment of group norms, to permit social monitoring and to provide cohesive support (Coleman, 1988).

In directed networks, there can be different types of network closure, in particular cyclic and transitive closure (Figure 2.4(d) and (e)). In a 3-cycle, all nodes have in- and out-degree 1 and in that sense are equivalent in this subgraph. So 3-cycles can be seen as a triadic version of reciprocity, encouraging exchange and cooperation (sometimes called *generalized exchange*). In a transitive triad, however, one node has in-degree 2 and is the most popular, so this may be an indication of local hierarchy. It is not uncommon to have negative cyclicity and positive transitivity effects in social networks, indicating local hierarchy as opposed to generalized exchange.

Research examples: Davis (1970) showed empirically that a large proportion of human social networks exhibit closure. Since then, pick up any issue of a journal such as *Social Networks* or *Network Science* and you are likely to find an example of an empirical study including network closure of some type.

Small worlds

A *small world* can be defined as a graph with low density, high closure but short average geodesic lengths (Watts and Strogatz, 1998). Translated into social terms, in such a network, actors tend to live in cohesive groups in the network (high closure) but can reach across the network in an efficient way (short geodesics). It is not obvious that this structure is possible when the density is low.

In an innovative and famous study, Milgram (1967) examined the connections among individuals in the United States. Participants communicated with acquaintances to try to reach a person of a given type. It is often forgotten that the majority of paths did not reach the target, but for those that did, the median path length was 6, leading to the popular notion of *six degrees of separation*. Watts and Strogatz (1998) reopened this issue by investigating small-world issues with computer simulations. They showed that the addition of a few random ties to a highly clustered graph with long geodesics could result in a rapid transition to a small-world graph.

Small-world ideas emphasize the balance between closure and connectivity and have become widely examined in the network literature. In real social network terms, this balance is between efficiency in the network (short paths) traded against the security and certainty of group cooperation (closure).

Research examples: Schnettler (2009a, 2009b) provided a fine review of the small world literature with guidance to those who wish to study small-world networks empirically. For those who want an even more comprehensive description, see Schnettler (2013).

Strong and weak ties

In a famous, much-cited article, Granovetter (1973) distinguished between strong and weak ties. He argued that strong social ties exhibited network closure, but weak ties did not. Weak ties, rather, provided connectivity between denser closed regions of strong ties. According to this well-known argument of the 'strength of weak ties', weak ties transmit new information and innovation across the network.

This idea has been prominent in network theory now for 40 years, but is not without its critics. Krackhardt (1992), for instance, pointed to the importance of strong ties, arguing that ties need to be conceptualized in more dimensions than just strong and weak. This argument about how best to characterize social ties continues today (e.g., Hite, 2003); but while strong and weak may seem somewhat simplified for many purposes, the distinction still serves a purpose.

Research examples: Granovetter's (1973) original empirical example related to finding a job. Bian (1997) gave a different sense to the argument, studying how strong ties also contributed to job search in China, invoking the Chinese cultural practice of *guanxi* relationships.

Network brokerage and structural holes

Drawing on Simmel's work on triads, Burt (1992) proposed *structural hole* theory, one of the most influential social network theories, especially in organizational contexts. Actors who bridge between different parts of the network are in a position to gain advantage as a *network entrepreneur* or *broker*. This hearkens back to Granovetter, although Burt ignores the distinction between strong and weak ties. The underlying idea is that ties that connect different sections of the network are particularly important and enable the spread of information and other resources. So actors involved in such ties have important advantages.

Again, structural hole theory is not without criticism. Krackhardt (1992) argued that actors in structural holes could experience more stress and, rather than reap reward, may find that competing pressures on them are too demanding. Nevertheless, Burt continues to extend and refine the theory (e.g., Burt, 2005).

Structural hole theory of course provides justification for the use of betweenness centrality. Actors in structural holes are likely to have higher betweenness centrality, irrespective of their degree centrality. So, the *status* of the actor in terms of degree centrality may not match the brokerage advantage that they can obtain from occupying a structural hole (Burt and Merluzzi, 2014).

Gould and Fernandez (1989) proposed five network patterns that indicated brokerage roles within and between groups. For instance, a person who brokers between two in-group members is termed a *coordinator*, while an actor brokering between two out-groups is a *liaison*. When the network study involves (say) two ethnic groups, actors may be classified into these different roles.

Notice how small worlds, strong/weak ties and structural hole theory each contrast closed structures and open paths in slightly different ways.

Research example: Burt (2004) argued that occupying structural holes in an organizational network enables managers to have better ideas.

Positive and negative ties: Structural balance

Frequently, social network researchers only measure what are termed *positive ties*, such as friendship, communication or collaboration. *Negative ties*, however, may be important in a social system: competition, dislike, working difficulty, and others. According to an old social network theory, *structural balance* (Cartwright and Harary, 1956), positive and negative ties tend to pattern into triangles in particular ways, reflecting old adages like 'My enemy's enemy is my friend', although the empirical support for balance theory is mixed (Doreian and Krackhardt, 2001).

Research examples: LaBianca and Brass (2006) set out good theoretical reasons to study negative relationships alongside positive ties. Good examples of negative tie research include research on bullying networks (e.g., Huitsing et al., 2012a study both positive and negative ties, including bullying).

Actor attributes 1: Social selection

Actors often choose network partners based on attributes, a process termed *social selection*. You choose a partner because you like that person's qualities. Network researchers frequently investigate selection process such as *homophily* where actors form a tie because they share one or more individual attributes (sometimes described by the old adage 'birds of a feather flock together'). *Generalized selection* (Wasserman and Robins, 2012) describes social processes where actors with certain attributes are predisposed to seek certain network positions (e.g., to have greater network activity or popularity, or to occupy structural holes).

Research examples: McPherson et al. (2001) set out theoretical arguments for homophily.

Actor attributes 2: Social influence and diffusion

For social selection, attribute values affect the presence of ties. In contrast, with *social influence*, actors change some attributes due to the influence of network partners. You may be influenced by your friends. This can often be seen as an individual-level quality or property 'flowing' through the network, for instance, network-based disease transmission, and is often also termed *network contagion* or *diffusion*.

Actors may change attributes because they occupy certain network positions – *generalized influence* (Wasserman and Robins, 2012). This is the nub of the structural hole argument, that network brokers gain personal advantage. Actors in the same structural equivalence class may also come to share certain attributes. For instance, Burt (1987) showed that innovations could spread through structural equivalent actors, not just through contagion by network partners.

Research examples: Those interested in network-based disease spread will want to read Morris's (2004) book which has plenty of good advice and examples about research design. There is a rapidly growing body of work on social influence in health behaviors. For instance, Christakis and Fowler (2007) made the controversial claim that obesity could be spread through friendship networks (more in Chapter 10). Diffusion of innovations has also been an important research area (Valente, 2005).

Network self-organization

Leaving aside attributes, network ties may also come into being because of the presence of other network ties. Reciprocity, closure and preferential attachment are all examples of *network self-organization* processes – processes that occur irrespective of attributes. So, these are *endogenous structural processes* (Wasserman and Robins, 2012), where the presence of some network ties sustains the ongoing presence of other network ties, or encourages them into existence. The structural outcomes are certain patterns (subgraphs) in the network (e.g., reciprocated arcs). So the presence of certain network patterns may be a clue about the structural processes that give rise to the network.

Research example: Again, let me refer right back to Moreno and Jennings (1938), who showed in a girls' school that mutual and triangulated ties were prominent network patterns, implying that the network self-organized through endogenous processes of reciprocation and network closure.

Dynamic network processes: Co-evolution of structure and attributes

Networks are seldom static; rather, they evolve as ties come into and out of existence. If strong network self-organization processes are present, however, cross-sectional data may give an indication of the mechanisms of evolution through the predominance of network patterns (e.g., reciprocated ties) typically associated with those processes.

Of course, there is no a priori reason why selection, influence and endogenous structural processes could not occur simultaneously. In that sense, network structure (i.e., the network ties) and actor attributes may co-evolve: network ties may change in line with selection and self-organization processes, at the same time that attributes may change due to influence. For instance, you can be influenced to like certain movies by your friends, and then choose new friends because they like certain movies. It is an empirical question whether one or both of these processes are occurring within the network, but for confident conclusions longitudinal network data is required.

Research examples: If you are interested in social network co-evolution, check out the two special issues on network dynamics in *Social Networks* (Snijders and Doriean, 2010, 2012).

Social capital

The literature on *social capital* goes beyond networks (e.g., Putnam, 2000), but network theory has a particular approach to the topic. Lin (1999) defined social capital as the resources embedded in a social structure accessed or mobilized purposely by the actors. In short, a social network may provide social capital to the actors within it, a capacity for social action or personal advantage that would not be available in the absence of a social system. Such a general definition, however, has led to conceptual differences, with important implications for measurement. Some researchers concentrate on degree-based options: for instance, Lin (1999) studied an actor's range of acquaintances across a variety of different social or employment categories (e.g., doctor, banker) to assess the social resources an actor can access. Van der Gaag and Snijders (2005) more directly focused on the types of resources that could be accessed socially, rather than on the variety of network partners (more on the measurement of social capital in Chapter 5).

An alternative viewpoint is to consider local structural position as the essence of social capital, exemplified by Burt's structural holes theory. A brokerage position is taken as social capital because there are benefits to be reaped from occupying the position. Sometimes this is called *bridging capital*. In contrast, Coleman (1988) considered that closed structures were indicators of positive social capital because they enabled more social support from close partners (sometimes called *bonding capital*).

Research example: Van der Gaag and Snijders (2005) showed in a Dutch sample that there were four different elements to social capital: prestige and education; political and financial skills; personal skills; and personal support. In the physics literature, Latora et al. (2013) discussed different social capital conceptualizations based on open and closed network structures, and showed how various indices of social capital were related.

Embeddedness

The concept of embeddedness is most frequently invoked in economic sociology. *Embedded ties* are often considered to be network ties based on strong relationships rather than market mechanisms. Uzzi (1996, 1997) studied these from a dyadic perspective, distinguishing embedded ties and *arm's-length ties*. Granovetter (1985), on the other hand, defined *structural embeddedness* as the extent to which a dyadic tie existed within closed triads. The argument is that the structural embedding of a dyadic tie creates additional opportunities and constraints for the dyadic partners.

Research example: Uzzi (1999) investigated how social embeddedness affected the cost of an organization's financial capital in the banking sector.

Multiplexity

A *multiplex tie* is a dyadic relationship that involves more than one type of relational tie between the partners. A *multivariate* or *multiplex network* study involves the simultaneous examination of different types of relational ties on the one set of actors. Human relationships involve a number of motivations and purposes, so it is hardly a surprising claim that different types of tie exist and that there can be advantage in studying them together. I will talk more about this in Chapter 3.

Research example: Multiplexity is often examined in organizational network studies. For instance, Soltis et al. (2013) studied both work flow and advice ties in relation to organizational turnover.

Network autocatalysis

John Padgett has proposed a radical new theory of societal change whereby multiplex social networks co-evolve and, in a process akin to chemical autocatalysis, produce spillover effects that lead to the emergence of entirely new production flows. This theory is sufficiently novel and radical that it is still being debated. I include it here to illustrate an ambitious network theory of very wide scope and implication. It is no less than a social network theory of history.

Research examples: In their book, Padgett and Powell (2012) provided many different examples, both historical and modern. Whether you buy into autocatalysis or not, I suggest you still read Padgett and Ansell's (1993) classic network study of how the Medici came to power in medieval Florence. This is a *tour de force* of network theory and exploratory social network analysis, illustrating multiplex networks, closed versus open structures, and structural equivalence.

In conclusion: The key point

This brief purview of network arguments is neither exhaustive nor extended. New ideas and theories keep emerging as network research becomes increasingly popular. The point of this chapter is to direct you to network concepts, terminology and arguments that will become your basic tools. The goal is for you to start thinking 'network-like', not just adding a vague idea of networks to your existing social science terminology.

In your research, you want to avoid merely employing the concept of a 'network' as a metaphor, a term without precise meaning but one that might be tossed into the interpretational mix. There is plenty of research that does only that, but the use of the network metaphor is not sufficient to count as a network study. Do not be fooled into thinking that networks cannot be measured or observed, nor treated as the object of empirical study (as I have heard some non-network researchers argue). The theoretical ideas in this chapter all use networks as quite definite empirical constructs: the ideas are testable, and the data can be analyzed, using empirical data.

There are many possible processes that could be occurring in a networked social system. Do not assume that your data is determined by one factor alone. You may need to control for a variety of different network mechanisms in order to draw definitive conclusions about the concepts at the heart of your research.

BOX 2.4

Pulling back the curtain: What goes on in real network studies

For the organizational collaboration network study, we decided that the principal interest was the nature of the network structure and how well the system of organizations collaborated to manage the water resources. This fundamental question led us to think about network self-organization and system performance along the lines studied by Robins et al. (2011). We also wanted to study both positive and negative ties because we felt that effective collaboration can be impeded by work difficulty as much as enhanced by positive cooperation. We were interested in the flows of resources through the network, and in which organizations were central in the network, using degree and betweenness centrality to examine both status and brokerage by organizations. We speculated about whether there might be important structural positions we could identify, and wanted to know which type of organization might occupy them.

So at best we had some guidance from Robins et al. (2011), but beyond that we had rather eclectic ideas about how to get an understanding of the social system. Nevertheless, the types of network arguments that we drew on gave us directions to pursue in terms of both measurement and analysis.

Given that our hypotheses were not too firm, we also planned to conduct qualitative interviews with our respondents to get a richer understanding of what they understood by effective collaboration, and their perceptions of the effectiveness of the organizational system as a whole.

For the sporting team, we had always proposed to collect attitudinal data on certain key cultural issues. We believed that attitudes would be associated with network structures, so we knew from the start that we would be looking at selection, influence and possibly co-evolution mechanisms. But we did not have clear guidance as to which types of network tie would best associate with the attitudes, so we planned to collect data on multiple types of tie, with a view to a multiplex explanation.

Hot topics and further reading

There are a myriad of hot topics that could be derived from any of the network ideas in this chapter. Here are just a couple.

In a review of small-world research, Schnettler (2009a) argued that future directions might focus more precisely on network diffusion, in ways that could affect the definition of 'smallness'. For instance, 'with regard to infectious diseases, the whole world could be small – but with regard to solidarity, and mutual support, six degrees might be a whole universe apart' (p. 177). What types of tie might enable easy diffusion (and hence easily produce 'small worlds') as opposed to the types of ties that could produce 'large' worlds even with small path lengths?

Granovetter's strong and weak ties theory has been pervasive. But a recent argument occurred within the social network community: how to understand latent ties, those that may have been strong but have not been activated for a long time. Is an 'old, strong tie' a strong tie or not? Are there better ways to carve out the types of ties that we should study?

Further reading

Here are some further readings related to social network theory:

- Peter Monge and Nosh Contractor have long argued that social networks are best researched from a multilevel, multi-theoretical perspective: that is, not simply assuming one network mechanism ('multi-theoretical'), and taking into account the possible multiple levels of a human social system.

  Monge, P. and Contractor, N. (2003) *Theories of Communication Networks*. New York: Oxford University Press.

- Charles Kadushin's text provides a good coverage of current social network theory.

  Kadushin, C. (2012) *Understanding Social Networks: Theories, Concepts and Findings*. New York: Oxford University Press.

- Steve Borgatti is a leading writer about general social network theory.

  Borgatti, S. and Lopez-Kidwell, V. (2011) Network theory. In J. Scott and P. Carrington (eds), *The SAGE Handbook of Social Network Analysis* (pp. 40–54). London: Sage.

THREE

Thinking about networks: Research questions and study design

What does a network perspective bring to your social science research study? What are the novel questions that can be addressed?

Now, after Chapter 2, you have basic network terminology, concepts and ideas in place. In this chapter, I want to present typical broad research questions that can benefit from network-based research. I will describe how to think about the building blocks of a network study and then go on to discuss specific social network research designs.[1]

Thinking about networked social systems, processes and structures

Social network research explicitly measures or observes a social environment, social context or social system.

Consider an individualized study of bullying in a school class. Participants might be asked whether they are victims of bullying, how they respond to bullying, what are their personal traits and characteristics, and so on. The focus is on the participant's internal response to the social environment and perhaps on the individual characteristics that predispose towards bullying.

In contrast, in a whole network study of bullying, every student in the class also nominates the other students who bully them. The goal is to understand the overall pattern of bullying, not just to study the behaviors, characteristics and feelings of

---

[1]Parts of this chapter draw on earlier versions in Robins et al. (2010).

bullies and the bullied. So the network study measures not just individual characteristics but also the relationships between bullies and the bullied. We want explicit observation of the social environment, not just an internal response to it (although that may be studied as well).

With a network study, you can begin to ask questions like: Do the bullied also bully? Are there groups of bullies who bully certain individuals? Is there a hierarchy of bullying in this classroom?

The point is: if bullying is not just an individual behavior but is embedded within the social system, then individual interventions may not be sufficient to eradicate it. In that case, we need to understand the social purposes of bullying, how that relates to other social processes (e.g., status achievement), and whether there is a culture of bullying in this class.

Importantly, such research can include both individual and network effects, so if the network effects are not apparent, we conclude that an individualized explanation is fine. But if network effects are important, then inferences based solely on individualized factors will be insufficient or even incorrect.

Often individual and network factors will both be present. Do not expect that an individual explanation precludes a network effect, or vice versa. The two explanatory factors may even interact. A predisposition to aggression may become bullying when there is a culture of bullying in the classroom (i.e., an individual factor may become active in a particular social environment).

In Chapter 2, I briefly introduced *egocentric network* or *egonet* studies (Box 2.1), where only that part of the network immediately surrounding participants is observed. Even in egocentric network studies, there is still a focus on the social environment, but this time as perceived by the participant: *ego*, the focal individual. In an individualized study of social support when the individual has a chronic illness, for instance, participants might describe whether in general they feel supported and under what conditions. In an egocentric network study, on the other hand, participants also identify the specific support of partners in their personal network, and provide information on the type of relationships with those partners and details about the partners themselves.

It should not be taken for granted that individualized or network studies will be better explanations: ultimately, that is an empirical question. Nevertheless, these examples illustrate how a network study may provide insights. Take the egocentric social support example: through careful examination of the social environment around an individual, we draw specific conclusions about the social aspects conducive to effective social support (e.g., the number and type of supporters). We decide whether it is the social environment that matters, rather than within-individual effects (e.g., how resilient an individual is in the face of the illness), or some combination or interaction of the two.

If we are attempting to intervene, does the social environment need to be changed, or does the individual need to respond differently? If social factors count, then individualized interventions may fail; if individual effects matter, then changing the social world alone may not have impact.

Research questions, complexity and parsimony

Common social network research questions broadly come under a few categories:

- How does the social environment affect individual outcomes? Specifically, how do network partners affect individuals? What flows through the network from one individual to another? (Generally, these might be thought of as influence or diffusion hypotheses.)
- How do individuals in certain network positions differ in their individual outcomes? (Generalized influence hypotheses.)
- How do individuals affect network structure? On what basis do individuals choose network partners or network positions? (Selection hypotheses, including generalized selection.)
- How does network structure come into being? What are the self-organizing processes involved? How can we best describe or simplify the network? (Structural hypotheses.)
- How do individual outcomes and/or network structure co-evolve over time? (Evolution and co-evolution hypotheses.)
- What are the global outcomes for a particular network structure? What makes a networked social system effective or responsive? (Hypotheses about global network outcomes.)

There are other types of research question, of course, but these cover a large slice of empirical social network research. If the list seems familiar, you have already met it in more intuitive form in Chapter 1 (Box 1.1).

To address such questions, we need to consider those elements of the social system or environment relevant to the research issue. Our theoretical thinking about the networked system is not trivial: there is no one abstraction that serves all studies.

Obviously, if our conceptualization of the social system is impoverished, we risk missing important effects. In Chapter 1, I wrote about dependence among actors as a central feature of social networks. Dependencies can lead to complex feedback mechanisms arising from the social processes we study. If we over-simplify, we might miss, for instance, important effects in the co-evolution of ties and attributes, the intersection of selection and influence. The interplay of endogenous network processes may not be evident in a simpler conceptualization.

But this is not a call for layers upon layers of complexity. Of course we want parsimonious explanations. Yet, because a social network conceptualization always carries some aspects of a social 'system', we need to be careful before breaking it down into constituent elements to be studied separately. The eminent organizational theorist, Karl Weick, criticized individualized arguments in organizational research as studying organizations 'one brain at a time' (Weick and Roberts, 1993: 358).

We need to be careful about studying a social system one person at a time, or one element at a time. Insights can certainly be gained by researching smaller system processes in isolation, but at some point we have to study the outcome when major processes are operating together and network dependencies come into play.

So, network research requires a balance between parsimony and complexity, a balance that will vary from issue to issue. That is why careful thought needs to be given to the theoretical conceptualization of the network systems and its processes. There is no template; rather, there are theoretical decisions to be made from a wide range of possibilities.

Building blocks for a network study

A social network study requires at the least a definition of social actors and social relationships among them. Starting from this point – the simplest ontology for our purpose – let us consider some practical building blocks for a network study.

Note that these are questions, not answers. You will need to make decisions in each of these areas, depending on the demands of your particular research and its theoretical basis. I will write about putting these building blocks together at the end of the chapter.

Who or what are the social actors?

Seemingly this is the easiest question to address and for much of social science the answer will be people. But depending on the research domain, it could also be animals, organizations, or institutions; and even socially inert entities such as websites could be treated as proxies for social actors. Of course, even with websites, the social 'action' might be due to an unseen human (the webmaster installs the hyperlinks for the website), but the nodes of the network might still most conveniently be considered as the websites among which the structure is observed.

The network boundary

In Chapter 1, I wrote of the network boundary. So for a given study we can ask where the network boundary is (or, indeed, if there is a network boundary at all). In short, which actors are to be included in the study? (Laumann et al., 1983).

Not every network study need have a clearly defined boundary. But sometimes the decision about the boundary is obvious: for instance, in the sporting team study described in Chapter 1, the actors were the professional athletes who were official members of the club at the time of the study. In other cases with more ambiguity, sensible theoretical or pragmatic grounds may assist in defining the nodes to be included.

Sometimes a decision on the boundary is not evident and even the notion of a boundary may not be well defined. In some cases, the study itself may be used to find the boundary empirically. For instance, in a study of a sex-worker network to investigate the spread of HIV, we probably do not know who will be in the network until we complete the study. So we may need to adopt a snowball sampling or respondent-driven sampling design (see below) to find the actors (or at least a subset of them). Such designs may also assist when drawing conclusions about an entire community (e.g., a town) where it proves impossible to obtain data from everyone.

In other cases, our focus may be on individual action within the immediate social environment, in which case egonet studies may be adequate. Then, individuals can be sampled randomly from a population in a standard way and the boundary in effect becomes the population from which the sample is drawn.

In short, the answer to the question whether there is a sensible network boundary affects the type of research design we adopt; and the answer to the question where the network boundary is, if it exists, affects the scope of the study we conduct.

Bipartite and multilevel social networks

But why should there be only one type of social actor? I am not referring here to different categories of the one kind of actor: for instance, males and females are different categories of *person*. Rather, I am referring to fundamentally different types of actors with no sensible higher-order category to encompass both of them. Organizations and people are social actors but they are fundamentally different entities, even though people are members of organizations and organizations are defunct without people. Ron Breiger (1974) famously wrote about this duality 40 years ago, a classic article always worth drawing on.

A popular representation of Breiger's dualism between organizations and people is a *bipartite network* with two types of actors, where ties between nodes of different types signify membership or affiliation. In this bipartite representation, ties are not included among nodes of the same type. An example is the extensive research into *interlocking directorships* where the two types of nodes are companies and directors (Kogut, 2012). It is also possible to extend the bipartite idea to *k-partite networks* with *k* types of nodes, although, in practice, empirical extensions even to tripartite networks are rare.

A newer but related abstraction is of *multilevel networks* where two types of nodes are construed as at different levels, a bipartite network represents associations between the two types of nodes, but unipartite networks exist among the nodes at each level (Figure 3.1). For instance, Lazega et al. (2008) studied researchers affiliated with laboratories (bipartite), where the two unipartite networks involved cooperation among laboratories and collaboration among researchers. In this case, we have two types of nodes and three types of ties.

Bipartite and multilevel extensions open the possibility that only one of the two types of nodes might be a social actor. This idea has led to new methods for studying *social-ecological networks* where one type of node is human and the other an ecological resource. Here the bipartite ties might indicate harvesting or management of the resource (Bodin and Tengö, 2012). Kathleen Carley's (2003) concept of a network *meta-matrix* is an earlier development but can be seen as a version of a multilevel network, with at least three levels: people, resources and tasks. People have resources and tasks, tasks require resources, and so on.

Researchers need to consider carefully whether the social processes they are examining are best conceptualized with a unipartite, bipartite or multilevel network.

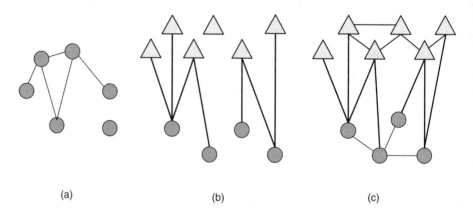

(a)   (b)   (c)

Figure 3.1   (a) Unipartite, (b) bipartite and (c) multilevel networks

What types of relational ties are relevant?

Once you have made decisions about the nodes and the boundary, you need to determine the relevant network relationships among the nodes. There is no agreed set of relational types to study, just as there is no agreed categorization of the types of relationships that humans have with each other. Fiske (1991, 1992) argued that human relationships come in four fundamental forms – *communal sharing, authority ranking, equality matching,* and *market pricing* – whereas Ibarra (1992), writing principally about organizations, proposed a typology of three different types – *prescribed relationships* (determined by external bodies, such as management), *instrumental relationships* dealing with purposes and goals, and *expressive relationships* focusing on emotional aspects.

What is clear is that a relationship between two humans can have many different aspects. A relationship can have both instrumental and expressive aspects, to use Ibarra's typology, and perhaps additional features as well. So we need to distinguish between a *relationship* (which may have many different facets) and *relational ties* (the different contents of social connections, of which there may be many in the one relationship).

It is seldom that network researchers content themselves with one rather generic type of relational tie that is not very precisely defined (e.g., *acquaintance* or *knows*). In social science, there is usually not much mileage in studying an undifferentiated relationship. So, several different types of relational tie are often used within the one study; and when only one type is studied, it is usually more specific than generic.

Frequently, the research topic will suggest types of relational ties rather obviously. For instance, in communication studies, a network of *who communicates with whom* or *information flow* makes sense. In studies of disease spread, a *sexual relations* network might be studied for HIV, *needle sharing* for hepatitis C, or simply *physical proximity* for influenza. In an inter-organizational network, *resource flows* or *equity* relationships might be important. In a workplace, an obvious relational tie is *collaboration* or *working together*.

But the obvious may not be sufficient. Workplaces, for instance, are domains not just of enlightened collaboration but also of musty non-cooperation, dark secrets and factionalized competition. That is why Ibarra emphasized expressive relationships. So, it not unusual for organizational network studies to include, for instance, networks of *friendship* or of *trust* to handle such factors.

In some cases, researchers also study *negative relationships*. People can of course *dislike* one another, school children can *bully* one another, and workers can find some of their colleagues *difficult to work with*. It should never be assumed that networks are always positive and helpful. Social networks can impede and dismay as much as they enhance and encourage. Network effectiveness and capacity are always empirical questions: just because a system is 'networked' does not mean it need be harmonious, effective or efficient.

Similarly, it should never be assumed that network ties are solely the conduits of rational instrumental exchange – the flow of information, for instance. Researchers coming to network analysis for the first time often think that information exchange, resource flow, or frequency of contact will be the important factors. They may be and it may be desirable to measure these types of relational tie. But it is also possible that friendships and enmities might be the driving social process in the system, and once taken into account wash out the effects of relational ties directed more precisely to 'rational' purposes. Do not presume your actors are only logical processors: we are dealing with human motivation here.

So, if possible, it may be a good idea to examine several different relational ties in the one study. As always, of course, this is dependent on context. If you are studying trade flows between countries, that is what you have and that will be your data. If you are studying email exchanges in an organization, then that may be the only type of relational data available to you. But more generally, the research topic may suggest some instrumental types of tie; and inclusion of expressive ties and where appropriate negative ties may also be desirable.

Of course, if the data is to be collected by respondent survey or interview where you can ask for different types of relationships, the desirability of collecting that information needs to be balanced against respondent fatigue. So, you may need to be discriminating in what you ask: not every type of relational tie can be studied at once. (More about measurement will appear in Chapter 5.)

How do you reach a final decision about the relational ties to examine? It is important to theorize carefully about the social processes you expect are operating and so decide which relational types are likely to be the most important. Review previous network research in your area to see which relational ties were studied. Look outside the network literature to understand other effects that have been studied in the research area, effects that may inform the types of ties to examine. (For instance, if a disease is transmitted through a certain physical process, that may inform the type of tie that will facilitate the spread.) Of course, an opportunity to pilot the study, or to interview key informants beforehand, may help considerably to sharpen an understanding of the relational ties to include.

BOX 3.1

Binary, valued and ranked ties

Is it desirable to have weighted data, where the network tie is observed at some strength instead of binary (present/absent)? For instance, data can be collected on frequency of contact, with the ties weighted by frequency. Another option is for categories of tie – for instance, strong and weak ties – with an ordering based on tie strength. Unless a weighted tie makes obvious sense (e.g., trade flows), or unless you think strong–weak tie theory is important to your research question, my personal bias is towards measuring several different relational ties with binary data, rather than a detailed weighted measure on one type of tie.

In some early social network research, social ties were occasionally ranked: for example, a student might be asked to rank all other students in the class in terms of their most important friend, the second most important and so on. Never do this! It makes for a nightmare in terms of analysis. Ask the respondents to choose, not rank.

To this point, I have referred to relationships and relational ties, which constitute the most common form of social network data. However, there is an increasing interest in *transactions* or *relational events* (Butts, 2008a). In contrast to a relationship of an indefinite duration, a transaction or relational event occurs between actors at a specific time-point (e.g., an email). There is a sequence of relational events across time among the actors. One approach is to collapse the time sequence of events into one or several cross-sectional networks, but recent methodological developments permit analysis of the sequence of events itself, predicting the next event from what has happened previously (Chapter 9).

Relational event models can be useful in several ways. First, the sequences of events can give fine detail on the dynamics of the social processes you are studying. In some cases, this might be exactly the type of conclusion you wish to draw. Second, the events might be seen as measures that indicate longer-term relationships (e.g., perhaps workers send more emails to colleagues with whom they collaborate), so conclusions about the sequence of events have implications for longer-term network structure and hence how the social system works. Finally, relational events may be recorded electronically (email is again a good example) which in the right circumstances can be a convenient data collection method.

Nevertheless, there is a strong theoretical distinction between relational events and relationships; and using relational events as the data suggests a commitment to investigating hypotheses relating to fine-grained social dynamics, as opposed to the structure of relationships.

Which actor attributes?

I am not going to say much about actor attributes at this point, because they are familiar fodder for most of social science: individual-level measures or observations on the actors in the network. These may be either explanatory factors, contributing to an explanation of the outcomes of interest – either network structure or other individual responses – or may be the outcomes themselves.

In short, there is no need to ditch your favourite individual constructs, just because you are doing a network study.

What are the outcomes of interest? At what level?

Research questions naturally determine the outcome variables of interest, but the systemic and potentially multilevel nature of a network opens up a wide choice of possibilities.

Outcomes for individuals

Many non-network social science studies are concerned with individual-level outcomes: for instance, organization behavioral research has investigated the factors that affect individual performance and job satisfaction; while organizational theory asks what factors influence organizational profitability and adaptation. These are individual-level research outcomes in the sense that they relate to outcomes for the individual persons or individual organizations. They do not immediately pertain to the entire company (in the case of the employees) or to the business sector (in the case of organizations).

Sometimes, individual-level results may be aggregated (e.g., a mean score) to apply at a higher level. For instance, average individual performance within a work group might be taken as a measure of work group performance. Sometimes this makes sense – the average running speed of the members of a relay team will indicate overall team performance – but in other cases, not so – in a football team the average number of kicks may not indicate overall performance when some defenders, for instance, are meant to concentrate on preventing an opponent from playing well, rather than kicking the ball themselves.

There are several distinctive aspects that a network study brings to the examination of individual-level outcomes:

- The presence of network ties in the study implies at least the empirical possibility of social influence, whereby the actors' outcomes are shaped not just by internal factors, or by general contextual features, but also directly by network partners. (*My knowledge is influenced by my friends' knowledge.*)
- Individual outcomes may be affected not just by network partners through social influence, but also by the network position that the individual occupies. For instance, an individual may obtain advantages by occupying a structural hole. (*I know more because I am associated with several distinct groups.*)
- The presence of a social network suggests that a simple average across individuals may not be the best way to combine individual-level measures to get an indication of system-level or group-level performance. Simple methods of aggregation may be unrealistic and inappropriate (White et al., 1976). If a system-level outcome is required, it may need to be an entirely different measure. (*The average of everything that I and my fellow group members know does not determine whether we combine our information effectively or not.*)

Outcomes for ties

The presence of network ties may itself be the research question: *What are the factors that create relationships among actors in this setting?* For instance, a bullying relationship in a school may relate to attributes of both the person bullied and the bully, perhaps personality factors or individual backgrounds. In this case, individual attributes may lead to the formation of ties, an instance of dyadic social selection. As noted in Chapter 2, a common dyadic hypothesis is that of *homophily* whereby social ties are more likely to be present when the actors share important attributes. This can be important for some types of attribute and tie – schoolyard friendships are usually strongly influenced by same gender – but perhaps not for others – the personal dispositions of bullies may well be different from those of their victims.

But network ties also can arise from *network self-organization* where the presence of some ties encourages other ties to come into existence. These processes create patterns in the network data, notably network reciprocity and closure. So possible research questions include understanding the self-organizational network processes and hence the nature of the global network structure: for instance, *is there significant closure in the network?*

Global network outcomes

The investigation of how structural effects may relate to system-level outcomes may follow rather naturally. For instance, Berardo and Scholz (2010) argued that in environmental governance networks, the organizations involved in managing the environmental resource will prefer more closed network structures in a risky situation; whereas, in less risky conditions, the system will be more efficient with open structures. The question, *'Is there significant closure in the network?'*, is again directly relevant.

The global network structure may also indicate different types of actors based on their structural position. *Blockmodelling* or *community detection* (Chapter 9) are methods designed to group actors depending on their network positions. One research question may then be: *Do people in different network positions or in different network communities have different qualities or outcomes?* For instance, are the popular network actors different in ways other than just popularity? Do these differences explain why they are popular, or are these features the outcomes of popularity? Do popular actors tend to like each other, or are they factionalized into distinct communities of fans and stars?

A potential issue arises with external outcomes for the system. For instance, suppose we investigate the Berardo and Scholz proposition that, in less risky conditions, system efficiency will be enhanced by more open structures. It is not always obvious how to measure *efficiency* at the system level. I will expand on this point in later chapters.

In short, we can have outcomes for the individual, for the dyad, and for the system as a whole. The outcomes for the system may be the network structure itself and the processes that lead to it or result from it; or how the network structure relates to external outcomes such as system performance, stability and efficiency.

Is time relevant?

As for other areas of social science, longitudinal studies have particular strengths but also usually require a more difficult and prolonged data collection. You have to decide whether the specific dynamics of the social processes require investigation, and of course you need to consider the resources you have available to do this. If you must disentangle selection and influence effects from each other, or make compelling inferences about other causal processes, you will require longitudinal data in some form.

Yet, the presence of network patterns does indicate possible network processes; so, many network studies are cross-sectional rather than longitudinal. As social network structure will seldom be fixed, we can expect changes to the networks we observe. But the structure may be relatively stable, as may be the fundamental social processes. In that case, although the network will evolve, the structural effects can be expected to persist across time, and the network observed at one time-point may be sufficient to address our research question sensibly.

Of course, if you have plentiful resources, a good supply of research assistants, time, cooperative respondents and sophisticated network analytic skills, then – in the best of all possible worlds – collect data longitudinally and collect plenty of it. There is no doubt that longitudinal data provides a richer description and enables stronger inferences.

Are there other exogenous factors?

There can be a number of other exogenous factors that affect network ties and structure, and also are relevant to influence-type mechanisms. Geographic location, for instance, may be a candidate for inclusion in a community-wide study, under the supposition that actors may develop social ties or experience similar contextual effects (e.g., environment, living conditions) due to geospatial factors. Spatial distance between pairs of actors can be introduced as an exogenous covariate of network ties, under the hypothesis that ties are more likely between proximate actors (adams et al., 2012).

What is the scale of the social system?

Social network research has a long tradition of research in smaller-scale social systems, for instance, schools or organizations. Recently, network studies of larger-scale systems, such as the internet or mobile phone exchanges, have become more common, in large part due to the ease of digital data collection. For such studies, the scale may even be on the level of the entire planet. However, such large-scale data are not usually collected to address specific social science research questions, and certain important variables may simply not be available.

In short, if the scale of your research is small, so that the boundary contains only a few hundred nodes (or even substantially fewer – network studies have been conducted with as few as ten nodes), then there are plenty of precedents. For larger-scale systems, you may need to consider whether secondary digital data gathered for other purposes will address your questions. If not, you may have to collect larger-scale data, for instance on a community.

To conduct a community-wide network study is not simply a matter of scaling up smaller network studies. Scaling up for whole network studies raises four conceptual and methodological issues:

1. Depending on resources, community-wide data collection may require techniques of network sampling, unless digital data is available to address the research question.
2. A larger-scale system may require more computational requirements when it comes to analysis. Large-scale analysis can be computationally expensive and often

increases in time with the square of the number of nodes (i.e., for any *n* actors, there are $n(n - 1)$ possible ties – the network *scale up* issue).

3. The increase in complexity across a larger-scale system may mean that the multilevel nature of the social system becomes more pronounced, and that methods attuned to multilevel settings may need to be considered, or variables that relate to societal groups and institutions included.

4. Larger-scale systems may mean that it is more difficult to ignore exogenous variables, such as geographical location, environmental differentiation, institutional agendas and policy initiatives.

There is a long-standing network research tradition of collecting community-level data through egonet studies. This design is described below. It is more akin to standard community sampling approaches and avoids some of these issues. However, it is limited to the extent it can investigate network connectivity and effects relating to influence and selection. For more ambitious community-level data collection with explicit attempts to get at connectivity, much thought should be given to the planning and scope of the study. I will provide some guidance in later chapters.

Social network research designs

I now turn to some important ways to do social network research. These research designs are included because either they are commonly used or they have distinctive and interesting features: they do not exhaust all possibilities.

Egocentric network studies

What is an egonet?

I described an egocentric network (or egonet for short) in Chapter 2. An *egonet* is the immediate social network environment of an individual (*ego*). Ego has network ties to other individuals (*alters*) who in turn may have ties among themselves. Egonet data usually includes individual attributes of both ego and alters.

An egocentric network study is based on a sample of participants who report their personal egonets. The data is entirely derived from these self-reports. Network data collection proceeds by asking participants, often selected randomly from a population, to list their important alters, and to describe the types of relationships they have with those alters, perhaps the relationships among the alters, and the attributes of themselves and of alters. The point of asking about alter–alter ties is to assess network closure around ego. Lower network closure may be indicative of a network broker occupying structural holes.

By definition, ego has a tie to every alter, but not all alters need to be tied directly to each other. Alter–alter ties alone (i.e., if ego and ego's ties are removed) constitute a whole network with the network boundary defined by actors tied to this particular ego.

Do not suppose that each ego has their 'own' network. This may seem slightly pedantic but a social network extends across a social system of actors, and does not 'belong' to any one of them. An egonet is a convenient measurement device to extract information from this larger network. A person can be said to have an egonet or a personal network, so use that terminology, but resist the temptation to think of a person as having a network in general. Serious network researchers do not talk about 'Mary's network', although they might mention 'Mary's egocentric network' or 'Mary's personal network'.

Strengths

A big advantage of egonet studies is that participants can be sampled in standard ways from a population. Egonets can be treated as a sample of independent observations, assuming that alters are not themselves respondents and are not shared across egonets. As a result, once summary indices about the egonet structure are calculated, these measures can then be analyzed using standard statistical approaches because observations are independent between egos. As we will see in Chapter 4, the egonet indices become variables pertaining to ego.

Issues

This design assumes that respondents can reliably provide information about alters, including alters' attributes and alter–alter ties. It may be problematic to use this design to study, for instance, social influence or diffusion, when we need good measures of behaviors or attitudes for both partners in a network tie. Moreover, an egonet design provides no observations of network ties beyond each egonet, and so is limited in assessing network connectivity. This becomes a problem where connectivity is crucial (e.g., disease transmission studies).

Examples

Egonet designs have been used in studies of subjective well-being or social support (Green et al., 2013), where the level of well-being or support is theorized to be associated with the respondent's immediate social environment.

Whole network designs

A *whole network design*, also called a *full network* study, requires a single set of actors within a well-defined network boundary. The data includes the ties that are present among all actors, sometimes referred to as a *network census*. Through a survey, actors may be asked to nominate network partners, but various forms of electronic and other types of data collection are also possible (Chapters 5 and 6). Individual actors are also typically surveyed about attribute variables. Both the sporting team study and the environmental management study (Box 2.4) are whole network studies. These are the staple of much empirical social network analysis.

Egonets can of course be extracted from a whole network design, simply by taking the immediate network environment around each node. But in a whole network design the egonets are overlapping and not independent of each other, so it does not make a lot of sense to analyze the whole network by converting to an egonet study.

A whole network design may involve several different types of relational ties (as indeed can an egonet study), in which case we can think of the data as representing a multivariate or multiplex network.

Strengths

With good measurement and a sensible network boundary, a whole network design is obviously superior to egonet designs in handling network connectivity. We are able to draw conclusions about the entire social system (within the boundary). Social influence can be better assessed, as we are not reliant on ego's reports of alter's attributes: each actor reports only on his or her own attributes. Network structure can be properly assessed because the data is fully available and does not have to be inferred from sampling procedures (either egonet or snowball sampling, below.)

Issues

Despite new methods for handling missing tie data (see Chapter 5), a whole network design typically requires a high response rate from the actors. So the design is not always useful for large-scale studies, unless perhaps the data can be collected digitally. As with other types of social science research, cross-sectional whole network designs can assess the associations between network ties and actor attributes but cannot differentiate selection and influence, or other causal effects, in a compelling way.

Examples

There are many examples in whole network studies in the social network literature, especially when the network boundaries are fairly obvious such as in school classrooms or organizational work groups. For an example of a whole network study of a top management team, see Lomi et al. (2014a).

Multiple network designs

By *multiple network* designs, I mean studies that involve several different whole networks. For instance, the famous National Longitudinal Study of Adolescent Health, known as Add Health (www.cpc.unc.edu/projects/addhealth), includes data on school networks across many different schools in the USA. In multiple network studies, network data is collected from several collective units (school or class), with each unit treated as creating a boundary and thereby a separate whole network. The networks are assumed to be distinct, without ties across boundaries to other units. The idea behind a multiple network study is to compare network effects across units with the goal of identifying major effects that apply to all units.

The multiple network design has some similarity to standard multilevel model designs (e.g., Snijders and Bosker, 2012) with the networks nested within the units. However, the within-unit dependencies created by the network mean that the standard multilevel statistical models cannot be used.

Strengths

A multiple network study is essentially many whole network studies combined, so this study carries the strengths and weaknesses of the whole network method. One important positive is that inferences can be made across many units, and not simply rely on a case study of one or a few.

Issues

The assumption is that the units are not connected by the types of tie under examination (in other words, that these networks can be treated as distinct). It is not always obvious how well this assumption is met, so care needs to be taken in sampling and selecting units.

Examples

I mentioned above the well-known Add Health study. School data are a common source of multiple network studies (see Chapter 6).

Cognitive social structure designs

Cognitive social structures are an extension of whole network designs. In addition to reporting on their own ties and attributes, actors also report what they perceive to be the ties among all the other actors within the boundary. The goal is to understand how *perceptions* of the whole network affect actual network structure and action within the network.

Strengths

This design – or versions of it – is necessary if the research question requires perceptions of others' network ties within a whole network.

Issues

The data collection is obviously demanding on respondents and can only be realistically applied to small-scale studies. The data analysis is complicated, with only a few methods available.

Examples

This type of design was introduced Krackhardt (1987b) who presented a now classic cognitive social structure dataset.

Bipartite and multilevel network designs

These designs are akin to whole network research, except that they involve two different types of nodes and (for multilevel networks) different types of ties within and between levels (Figure 3.1). Much bipartite data arises from archival records: for instance, data from the extensive research on interlocking directorships (e.g., Kogut, 2012) usually comes from databases of annual company reports required by national financial authorities. The network boundary may then be taken as the nodes described in these databases. In other cases, the network boundary needs to be determined. For these types of studies, action sometimes only occurs at one level: for instance, people may choose to attend certain places (the places do not choose people); or in social ecological networks (Bodin and Tengö, 2012), people may harvest certain ecological resources (not the other way around). In these cases, the network boundary may be determined from the actors (e.g., the people) and the 'passive' nodes decided by the actors' choices. Care needs to be taken in making this decision because action can indeed take place at both levels in many cases: directors agree to sit on company boards, but boards also recruit new directors.

Strengths and issues

Bipartite data are often easier to obtain if a database can be readily accessed. Bipartite studies do not have within-level (e.g., people to people) social ties, and in some cases a fuller multilevel network dataset may be desirable. One of the advantages of a multilevel design is that the within- and cross-level tie data are differentiated but obviously there are greater demands in collecting several different types of tie at different levels.

Network sampling designs

Apart from egonet designs, traditional random or stratified sampling may not make a lot of sense for a network study. Dependencies among individuals are lost by random sampling and an understanding of network connectivity is better obtained with some form of snowball sampling or link tracing design.

Handcock and Gile (2011) examined the history of snowball sampling and link tracing designs (see also Heckathorn, 2011). They distinguished (at least) two broad motivations: to obtain information about network structures in larger communities, and to obtain information about individuals in populations that are 'hidden' or 'hard to reach' (e.g., drug users).

Snowball sampling

Snowball sampling is usually the preferred approach for investigating network structure using sampled data. I describe the data structure of a snowball sample in more detail in Chapter 4, but let me offer a brief description here. A snowball sample is obtained by starting from an initial set of respondents (the *seed set*), determining their network partners (*wave 1*), determining the new network partners of wave 1 respondents (*wave 2*) and so on until stopping at an agreed number of waves. In the social networks literature, an earlier version of snowball sampling was referred to as *random walk sampling* (McGrady et al., 1995), where the basic snowball approach was applied but only a random sample of network partners for each actor was sampled.

Snowball sampling to determine the network boundary

Sometimes it is not clear which actors should be included within the boundary for a whole network study. For instance, in a health policy network (e.g., Lewis, 2005) prominent policy-makers obviously need to be included in the study. But who else is within the boundary? The set of known actors can be taken as the seed set in a snowball sample: they can be surveyed to determine their major network partners, with partners not in the seed set taken as wave 1. The snowball can continue across multiple waves until no new partners are named. Often additional constraints are included to keep the process manageable and the node size limited: for instance, previously unnamed partners might be included in a new wave only if they are named by more than a certain number of current actors.

Once the boundary is so determined, the entire set of actors may be surveyed again as in a whole network study. If the survey instrument is well designed, the actors may even be surveyed as part of the snowball sample process, with no need to return for a second data collection.

Snowball sampling to determine structural effects in a large community

A snowball sample – or versions thereof – may be used to investigate network effects in a large community. Recent statistical models for social networks have demonstrated that estimated effects from a snowball sample can be consistent with the entire network structure. (More in Chapter 9.)

Respondent-driven sampling

Respondent-driven sampling (RDS), on the other hand, is typically used to identify the characteristics of a hard-to-reach population (i.e. actor attributes), and is not so relevant to investigations of network structure. Rather, it uses network structure to obtain the information about the population. Again, random walk sampling can be seen as an earlier version. RDS is often applied in disease studies where disease status (e.g., HIV) of actors in a hard-to-reach population is the research question. Nevertheless, there is growing interest in RDS for other populations as well, and there are indications that it can perform well in a variety of circumstances (Dombrowski et al., 2013).

The basic idea behind RDS is a *chain referral* or *link tracing* method, whereby respondents themselves try to recruit one or more of their network partners (Heckathorn, 1997). A difference from snowball sampling, however, is that some chains of referrals may be very long, but others very short when some respondents do not recruit or recruit only a few partners.

Data collection requires some thought because actors need to be motivated both to participate and to recruit. I shall say more about RDS data collection in Chapter 5, and about methods in Chapter 9.

Internet studies

Many internet studies have versions of network sampling designs. Often a webcrawler is sent out from certain websites to provide data on hyperlinks to other websites. The relative ease of electronic data collection means that in some cases the data could be so large that the notion of a 'sample' is not entirely relevant. Indeed, many studies of the internet claim to be studying the entire internet, or at least the most important parts of it. In Chapter 6, I will describe some huge internet datasets. Nevertheless, smaller-scale internet studies on specific topics may also use the webcrawler approach.

Network structure derived from egonet sampling

As described above, egonets are limited in providing information about important network properties. However, new methodological developments based on a combination of statistical modelling and simulation may enable an understanding of certain whole network properties consistent with the egonet sample (Smith, 2012). Because egonet sampling is much simpler in terms of data collection, these new methods open possibilities for understanding structural properties of large networks in a relatively efficient way. See Chapter 9 for more.

Strengths and issues

Network sampling can provide direct evidence about network effects in a larger context not well suited to whole network studies. Even so, the data collection demands can be substantial, depending on the nature of the study. I discuss these issues further in Chapter 6.

Longitudinal designs

Panel relational data

Egonet, whole network and bipartite network designs can be readily adapted to a panel approach simply by collecting data at multiple time-points. If the dataset is not too large, so that computational requirements are not overly demanding, inferences differentiating selection from influence can be made using sophisticated statistical models (Chapter 9). This has become a major theme in much current social network research.

Relational event designs

As discussed earlier in this chapter, we now have new and exciting methods for dealing with event-based data. The design here is straightforward: a network boundary is established, and the data comprises a sequence of transactions among the actors across time. The next transaction (event) is predicted from the past patterns of events. This design is well suited to email and other electronically collected data, where it is a simple matter to collect the timing of the event (e.g., an email from i to j). Much work on social media (e.g., Twitter) is a variant of an event-based design.

Strengths and issues

The strengths and weaknesses of panel network studies are similar to those of longitudinal studies more generally: more compelling inferences about causality, including about selection and influence, are available, but data collection costs are likely to be greater. Event-based designs often involve automatic electronic data collection, in which case additional costs may not be substantial. But they are focused on the specific dynamics of time-stamped transactions, so that inferences about longer-term relationships may be more difficult.

How to put it together

Beware checklists! But, even so, here is a guide to how to consider your network research design.

Always start from your research question and be guided by past theory and research. Consider carefully why social networks are important and how they relate to the outcomes relevant to your research question. Your answers constitute the theoretical base of your network research. But also consider non-network theories or processes that might be relevant and need to be studied alongside your networks.

Then you have some overlapping decisions to make. The answers depend on your theorization, but also on your resources and timing.

- What are the outcomes of interest? How will you measure or observe them?
  - How does the network relate to the outcome? Do you have specific expectations or hypotheses?
  - At what level is your outcome (individual, dyad, system)? Are there interesting outcomes at the other levels that may also be studied?
- Who are the actors?
  - Are there multiple types of actors, so that you will follow a bipartite or multilevel network design?
- Is there an obvious network boundary?
  - If so, are you undertaking a whole network design? Will it be a single network study (akin to a case study – Chapter 10), or a multiple network design?
  - If not, do you need to find the boundary using a snowball?
  - Or are you going to undertake some form of network sampling: an egonet study, or snowball or respondent-driven sampling?
- What are the important relational ties?
  - Are you studying relationships or relational events?
  - Do you need both expressive and instrumental ties in your network? Which types, specifically? Will you study negative ties?
- Is time important? Will this be a cross-sectional or longitudinal design?
  - Are you seeking to disentangle selection from influence?
  - If it is longitudinal, will it be a panel, or event-based design?
- Are there other exogenous factors that might be relevant?
- What is the scale of your research context?
  - If it is large-scale, do you have the resources to obtain good data? Are there additional factors that need to be considered because of the larger scale? Are the methods to analyze your research question tractable for very large data?

Once you have the answers to these questions, you will be ready to think about the specifics of measurement and observation.

Conclusion: The key point

There is no single correct network research design; rather, there are many decisions to be taken in setting up the study. These decisions will enable you to address one or more broad categories of network research questions. You need to have a clear idea of how a network conceptualization assists in addressing your particular research issue and then tailor your decisions to that idea. These decisions will address who are the actors, what types of tie to study, what are the relevant outcomes and at what level, whether time or other exogenous factors need to be included, and what is the scale of the social system you are studying. Ultimately these are theoretical decisions, although they may be guided by previous empirical work. The answers to these questions lead naturally into selection of a sensible design. By this point, in effect you have constrained what you can and cannot address in your research, because these decisions determine what data you will collect and the form in which it is collected.

BOX 3.2

Pulling back the curtain: What goes on in real network studies

For the sporting team study (Figure 1.2), a network boundary based on club membership was a natural and easy decision. It was more difficult to decide which relational ties and which actor attributes to study. Some attributes were again obvious: official leadership positions, games played, age and so on. As we were interested in club culture and player attitudes, and we could not find a ready-made attitudinal scale for our purposes, we spent a lot of time (including pilot studies) developing our own. Our final articles do not convey the months of work in item development and testing, psychometric analysis and confirmatory factor analysis that occurred even before we got to the actual network study. This emphasizes that you should not surrender your standard social science skills when undertaking network research – poor measurement of attributes will still lead to poor results.

Which relational ties to include? There is little theoretical guidance about the types of ties implicated in team culture. We decided to ask players about a number of different networks, including standard network items such as friendship and trust but also networks more specific to our interests, such as socializing outside of training and competition. We also asked about negative ties, including ties relating to aggression in training. Not all of these network questions proved to be fruitful, and our reports tend to include only those in focus for a particular analysis. This point illustrates that, if possible, it is often worthwhile to collect data on several types of ties, because it is not always evident which relational tie will give best leverage on your research question.

For the organizational collaboration network (Figure 1.1), we employed a version of a snowball sample design to determine the network boundary, using a seed set of core organizations, asking them about their important collaboration partners, and then snowballing out until we had a set of organizations that constituted the key players. In addition to standard organizational attributes (e.g., size, sector), we interviewed respondents about their organizations' policies and attitudes to central issues, so that the research included a strong qualitative component. Again, there is not a lot of theoretical guidance on the type of network tie for effective network governance. We focused on collaboration ties, which surely must be at the heart of a good network governance system, but we also included information and resource-flow ties because of their importance to organizational interaction. We also added a negative tie network, asking for nominations on other organizations that were difficult to work with.

Hot topics

Network effectiveness. Researchers coming to networks for the first time often think that they will be able to determine whether a networked system is effective or not. While there are some clear ideas about outcomes for individuals (e.g., structural hole theory), outcomes for the network as a whole are not that obvious. Read Berardo and Scholz (2010) about the performance of governance networks. Notice how their ideas about the effectiveness of certain network structures relate to long-standing notions about network closure. Think about system performance in other domains (organizations, political parties, sporting teams). Are ideas about network closure and performance of the network as a whole likely to translate to such examples? If not, what other network structures or ideas might be relevant?

Berardo, R. and Scholz, J. (2010) Self-organizing policy networks: Risk, partner selection, and cooperation in estuaries. *American Journal of Political Science*, 54, 632–649.

FOUR

Social systems and data structures: Relational ties and actor attributes

In Chapter 3, I wrote that there was no unique network abstraction to be universally applied. We need to think carefully about how best to represent the features of the particular social system or social context that we are studying, and adapt our network conceptualization accordingly.

In this chapter, I present different types of data structures applicable to the types of research designs and questions in Chapter 3. The research question obviously has implications for the appropriate data to be collected. A given data structure is integral to the design of the study and to the method of data collection.

Following this chapter, I will take up general issues for network data collection in Chapter 5, and different contexts in which network data may be collected in Chapter 6. The data structures presented in this chapter can be used for network visualization (Chapter 8) and for subsequent analysis (Chapter 9).

Qualitative and quantitative data

Much network research has a strong quantitative aspect, but that does not mean that qualitative methods are not applicable. I will discuss qualitative network studies in more detail in Chapter 6. The current chapter concentrates on the structure of numerical network data, but that is not to privilege quantitative methods. Indeed, qualitative research based on careful interviews, if it is network-based, will need to extract relational information that can then be translated into the data structures of this chapter. This will be necessary, for instance, if the qualitative researcher wishes to visualize the networks using standard software. So, if you are a qualitative researcher and prefer to exclude quantitative inference, you may still want to produce the binary edge lists or matrices described below. Because I talk of data, matrices and vectors, that does not mean that this chapter is irrelevant for qualitative research.

Qualitative network research often uses an egonet design, where ego is the interviewee from which qualitative data is obtained. The structure of egonet data is described at the end of this chapter. It is important for the qualitative researcher to understand this data structure if an explicit network framework is to be used, even when the original data is not numeric. For network mixed methods approaches, where qualitative and quantitative research are integrated, all the data structures of this chapter are potentially relevant.

Some network notation

Not everyone is keen on mathematical notation, so I will keep it to a minimum. Nevertheless, it is helpful for this and following chapters to have some simple mathematical descriptors of the network structures we examine. My notation is presented in Box 4.1. (Note that there is no one standard notation, and different authors have different practices.)

From this point, I will start to use terminology such as tie or attribute *variables*. The use of the term *variable* is again not intended to privilege a quantitative, or more particularly, a statistical point of view, although some but certainly not all of the methods described in Chapter 9 are statistical. A tie is possible between pairs of actors, but need not be present. Hence the presence of a tie can be said to vary across pairs of actors. Similarly, an actor may or may not have a particular attribute (e.g., be female), so that attribute can be said to vary across actors. At this point, I intend no more than this in the use of the term *variable*.

Often, but not always, tie variables are binary, so that they take the value of 1 or 0 depending on whether the tie is observed or not. As usual, a variable needs to be distinguished from the value it may actually take. For instance, *age* may be a variable in a study, and an actor, John, may have an age of 37. The variable here is *age* and its value for John happens to be 37.

BOX 4.1

Some network notation

- X_{ij} denotes a network tie variable between actor i and actor j. If the network is directed, X_{ij} denotes an arc variable from i as sender to j as receiver. For binary networks, $X_{ij} = 1$ if the edge or arc is observed, and $X_{ij} = 0$ if not. If the tie is *valued*, then

X_{ij} may take a value in whatever range is permissible. To differentiate the variable from the value it may take, sometimes I write $X_{ij} = x_{ij}$ to signify that, in the observed data, the tie variable X_{ij} takes the value x_{ij} for the pair of actors (i, j). In a unipartite network, it is usual (though not universal) for self-ties from a node to itself to be excluded, so that x_{ii} is forced to be zero.

- Y_i denotes an actor attribute variable for the actor i. To differentiate the variable and its observed value, sometimes I write $Y_i = y_i$.

- The set of all the tie variables (i.e., all of the X_{ij}) may be written as X, which then represents a variable that describes the whole network (not just for an individual (i, j) pair). Sometimes I write x to represent actual network data, so that x is the collection of all observed values x_{ij}.

- Suppose there are k types of relational ties in a multiple or multiplex network study. Then I write X_{ijm} to denote a tie variable between actor i and actor j on the mth type of relationship.

- In a longitudinal network study, I write X_{ijt} to denote a tie variable between actor i and actor j at time t.

Relational data structures

Now let me describe various network data structures. An understanding of the data structures will help you appreciate the possibilities of the designs in Chapter 3. I then introduce actor attribute variables. I postpone egonet data structures until late in the chapter, because they typically include attribute variables.

Many social science researchers will be used to entering the data into a spreadsheet or perhaps a favorite statistical package. While this is possible for network data, it is quite common to enter the data into simple text files. Most network analytic software can read in text files in a straightforward way, although the precise format depends on the program.

Whole network data

I begin with a whole network research design because this is so often the standard way in which network data is described. Recall that in a whole network we have a subset of actors defined within the boundary of the study. The data then comprises relational ties among the actors. In short, we represent data as observations x_{ij} among pairs of actors.

To begin, we give each of the n actors an identification number (ID), usually sequentially from 1 to n. Then there are two standard and equivalent ways to enter the network data.

- An *adjacency matrix* (sometimes called a *sociomatrix* for social network data): Here each of the rows and columns represent the actors, and the cell in row i and column *j* takes the value x_{ij}. For a binary network, then, the adjacency matrix is a matrix of 0s and 1s representing the absence or presence of a tie.

- An *edge list*: This is simply a list of all the edges present in the network (i.e. where $x_{ij} \neq 0$) in three columns, describing the sender *i*, the receiver *j* and the value of the tie x_{ij}. If the network is binary, the third column x_{ij} is often dropped because it is 1 for all rows in the list.

Figure 4.1 depicts a small example of an undirected four-node network, with both its adjacency matrix and edge list. Figure 4.1(a) visualizes the network with the nodes labelled by numbers. Figure 4.1(b) shows the adjacency matrix where the first row and column in the table are headings for the node numbers. So, for instance, cell (1,1) is 0, because self-ties are not permitted; whereas cell (1,2) is 1 because there is a tie between nodes 1 and 2. Because $x_{ii} = 0$ (no self-ties), the diagonal of the matrix is forced to be 0. Notice that because the network is undirected the matrix is symmetric (the top right of the matrix above the diagonal is the same as the bottom left below the diagonal).

Figure 4.1(c) presents the same matrix without the row and column headings of node numbers. This is how it is usually presented in network data, where the first column is assumed to apply to node 1 and so on (it is for this reason that it is often convenient to label the node IDs sequentially from 1 to *n*). Figure 4.1(d) provides the edge list. Notice that because the network is undirected, the order of *i* and *j* does not matter. It is common for the full adjacency matrix to be included as in (b) and (c) even though it is symmetric (so some of the information is redundant), but it is not usual in the edge list to repeat the same undirected tie for *i* and *j* and for *j* and *i*. In other words, for an edge list, if there is a tie between nodes 1 and 2, it is entered once, and not repeated for nodes 2 and 1. Notice that in the edge list in Figure 4.1(d), the last column x_{ij} has been dropped because this is a binary network.

Figure 4.2 now presents an example where there are values on the edges. In this case, the ties may be weighted 1, 2, or 3. Now the adjacency matrix is no longer binary and the edge list includes the third column x_{ij} to indicate the values on the edges. The thickness of the lines in the visualization indicates the weights.

Figure 4.3 depicts an example of a binary directed network. Note now that the adjacency matrix is not symmetric and the order of actors in the edge list is important. (Strictly speaking, it is now an *arc list*, although the term *edge list* is still often used for directed networks.) We can see from Figure 4.3 (a) that there is an arc from node 2 to 1 but not from 1 to 2. This is represented in the matrix as a 1 in cell (2,1) but a 0 in cell (1,2). In the edge list, there is an entry for '2 1' but not for '1 2'. The presence of an arc from *i* to *j* as well as from *j* to *i* means that there are *reciprocated* or *mutual* ties between those two actors. We can see this with ties from actors 2 to 3 and from 3 to 2, with both cells in the matrix entered as 1 and both arcs entered in the edge list.

Commonly, network analysis software will require an adjacency matrix or an edge list to enter network data. The edge list seems a more efficient way to enter the data

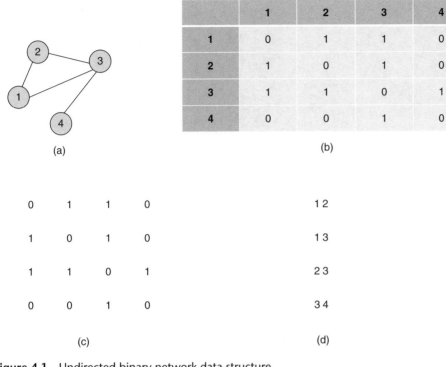

	1	2	3	4
1	0	1	1	0
2	1	0	1	0
3	1	1	0	1
4	0	0	1	0

(a)　　　　　　　　　　　　　　　　(b)

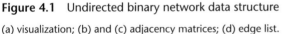

0	1	1	0
1	0	1	0
1	1	0	1
0	0	1	0

1 2
1 3
2 3
3 4

(c)　　　　　　　　　　　　　　　　(d)

Figure 4.1 Undirected binary network data structure
(a) visualization; (b) and (c) adjacency matrices; (d) edge list.

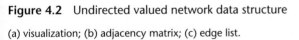

0	2	1	0
2	0	3	0
1	3	0	2
0	0	2	0

1 2 2
1 3 1
2 3 3
3 4 2

(a)　　　　　　　　　　　(b)　　　　　　　　　　　(c)

Figure 4.2 Undirected valued network data structure
(a) visualization; (b) adjacency matrix; (c) edge list.

because, of course, by definition it does not require any 0s to be entered, whereas in the matrix both 0s and 1s are included. However, it is easy to see that certain features of networks can be extracted from the adjacency matrix. In a binary undirected network, the degree of each actor is the sum across the rows (or the columns). For those who like mathematical formulae, the degree for actor i then is simply $\sum_{j=1}^{n} x_{ij}$.

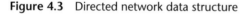

	1	2	3	4
1	0	0	1	0
2	1	0	1	0
3	0	1	0	0
4	0	0	1	0

(a)   (b)

0	0	1	0
1	0	1	0
0	1	0	0
0	0	1	0

1 3
2 1
2 3
3 2
4 3

(c)   (d)

Figure 4.3   Directed network data structure

(a) visualization; (b) and (c) adjacency matrices; (d) edge list.

Again for a binary undirected network, the total number of edges L is the sum of all the cells in the matrix, divided by 2 for an undirected network because the top right of the matrix is the same as the bottom left – in short, just count all the 1s in the matrix and divide by 2 (i.e., $L = \frac{1}{2}\sum_{i=1}^{n}\sum_{j=1}^{n} x_{ij}$).

The number of cells in the matrix is obviously n^2, but n of these are along the diagonal and forced to be 0, so cannot be edges. Because the cells below and above the diagonal are symmetric, only half of the non-diagonal cells represent distinct data, so the largest possible number of edges is $(n^2 - n)/2 = n(n - 1)/2$. Hence, the density of the observed network – the proportion of observed ties to possible ties – is $2L/n(n-1)$, as noted in Chapter 2.

In Figure 4.1(b), as $n = 4$, we have $n(n - 1)/2 = 6$, which means there are six cells above (or below) the diagonal, as can readily be seen from the figure. As four of these contain 1s, the density is $4/6 = 0.67$.

For directed networks, on the other hand, row i in the adjacency matrix represents the choices of network partners made by i as sender, so that the sum of the row is the out-degree of $i(\sum_{j=1}^{n} x_{ij})$. The sum of the i-th column is the in-degree of i ($\sum_{j=1}^{n} x_{ji}$). Now there is no symmetry, so the total number of arcs is $L = \sum_{i=1}^{n}\sum_{j=1}^{n} x_{ij}$ and the density is $L/n(n-1)$.

So just by looking at Figure 4.3(c), we can see that the out-degree of node 1 is 1 (i.e. the number of 1s in the first row), and the in-degree is also 1 (the number of 1s in the first column). Node 3 has an in-degree of 3 (the third column). Here the number of possible ties (non-diagonal cells in the matrix) is $n(n-1) = 12$. There are five arcs in this network, so the density is 5/12.

If you have some basic programming skills, it is not difficult to convert a binary edge list into an adjacency matrix. Box 4.2 describes a simple algorithm to do this. If you do not have programming skills, do not worry: if ever you need to do this, there is software that will do it for you (Chapter 9).

BOX 4.2

Creating an adjacency matrix from an edge list

1 Determine the number of nodes n and check that the nodes are numbered from 1 to n in the edge list (change the coding of the node IDs if not.)
2 Determine the number of edges L in the edge list.
3 Create an $n \times n$ matrix G with cells $G(i, j) = 0$.
4 Read in the edge list E as a $2 \times L$ matrix.
5 Loop though the L rows of E.

   o For each row r in E, set $i = E(r, 1)$ and set $j = E(r, 2)$.
   o Set $G(i, j) = 1$.
   o (If the network is undirected) Set $G(j, i) = 1$.

6 Finish when the loop in step 5 is complete.

There is an additional method of recording binary network ties – that of a *node list* or an *adjacency list*. In this method, the 'focal' node is placed in a first column and then every node connected to it is listed in subsequent columns. A new row presents a new focal node. The node list method is convenient for data entry, but usually needs to be converted into an edge list or adjacency matrix for entering into network software.

Multiplex networks

In a multiplex network study, there are several different types of relational ties on the same set of nodes. For instance, an organizational network study might examine collaboration, trust and friendship among a set of managers (e.g., Rank et al., 2010).

This case is a simple extension of the whole network data structure, except that there are now multiple adjacency matrices or edge lists, one for each type of relational tie (X_{ijm} where m goes from 1 to k for k different types of relational ties). These may be entered into k different files, or in some cases, if required, the matrix can be 'stacked' into one $kn \times n$ matrix in the one file as described below for longitudinal networks. (The choice here often depends on how the data will be processed after entry, in particular the form in which different software tools require the data.)

Cognitive social structures

Cognitive social structure data is an extension of a whole network study, but actors within the network boundary are asked about not only their own ties but also their perception of the ties among all other actors. In this case there is one adjacency matrix or edge list for actors' reports of their own ties, but each actor also has his or her own adjacency matrix reporting knowledge of ties among other actors in the network.

If there are many actors in the network, this may be a demanding task for the participant. The number of possible ties for an undirected network is $n(n - 1)/2$, which increases with the square of n, so for large n there may be very many possible ties for participants to report on. It is perhaps for this reason that this design is not very commonly used. The data structure for this design is similar to a multiplex design, except that now X_{ijm} indicates actor m perceiving a tie or not between actors i and j.

Snowball samples

Figure 4.4 depicts a two-wave snowball sample design. The first wave of data collection involves starting from a seed set of actors (perhaps from a random sample of nodes) and collecting data on their network ties. Pattison et al. (2013) referred to the seed set as *zone 0* nodes: in Figure 4.4 they are represented by the dark grey nodes.

The ties from zone 0 nodes include ties among the seed set, but also to another set of nodes not in zone 0. In the figure, these are represented by the grey nodes (zone 1). The second wave of data collection involves ties from the zone 1 nodes. These identify additional ties among zone 1 nodes but also ties to new nodes not in zones 0 and 1: zone 2 nodes (light grey in Figure 4.4). Because this is a two-wave design, network data is not collect from the zone 2 nodes, so we do not have data among those nodes, or among other nodes beyond zone 2. If there were more waves, we would continue to collect network data from each zone of actors until we reach the requisite number of waves. The dotted lines in the figure represent the boundaries of the different zones. Notice that a full two-wave snowball sample necessarily reaches all nodes within geodesic distance 2 of a seed set node. More generally, if there are k waves, the snowball sample comprises all nodes within geodesic distance k of a seed set node.

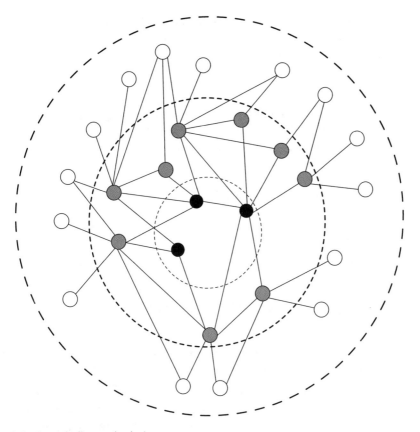

Figure 4.4 Snowball sample design

For a snowball sample, the data can still be presented as an edge list or an adjacency matrix, but an additional variable should be included for each node: namely, its zone. In data entry terms this may be included as an attribute variable, as discussed below when we come to attributes.

It is particularly important to note that in a snowball sample there are additional forced zeros and unobserved ties. For instance, by design in the data collection, it is impossible to have ties between zone 0 and zone 2, so they must be zeros in the adjacency matrix. None of the ties among zone 2 nodes are observed. Just as with the diagonal in a whole network adjacency matrix, they should not be included in any relevant calculations (such as the calculation of density). This shows that simply collecting snowball samples, entering data into an adjacency matrix and performing standard calculations (e.g., for density) without taking into account the snowball sample design is a serious error.

Figure 4.5 represents the adjacency matrix data for an undirected network (hence only the matrix above the diagonal is presented) showing what is known when a two-wave snowball is used. The nodes in the network are blocked and ordered by zones. Ties among zone 0 nodes and between zone 0 and 1 are observed, as are ties between zone 1 and 2 nodes. By design there are no ties between zone 0 and zone 2 and remaining nodes (i.e. beyond zone 2), and between zone 1 and remaining nodes. All other ties are not observed.

	Zone 0 nodes	Zone 1 nodes	Zone 2 nodes	Remaining nodes
Zone 0 nodes	Observed	Observed	0	0
Zone 1 nodes		Observed	Observed	0
Zone 2 nodes			Not known	Not known
Remaining nodes				Not known

Figure 4.5 Regions of an adjacency matrix for a snowball sample design

The point of collecting a snowball sample is to make inferences applicable to the whole network using just the snowball data. Figure 4.5 shows that the zone structure of the nodes is a crucial part of the data, and if it is ignored incorrect results will follow. In Chapter 9, I will discuss some methods for the analysis of snowball samples.

The data structure for respondent-driven sampling has some similarities to snowball sampling but can differ in that some chains of referrals can be much longer than others. In this case, the data is best not conceptualized as a neat square matrix (albeit with gaps) as in Figure 4.5. You are more likely to have a tree-like structure, possibly with some intersecting branches (Heckathorn, 1997). Some branches in the tree will be short (or non-existent) when respondents do not recruit or recruit few partners. It is very important, however, to know who has recruited whom and for this to be recorded in your datafiles. Because RDS is typically applied to actor attributes rather than to network structure (the network structure is used as a sampling device to get at the attributes), this recruiting information will usually suffice in drawing sensible conclusions about the attribute distribution (Chapter 9).

Bipartite network data

Recall that a bipartite network has two types of nodes with ties between nodes of different types but not between nodes of the same type. Bipartite data often represents memberships, participation or attendance. For instance, bipartite data on company directors has ties from directors to their various company boards (reflecting membership), but no ties between companies or between directors.

Suppose that there are *m* and *n* nodes of the two different types. It may be more convenient to code IDs for the nodes from 1 to *m+n*, rather than have two separate codings for different node types. Bipartite data can then be represented in edge list or adjacency matrix form. In edge list form, it is probably best that the two columns (assuming binary data, i.e. no third column of tie strength x_{ij}) consistently represent the two different types of nodes (i.e. nodes of one type always in the first, and of the second type always in the second). The adjacency matrix is an $m \times n$ matrix and no longer square (unless it so happens that $m = n$), with no forced zeros on the diagonal.

Figure 4.6 presents an example of a bipartite network, together with its associated edge list and adjacency matrix. Suppose this is a network of two people (nodes 1 and 2) attending three events (nodes 3, 4, 5). The first row of the 2×3 matrix in Figure 4.6(c) represents the attendances by person 1 (i.e., at all three events), while the second row shows that person 2 did not attend event 4.

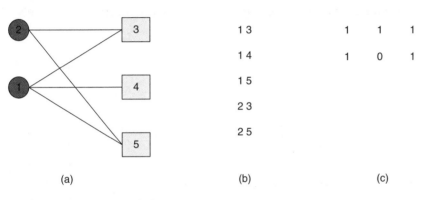

1 3	1	1	1
1 4	1	0	1
1 5			
2 3			
2 5			

(a) (b) (c)

Figure 4.6 Bipartite network data structure
(a) visualization; (b) edge list; (c) adjacency matrix

Again, many simple network properties can be calculated from the matrix. The sums of the rows still constitutes a degree distribution as for unipartite networks, but here each row sum indicates how many events were attended be each actor (3 for person 1, and 2 for person 2). The sum of each columns shows how many people attended each event (2 for events 3 and 5, and 1 for event 4). There are no forced zeros in this matrix, so the total possible number of ties is the number of cells ($2 \times 3 = 6$). As there are five 1s in the matrix, the density of the bipartite network is 5/6.

It is relatively rare for a study to collect *k*-partite data with $k > 2$ – that is, with *k* types of nodes. Mische (2008) provided an example of tripartite data, when she studied a Brazilian political movement with three types of nodes: political activists, organizations and events. Activists could be members of (multiple) organizations and attend events; organizations could be officially represented at events. Formally, in this case there is a three-way data array, rather than a two-way matrix as in Figure 4.6(c). More conveniently, tripartite data can be represented by three two-way matrices: for the Mische data, these were activist × organization, activist × event, and organization × event.

Multilevel networks

Recall that multilevel networks have two types of nodes (thought of as at different levels) with a bipartite network representing associations between the two types of nodes, and unipartite networks among the nodes at each level: that is, two types of nodes and three types of ties.

Figure 4.7 shows an example bipartite network and how it can be represented in three matrices. Here, following Wang et al. (2013), I have labelled the two types of nodes *A* - circular in the visualization in Figure 4.7(a)) – and *B* (square), so that we have an *A* network among the circular nodes, a *B* network among the square nodes and an *X* network of bipartite ties between *A* and *B* nodes. The *A*, *X* and *B* adjacency matrices are presented in Figure 4.7(b), (c) and (d), respectively. The

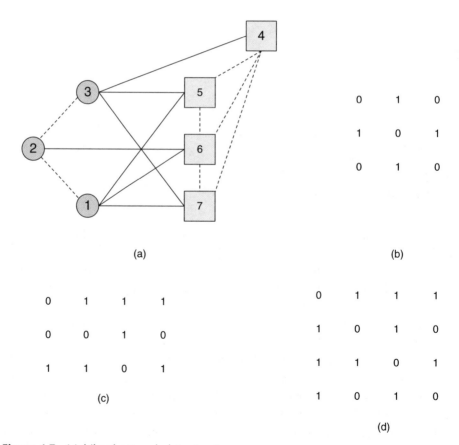

(a)

(b)

(c)

(d)

Figure 4.7 Multilevel network data structure

(a) visualization; (b) A-matrix (circular nodes); (c) X-matrix (bipartite); (d) B-matrix (square nodes)

A and B matrices are square with 0s down the diagonal, just as one would expect for unipartite whole networks. The X network is rectangular as for a bipartite network.

Of course, the three matrices in Figure 4.7 can be combined into one larger 7 × 7 matrix with the cells representing the links present in the visualization. In organizational and defence network research, Kathleen Carley (2003) proposed such a *meta-matrix* where the nodes represented people, resources and tasks: people have resources and tasks (as well as social ties), tasks require resources, and so on.

Longitudinal panel network data

The most commonly used network longitudinal design is for whole network data to be collected at multiple time-points. For instance, for the four-node network in Figure 4.1(a), the ties among the four nodes might be measured across three time periods. This assumes that the network ties change but the nodes are present throughout.

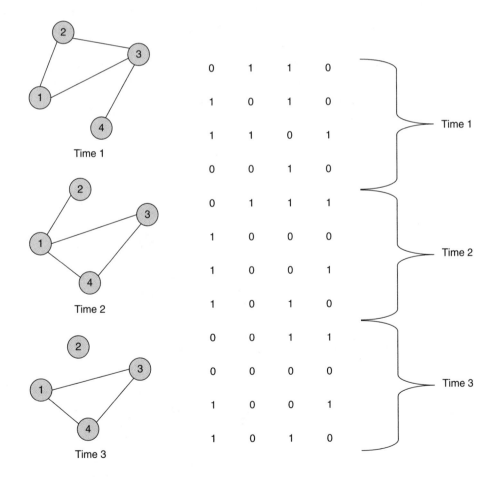

Figure 4.8 Panel longitudinal network data structure

This assumption may be appropriate in certain contexts, but not in others. In a school classroom, for example, the students may be unchanged across the one term, but their friendships may change.

In this case, we have three adjacency matrices, one for each time-point, which can be 'stacked' into the one rectangular matrix, as long as it is understood that the first n rows belongs to the first time-point, the second n to the second time-point, and so on (Figure 4.8). Alternatively, the three matrices can be stored in three separate data-files. In Figure 4.8, supposing that the relationship is friendship, we see that from time 1 to time 2, actor 2 ceases to be a friend with actor 3, and a new friendship is formed between actors 1 and 4. By time 3, actor 2 has ceased to be friends with the other actors.

Further complexity is introduced when the node set is not constant across time. For instance, a student may leave the school or a new student may arrive; or a company may cease to do business, or a new company may start up operations. So nodes can come into and out of existence. There is no unique method to enter network data with a changing node set: much depends on the proposed method of analysis. Sometimes researchers simply enter distinct panels for each time step, including both the adjacency matrix and a listing of the nodes present at that time. This would enable, for instance, calculation of the density at each time-point, irrespective of the nodes present. Sometimes it may be convenient to treat the boundary of the network as all nodes that appear at any time-point, but for a particular time the rows and columns for 'dead' nodes are forced to be zero.

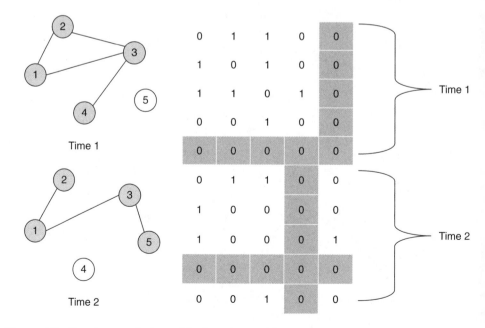

Figure 4.9 Panel network data with changing node set

For instance, in Figure 4.9, a two-panel longitudinal study, node 5 is not present at time 1 and node 4 is not present at time 2, as indicated by the non-filled nodes in the figure. There are some changes to ties among the nodes that are present across both time-points, and of course if a node is 'dead' at a particular time-point it can have no ties. Here the stacked matrix comprises two 5×5 adjacency matrices, but with row and column 5 fixed at 0 for time 1 and row and column 4 fixed at 0 for time 2 (these are shaded grey in the figure). The forced zeros need to be taken into account in doing any calculations: for instance, these cells need to be excluded when calculating the density, just as we excluded the diagonal cells from the original density calculation.

Event-based and other time-stamped relational data

Sometimes, instead of having panel network data, we have transactions between actors at a given time-point. For instance, the data might comprise telephone call data, where actor i phones actor j at time t. At its simplest, only the sequence of events might be recorded, perhaps in an edge list, where the first edge is the caller and receiver for the first phone call, the second edge the caller and the receiver for the second phone call, and so on. If the times that the calls started and ended are recorded, these would usually be entered as a third and fourth column, perhaps minutes or seconds after time 0, where time 0 could be the start of the first phone call.

Often event-based relational data need to be further processed for analysis. For instance, in some event history models, the number of possible phone calls at the given time (the 'risk set' of possible events at t) needs to be included in the dataset before analysis. This requires knowing which nodes are active at which time. Special purpose software is often used for this additional processing of the basic data structure.

Actor attributes: Putting individuals back into the network

Social networks are representations of social systems. Social systems are not just a collection of relational ties but also include individual actors. The best of social network research captures a balance between the individual and the system, between actor attributes and social structure. While much network research might focus on the network structure, it would be an unusual *social* network study that did not take into account individual variables of some type. Of course, the precise nature of the individual observations depends on the research question, the theoretical impetus behind the study, and the effects that need to be controlled in order to draw correct inferences about the processes at the centre of the research.

In this section, I describe the types of individual measures that can be used, the types of construct that might be considered, and appropriate data structures. I also make a few comments about dyadic covariates, which are network-like data structures that might help explain the network data under consideration. Often these are derived from observations on individuals. I will conclude the chapter by describing egonet data, a particular combination of individual and network variables.

Before we proceed, however, it is worth noting that sometimes research decisions need to be made about what counts as an individual, a node in our network. This is not a matter of defining the network boundary; rather, sometimes the definition of a node itself may be ambiguous. For most studies this issue is irrelevant and so is usually overlooked in texts on network analysis.

Let me explain. If the study is of students in a classroom, then the nodes are obviously the students. A study of organizations, however, is not always so clear-cut. Should a local government be seen as one organization, or should its different departments be treated as separate nodes? Should a bank be seen as one node, or separate bank branches? In a study of social ecological systems, Bodin and Tengö (2012) treated forests as separate nodes, but some forests were in close proximity, almost to the point of overlap. In this case the researchers could rely on distinctions between forests made by the local people, but in other contexts it may not be so clear-cut. When node definition is vague, there is no hard and fast solution, nor is there a general method. Rather, a careful research decision needs to be made based on theoretical grounds, knowledge of the specific context, or reasonable pragmatic considerations.

Types of individual constructs

The constructs to be considered are of course entirely dependent on the research question and include any individual effect relevant to the social system. In short, any construct used in other areas of social science is potentially applicable. Box 4.3 describes some of the types of individual constructs used in social network research, where the actors are people. Several different types may be relevant to the one study. There would be a different set of constructs for organizations, animals and so on.

These types of constructs will be familiar to social science researchers. It is at this point that other areas of social science most directly intersect with network research. If you have a carefully designed scale of attitudes, for instance, with reliability tested and the factor analytic structure of the scale well understood, this can still be used in social network research. Indeed, network researchers could learn much from the careful approach to observation of individual attributes adopted in other areas of social science. Too often, network researchers think that the skill lies in the network analysis, not in the observation and measurement. But with poor measurement of actor attributes, the finely tuned analysis is likely to prove meaningless in drawing conclusions about the individuals and possibly about the network structure.

BOX 4.3

Common types of individual constructs

1. *Demographic*: It is usual in social science research to collect some simple demographics on participants, such as sex or age. These remain relevant in social network research. For a start, it is good to report descriptive statistics about your actors, just as we would with a more traditional sample. But, additionally, the possibility of homophily effects for sex or age means that such attributes may be important factors in network structure.

2. *Social (or other) categories*: Individuals can belong to various groups that might be relevant in the network. Sometimes these might be considered demographic (e.g., ethnicity), but on other occasions the categories might be important aspects of the social setting within which the research takes place. For instance, in an organization, workers might be part of different divisions or work teams.

3. *Physical*: Certain physical attributes of the individual may be relevant, depending on the study. For instance, disease status is obviously relevant when studying the spread of contagious diseases. De la Haye et al. (2010) used the Body-Mass Index of adolescents in a study of eating behaviors in networks. External physical attributes may also be considered, such as the physical location of individuals if geospatial effects are considered.

4. *Behavioral*: The behavior of the actors can be relevant: for example, adoption of an innovation (Valente, 2005); a health-related behavior such as smoking or drinking (Light et al., 2013); teenage delinquency (Snijders and Baerveldt, 2003).

5. *Attitudinal*: The attitudes of individuals may be the topic of an influence study, where attitudinal change may be influenced by network partners. Attitudes may also affect other individual variables in a study, or the network structure itself.

6. *Psychological*: There is a small but growing body of work on the intersection of psychological factors, such as personality traits, and network structure (for more, see Chapter 6).

Types of individual measurement and data structures

There are basically three types of observations that can be applied to actor attributes. These are familiar from regular social science research.

- *Binary*: Binary observations include variables such as sex (male/female). It is often good to code these as 0 or 1.
- *Categorical*: Actors may be grouped into certain categories: for instance, ethnic group or work division. Numbers may be assigned to these categories but they are no more than indicators of similarities or differences (i.e. actors may be members of the same or different categorical group) and the actual values should not be considered.

○ Sometimes in social science, the categories may be ordered (*ordinal measurement*) so that a larger number does indicate a difference in a particular direction. Ranks are a good example: for instance, ordinal measures of a horse race indicate which horse comes 1st, 2nd, 3rd, ... Ordinal actor attributes are not as common in social network research.

- *Continuous*: Actors will have different ages, for instance, where the numbers represent a continuous measure of time.

Irrespective of the type of measure, each actor attribute variable can be entered into a dataset as a separate column, as is the standard practice in social science research. Mathematically, each attribute variable can be thought of as a *vector* (a single column of numbers). It is important that the row numbers coincide with the numbering of the nodes and hence with the row numbering of the adjacency matrix. In network visualizations, binary and categorical attributes are often represented with different colors on the nodes, and continuous attributes by different node sizes.

Figure 4.10 shows an example of the three different types of attribute variables for the network of four nodes in Figure 4.1. Here, the binary variable 'Sex' represents males (0) and females (1); the categorical variable 'Dept' represents three different departments in an organization; and the continuous variable 'Age' represents the age of the actors.

Node ID	Sex	Dept	Age
1	1	1	27
2	0	3	36
3	0	2	25
4	1	3	27

Figure 4.10 Attribute variables

For those who know some basic matrix algebra, simple results can be derived from a combination of the adjacency matrix and the attribute vector. For instance, multiplying the adjacency matrix by a binary attribute variable (coded 0 and 1) gives a vector with each row signifying how many network partners with attribute value 1 the row actor has. So, for instance, multiplying the adjacency matrix in Figure 4.1(c) by the vector for the attribute 'Sex' in Figure 4.10 gives the number of female network partners for each actor, as shown in Figure 4.11. We see, for instance, that actors 1 and 4 are female; actor 1 is a network partner of actors 2 and 3; so actor 1 has no female network partner. Actors 2 and 3 have one and two female partners, respectively, and actor 4 none. The entry for each row in the final vector is $\sum_{j=1}^{n} x_{ij} y_j$.

0	1	1	0		1		0
1	0	1	0	×	0	=	1
1	1	0	1		0		2
0	0	1	0		1		0

Figure 4.11 Matrix multiplication of binary adjacency matrix and attribute vector

Matrix multiplication can also be used for other purposes in network analysis: for instance, multiplying an adjacency matrix by itself gives a matrix where each cell contains a count of the number of 2-paths between the two nodes. There are other different results, depending on the power and order of multiplication. These are the domain of network algebras. Mathematically inclined readers who are interested in following the topic further will find some directions in Chapter 9.

For most empirical network studies, however, we need not be too bothered by these details and you will typically not have to worry about matrix algebra.

Dyadic covariates

A study may include dyadic variables that, strictly speaking, do not constitute a social network, but do have the same data structure as a network. Such data are typically not at the centre of interest in a study but may be treated as 'covariates', in that the network structure that is the focus of attention may be affected in some way by the dyadic covariate. A good example is geospatial distance between actors. In some studies, the distance between actors (e.g., between the locations of their homes) may be theorized to affect the social network relationship between them. Current work on the integration of social networks in space is exemplified by articles in a recent special issue of the journal *Social Networks* (adams et al., 2012).

Dyadic covariates may also be derived from actor attribute data. For instance, if our interest is in age homophily, then the absolute difference in ages between pairs of actors can be treated as a dyadic covariate of the network tie. The age difference between each pair of actors is calculated, signs ignored, and the results placed in a dyadic covariate matrix as in Figure 4.12(a), which uses the age data from Figure 4.10 (mathematically, $|y_i - y_j|$). In this case, given that the data is an absolute difference, the matrix is naturally symmetric. In Figure 4.12(b), the categorical attribute variable 'Dept', describing an actor's department, is used to derive a binary dyadic covariate, 'Same department'. Figure 4.10 shows that only actors 2 and 4 come from the same department, so there is a 1 only in cells (2,4) and (4,2) in the matrix. Again the resulting matrix is naturally symmetric. A study involving such data could investigate whether friendship was related to age difference or working in the same department, using these dyadic covariates.

Notice that a positive association between a network tie and age difference implies that a tie is more likely to occur when there is a larger difference in age: that is, in situations of heterophily (the opposite of homophily). So the direction of effect needs to be taken into account when interpreting the result.

0	9	2	0		0	0	0	0
9	0	11	9		0	0	0	1
2	11	0	2		0	0	0	0
0	9	2	0		0	1	0	0
	(a)					(b)		

Figure 4.12 Dyadic covariate matrices

(a) absolute difference in ages; (b) same department (derived from Figure 4.10)

Of course, there can be additional transformations applied in creating dyadic covariates. For instance, given that some spatial distances may be very large and some comparatively small, it may be helpful to use a logarithm of the distance between actors in analysis (Daraganova et al., 2012).

Egocentric network data

I have saved a description of egocentric network data structures until the end of this chapter, because although egocentric data are often the easiest to collect, several of the features discussed above are relevant.

Recall that an egonet comprises the network neighborhood around an actor (*ego*), including the network partners of *ego*, referred to as *alters*. The neighborhood includes the ties from ego to each alter, and often alter–alter ties. An egonet is akin to a one-wave snowball sample with a seed set size of one (ego). This data can be collected by survey, but may also be available by other means (electronically, or egos might be extracted from larger whole network data.)

There are several different levels of data here and it is often helpful to enter the data into three different files:

- An ego-level file which will contain all the attribute data collected on the *egos;*
- An alter-level file which will contain attribute data about each alter, as well as the ego to which each alter refers (this variable links cases across the different files), and data about the relationship between ego and alter (e.g., type of tie, strength of tie);
- For each ego, an alter–alter file containing data on the network ties between alters (if this data is collected).

Figure 4.13 illustrates the type of files from a small example with three egos (usually, of course, there would be many more). Here the ego-level file contains an ID for each ego and a variable for the sex of each (1 for female, 2 male). In a real study, of course, there may be many such variables.

The alter file contains ID variables for the alters as well as for the relevant ego. For instance, alter 11 is an alter for ego 1. In this case, I have coded the alter ID as a two-digit number with the first digit representing the relevant ego. Of course, this only works here because there are fewer than 10 egos and fewer than 10 alters per ego; more generally, some thought should be given to the most convenient method for numbering alter IDs. In an egonet study, it is typically assumed that the alters are different from one another (i.e. that the egonets do not overlap), so the coding is unique (e.g., alter 13 is not the same as alter 32). The ego-ID variable is important here because it links the alter and the ego files. In this particular example, there are three alters for each of the three egos, but of course that does not have to be so, and usually egos will differ in the number of alters.

Additionally, in the alter file we see a variable for sex of alter with the variable name 'Sex-A' to emphasize that this variable relates to alters, not to egos. There is also a variable named 'Close' for the closeness of the relationship, here measured as binary where '1' indicates a close relationship. Notice how the tie between ego and alter becomes an attribute variable for alter: this is a peculiarity of an egonet study.

Ego-ID	Sex
1	1
2	2
3	1

Alter-ID	Ego-ID	Sex-A	Close
11	1	1	1
12	1	2	0
13	1	2	0
21	2	2	1
22	2	2	1
23	2	2	0
31	3	1	1
32	3	1	1
33	3	2	1

0	1	1
1	0	0
1	0	0

| Ego file | Alter file | Alter-alter file for Ego1 |

Figure 4.13   Data structure for an egonet study

Figure 4.13 also presents the alter–alter file for ego 1 in the form of an adjacency matrix. In this egonet, alter 11 is tied to alter 12 and 13 but there is no tie between alters 12 and 13. The egonet for ego 1 is visualized in Figure 4.14. The node for ego is a box, and nodes for alters are circles. A filled node indicates *Sex* and *Sex-A* = 1, and a thicker line represents *Close* = 1. Ego is of course tied to all alters but only to alter 11 with a thick line. Alters 12 and 13 are not tied.

There could be separate alter–alter files for each ego, but sometimes it is more convenient to enter this data into one file with an additional variable to indicate which matrix belongs to which ego. It is also possible to code this as an edge list, rather than a matrix. An edge list might include three columns, one for the ego and one each for the relevant pair of alters.

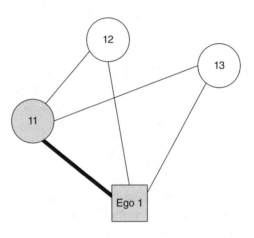

Figure 4.14 Egonet

For ego 1 from Figure 4.13

What is often done in terms of analysis is to create some additional variables from the alter–alter file to add to the ego file. For instance, the density of the alter–alter network indicates the extent of closure in ego's social environment: conversely, a lower density suggests that ego is in more of a brokerage position. Ignoring the variable *Close*, the alter–alter file for ego 1 is an undirected network and has two out of a possible three ties (remember ego and ego's ties are not included), so the density is 0.67. Let us suppose that the densities for the alter–alter networks for egos 2 and 3 (not shown in Figure 4.13) are 0.33 and 1.00, respectively.

In Figure 4.15, I have added these densities as a variable *Dens* to the ego file. Similarly, variables from the alter file can be aggregated into the ego file. I have also included additional variables: proportion of same sex alters (*Samesx*) and proportion of close partners (*Nclose*). For ego1, only one alter is the same sex and only one is close, so these proportions are 1/3.

Ego-ID	Sex	Dens	Samesx	Nclose
1	1	0.67	0.33	0.33
2	2	0.33	1.00	0.67
3	1	1.00	0.67	1.00

Figure 4.15 Expanded ego file

Including variables aggregated from the alter file and alter–alter files from Figure 4.13

There are usually important decisions to be made about the method of aggregation. In Figure 4.15, I could have used the number of same sex and close partners, rather than the proportion. Such choices are theoretical decisions that need to be thought through carefully. In this particular case, it makes no difference because each ego has three alters, but in reality the number of alters will differ and quite often dramatically. In that case, the counts of particular alters (e.g., females) may vary considerably from the proportion. Suppose, for instance, your egonet study is about social support. In order to feel well supported, is it sufficient to have a small number of strong friends who offer support, irrespective of how many friends you have, or is it necessary to have a high proportion of all your friends as supporters? The number and proportion have different theoretical implications.

Often the analysis will then be conducted using standard statistical techniques on the expanded ego file: for instance, in Figure 4.15 correlations and regressions could be conducted among the continuous variables and differences in means compared between sexes. Those readers familiar with hierarchical linear modelling (Snijders and Bosker, 2012) will note, however, that the datafile in Figure 4.15 and the alter file in Figure 4.13 are jointly suitable for multilevel modelling, with alters nested within egos. A multilevel model could then be used to predict alter attribute variables[1]. This could include predicting the type of relationship between ego and alter, given that in egonet studies the type of ego–alter tie (close or not close, in our example) becomes an attribute variable in the alter file.

In conclusion: The key point

As researchers, we all need to know how to enter data in the right form, but the right form itself reveals important aspects of the research design. So this is not just a *how*

---

[1]Do not confuse a *hierarchical linear model* – often called a 'multilevel model' – with multilevel networks. In this context, a multilevel model is a statistical model for nested data more generally, not specifically for networks. A multilevel network is a particular network data structure as explained earlier.

to do it chapter. Rather, an understanding of these different data structures will give an understanding of network-based research design.

The chapter also emphasizes – albeit, implicitly – *choice*. We have a variety of data structures. The first step is to decide which best applies to our study. This is not just a personal preference but crucially determines, and is determined by, our theoretical position. If we adopt bipartite data when the theoretical context demands a unipartite representation, we risk making horrible mistakes in inference. Once we have made the serious decision about why we should adopt a particular data structure, then we have to engage with the difficult question of which types of tie to investigate, which types of attributes and so on. These are not decisions based on numbers or measures, convenience or habit: these are matters of theory. I do not mean a 'Theory of X, Y or Z' but, rather, a theoretical argument which involves an understanding of the research context, previous work and existing knowledge. Then the decisions about the right data structures and the right variables can be made on the most solid ground.

BOX 4.4

Pulling back the curtain: What goes on in real network studies

For the sporting team study, we used a whole network approach. We had a complete list of current athletes in the club, so – as explained in Chapter 3 – the network boundary was relatively unambiguous. In Chapter 3, I described the difficult decisions made about the types of ties and attributes to measure. In the end we had several different types of ties, each of which were entered into a separate adjacency matrix analogous to that shown in Figure 4.3(c), with attribute variables entered into a datafile in the form shown in Figure 4.10.

For the organizational collaboration study, as explained in Chapter 3, the boundary was uncertain, so we employed a snowball sampling strategy in an effort to determine a sensible boundary. As in Figure 4.4, we had a core set of organizations that we knew were definitely relevant: these became our seed set. By asking informants from each of these organizations which other bodies were major collaboration partners of their own organization, we uncovered the collaboration ties among our seed set and snowballed out to a first zone of other organizations. We then sought to interview informants from those organizations, and so on. There is an issue of how many waves of snowball sampling are necessary. Ideally, there should be as many waves as required until no new organizations are named, but there are usually funding and timing constraints that need to be taken into account. For instance, if an organization is nominated by only one, or a small number, of the more central organizations, then perhaps that organization could be treated as peripheral and not interviewed. What counts as a 'small number' needs to be decided: there is no established rule.

In our case, the snowball approach after one wave seemed to capture the most central actors, with other actors more peripheral and of lower degree. Due to resource constraints, we concentrated our analysis on these central actors. At this point we reverted to a whole network study among these central actors, so did not explicitly invoke the data structures of Figures 4.4 and 4.5.

A question arises about whether we can find the entire boundary if the network is disconnected and our seed set only includes nodes that are likely to be tied to each other. Then it may be impossible to find separated components. In our case, due to local knowledge and the specific context, we were confident that major players would have some connection – perhaps indirect – to our seed set nodes, so this was not an issue for us. More generally, the extent of such a problem may be investigated by sampling some actors who seem more remote and disconnected from the original seed set, to see whether a snowball from them may eventually reconnect. The choice of such actors may not be obvious, however, and resource constraints in data collection need to be taken into account.

FIVE

Network observation and measurement

This is the first of two chapters on network data collection. In this chapter, I review general issues about network observation and measurement. In the next chapter, I discuss data collection in specific empirical contexts.

I will often use the three terms 'observation', 'measurement' and 'data collection' interchangeably, although to be precise there are important differences among them. In particular, *measurement* implies the assignment of numbers to the objects of study. *Measurement* seemingly implies quantitative rather than qualitative work, but, as I noted in Chapter 4, a qualitative researcher at least may wish to use a binary tie measure as input into software to visualize an egocentric network. Later in this chapter, there are sections about the use of name generators and the like relevant to qualitative researchers. And the argument that I will make in the next section, although couched in terms of measurement, can also be translated to qualitative data.

Some network measurement theory

Network measurement has similarities with measurement in other areas of social science, but also some striking differences. For much social science, the 'objects of study' are individuals from a population, studied through data collection from a sample. As will now be apparent, the 'objects of study' for network research may be individual actors but also include social ties between actors, and possibly the network system as a whole (or systems, if multiple networks are studied). The fact that measurement may occur at different levels simultaneously (individuals, dyads, the whole network) is a complicating factor that distinguishes network studies from some other areas of social science.

But there are deeper arguments about the distinctiveness of network research. In Chapter 1, I noted the Brandes et al. (2013b) argument about how network science differs from more standard social science. Let us now be a little more precise.

In doing so, I will present a theoretical argument about network measurement. If that argument proves overly abstract to your taste, there is no need to wrestle with the detail of this section. My basic point is to show that network research goes beyond standard social science by making some strong theoretical commitments that are bound up deeply with network measurement and observation. In that sense, measurement and observation of networks is at the heart of what we do in our social network science.

Social science measurement

In much social science, we observe a sample of individuals and apply a measure to them (for instance, suppose we measure their IQ, their gender or their cultural background). Formally, we apply a measurement function μ from the set of sampled individuals to a set of numbers. Any function has a *domain* and *range*, which in this case are the individuals and the set of numbers, respectively. The function 'translates' something from the domain into the range (i.e., it translates from the individual to the appropriate individual score for the construct measured).

Stevens (1946) introduced a typology of measurement scales: *nominal, ordinal, interval* and *ratio*. A nominal scale is simply a categorization, with ordinal a set of ordered categories (akin to the order of finishing in a race). Interval and ratio scales are both continuous, with a ratio scale having a real zero, where 0 does indeed mean that there is no quantity present. Measurement of temperature in degrees Fahrenheit or Celsius is ordinal because 0 does not indicate the total absence of heat; measurement of my bank balance is a ratio scale as zero means no money.

IQ is measured on an interval scale, where the intervals among the numbers are meaningful. In theory, IQ can range between 0 and a very large number, but in practice an IQ score falls between 70 and 130 for most people. Given an interval scale, it makes sense, for instance, to calculate an average, so that the numeric operations of addition and division are possible. Hence we can talk of average IQ. But because 0 is an arbitrary IQ score, it does not make sense to speak of ratios: so your IQ might be larger than mine, but we cannot say it is twice as large.

With a ratio scale, on the other hand, we can also take ratios between different measures, so that your bank balance might indeed be twice as large as mine. Such a ratio is not sensible without a real zero. Gender and cultural background, in contrast, are measured on a nominal scale, where numbers are applied simply to signify categories. In this case, the researcher chooses certain numbers, and hence determines the range of μ. The only 'numeric' operation that is appropriate is '=', where the equality of two numbers indicates two individuals with the same gender or cultural background. Calculation of a mean or a ratio makes no sense at all.

So, the type of scale we use imposes a particular structure on the numbering system and that structure affects the operations that make sense.

Whether we choose Stevens's typology or some other (Stevens is not without his critics), the point is that a structure on the range of μ determines the 'level of measurement'. In short, typical social science research imposes a structure on our measurement: but only on the *range* of μ, not the domain. With no structure on the domain, the individuals are assumed to be independent of each other. Much research design goes to great lengths to ensure this, often through random sampling of participants.

Network science measurement

According to Brandes et al., on the other hand, network science explicitly assumes dyadic structure on the *domain* of μ. Dependencies arise from the network ties that are assumed to constitute that structure. Hence, independence among individuals is explicitly denied and random sampling irrelevant (and sometimes downright wrong, as I argued in Chapter 1). In network terminology, the measurement function μ is now a measure of actor attributes.

But now the network ties are themselves available for empirical observation and analysis. So a separate measurement function μ' maps these dyadic dependencies onto a two-way array (actor-by-actor), the adjacency matrix. Hence, as in Chapter 4, we have separate data structures for network ties and for actor attributes, but data structures that can be linked as shown in that chapter.

This account about the distinctiveness of network science emphasizes an underlying theoretical base (structure on the *domain* μ is assumed and then empirically investigated through μ') integrated with a deep linkage to measurement (both μ and μ' are specifically measurement functions). What happens, you may ask, if the theoretical assumption of the presence of the structure, the network, is wrong? Well, if our analysis shows that the network ties bear no relationship with the attributes, then the network structure is irrelevant, and we can revert to the simpler procedures of standard social science. The network assumption can be tested and rejected.

I noted in Chapter 1 that just as there can be dependence among actors through network ties, there can also be dependence among network tie variables. These create tendencies toward certain network patterns, such as reciprocity and network closure, exemplified in some of the network theories described in Chapter 2. As we will see later, there are analytic methods to search for these patterns, and a number of hypotheses about such network tie dependence are available (Pattison and Snijders, 2013). This is rather deep social network theory which readers can safely avoid at this point – but some of the more enthusiastic may wish to follow up.

This abstruse theorizing about network science and network dependence may seem a little remote for a book that is meant to provide a practical approach to network research design. Most readers can ignore these abstractions and focus on the pragmatics. Nevertheless, the argument emphasizes how a network approach is not merely an add-on to existing methods, but rather entails strong theoretical commitments that are bound up quite deeply with observation and measurement.

As a corollary, let me add that to undertake social network research is not just to do *social network analysis* (SNA). Even to conceptualize such research is to adopt social network theory, at least implicitly, long before there are any data. Collecting the data entails strong network theoretical commitments, whatever our analysis may eventually be. So, beware the use of 'SNA' as an umbrella acronym: leave it for the actual analysis. The measurement of social networks is not SNA.

Populations and samples

Let me briefly return to an issue introduced in Chapter 1: populations and samples. Because social science often relies on careful sampling from a postulated population of individuals, we need to think carefully about how these ideas play out in a network study. In Chapter 1, I pointed out how difficult it may be to translate the usual approaches to populations and samples into network terms.

Sampling of networks

But this does not mean that these ideas are irrelevant or never applicable. For instance, you may need to sample networks themselves. Egonet studies provide a good example. Often egonets are studied across a sample of individual respondents who come from a population of egos. A multiple network study also involves a sample of networks. Within each *unit* (Chapter 3) there is a separate network. The units are typically assumed to come from some population of units: a sample of school classroom networks comes from a population of classrooms.

In these cases, thought needs to be given to how the population is defined. For instance, is the population of classrooms based on the one education system, or one region, or is it more universal? These decisions will enable a sampling frame from which to sample units or egos, with the usual considerations given to random sampling, stratified sampling and so on. Here there is no distinction from familiar social science sampling methods, with the exception that some care may need to be given to ensuring that the units and egonets do not overlap or are not connected directly to one another.

How large a sample is required? For egonet studies and multiple network studies, you should be guided by sample size considerations applicable to your area of social science. An egonet study can be treated like a study of individuals in this sense. When it comes to multiple network studies, the usual suggestion in standard multilevel studies is that there should be at least 20 or 25 units (Snijders and Bosker, 2012), although this rule-of-thumb from hierarchical linear modelling may not be entirely relevant to a network study. If you have only a few networks in a multiple network study, then you are in effect dealing with comparative case studies.

Even when we sample the units or egos, we may still apply whole network data collection within the unit or ego. In other words, sampling between units does not imply that sampling within units is appropriate. It is a separate question whether or how to sample within networks.

Sampling within networks

Within a whole network with a well-defined boundary, the idea of a population starts to become ambiguous. Do the actors within the boundary constitute the population, or are they meant to be representative of actors elsewhere? And if the object of study is the network structure, then perhaps the network ties constitute the population, rather than the actors? Or perhaps it is the network system as a whole? These questions seem sufficiently arcane that many network researchers ignore the question of *population* entirely. Nevertheless, the idea of sampling within a large network, rather than collecting whole network data, has appeal, if for no other reason than to manage resources and time.

Of course, if the network is small enough (i.e., a small number of actors), then sampling is probably not necessary and a *tie census* of the whole network should be attempted, the classic unipartite data structure. In that case, ideally you want a 100% response rate, often not practical. I will say more about that when I deal with missing data below.

What counts as *small enough* for a network census? This decision needs to be tailored to each study and often depends on the pragmatics and resources of data collection. For instance, if network data is collected by respondent survey or interview, we need to avoid respondent fatigue: asking respondents to describe a huge number of possible network ties is not going to result in good data. It may be helpful to conduct a pilot study to check how well respondents manage the network census. If, on the other hand, the data is automatically collected by electronic means there may be few such issues but other pragmatics may still intervene to require a sample. For instance, in some social media research a sample may be all that is available for collection based on what the social media organization is prepared to release.

Snowball sampling, respondent-driven sampling and related methods – as described in Chapters 3 and 4 – are a natural way to sample within a network with a view to understanding or controlling for network structure. In contrast to a random sample of actors, these methods better capture structural features because they sample by utilizing the network connectivity. Still, they present their own problems in terms of manageability and difficulties in analysis, as I discuss below. Box 5.1 presents some other approaches.

Big data

To this point, I have discussed sampling as a data collection method, but it may be a computational device. For very large network datasets where all the data is already available, certain calculations are computationally very demanding, even for modern computers. In Chapter 2, I introduced *scale-up* issues for networks, where scale-up refers to changes as the number of nodes n increases. Different network properties scale up in different ways; that is, they depend on n differently and so may behave differently in large networks. This situation extends to the calculation of different network properties. Even for very large networks, it is not problematic to work out degree distributions, average degree and the like, whereas calculation of network closure is more computationally demanding.

So, with modern *big data* – network-based datasets that are collected electronically and automatically – the complete data (in a sense, the population data) may be available but certain analyses may be intractable or computationally too exacting for complete analysis. In this situation, sampling strategies might be used for efficient analysis.

BOX 5.1

Simple methods for sampling within networks

Methods related to network sampling that may help but are not always ideal:

- *Restricting responses to a maximum number of alters*: For a survey or interview, respondents may be asked to identify a *maximum* number, k, of network partners. This is usually not good practice, especially if k is small (say, 3 or 4). The method will produce strong tie partners and privileges respondents with fewer strong partners (all of their data will be collected, but only part of the data of actors with many partners). If k is sufficiently large (say, 12, 15 or more), and the average degree turns out to be substantially less than k, then there is less cause for concern.

  o If using this method, it should be emphasized to respondents that they do not have to nominate the full number of k partners.

  o And they should be instructed that there is no 'correct number' of partners to nominate: different people nominate different numbers.

- o The problems with small *k* are probably more acute when the research is about network structure, rather than social influence.

- o With small *k* the method is best applied when the researcher wants a deep examination of the nature of relationships, preferring lots of information about a few relationships, rather than a little information about many. Here one is trading detailed structural data against rich dyadic information.

- *Sampling using common names.* To avoid respondents nominating only strong tie partners, McCarty et al. (1997) proposed a novel method to sample both strong and weak ties, the *first name cue method.* Participants were presented with a list of common first names and asked whether they knew someone of that name, to a maximum number of alters. With this methodology, participants are more likely to nominate at least some weak tie partners.

- *Cognitive social structures.* A full cognitive social structure design is very demanding on participants if the number of actors is much beyond 10 or 20. With larger sets of actors (around 60), Flynn et al. (2006) randomly selected eight other actors for each participant and asked them to delineate the relationships among them. In separate work, Siciliano et al. (2012) estimated network structure based on a cognitive social structure design using only a sample of actors.

Practical issues about the network boundary for whole network studies

Let us now turn to a network census for a whole network study. To begin, there are some practical steps to be taken about the network boundary and how the actors within the boundary are to be identified (Laumann et al., 1983). Then decisions are required about the general method to collect network tie data within the boundary.

Suppose the study is of a top management team within an organization and data on trust ties are to be collected by survey or interview. The definition of top management in this organization needs to be clear to both the researcher and the participants. Prior to a survey, for instance, you might determine – by seeking expert advice, perhaps from the CEO or another senior figure – which people are in the top management team.

Then a list of these names can be presented to every top management member, each of whom is asked to nominate those whom they especially trust. This *recognition* method only requires respondents to recognize individuals, and so is not usually very demanding.

Alternatively, if the researcher is confident that there is no ambiguity among participants about the boundary, then they can simply be asked to *recall* those whom they especially trust without being presented with a list of names. In this case, respondents themselves list their trust partners. I discuss important differences between recognition and recall methods later in this chapter.

Even using the recall method, the researcher still needs to know who is in the top management team, in the first place to identify to whom to deliver the survey. Moreover, even if someone in the top management team is trusted by no one and trusts no one, and so does not appear in responses at all, the presence of a network isolate is likely valuable information. The isolated actor needs to be included in the data, even though he/she is not mentioned or identified in the data collection. So a researcher needs to check the responses against a pre-existing list of actors within the boundary. Then it becomes a practical necessity for you, the researcher, to have such a list. Of course, depending on context, the list may not be of names but may be of some other form of identifier that can be used in collecting the data (e.g. email addresses if the study were of email exchanges within an organization).

Name generators

So how do we collect survey data for a tie census in a whole network study within a well-defined boundary? The basic idea is described in the previous section: use one or more *name generator* items. A *name generator* is a survey item that asks respondents to nominate network partners. A name generator can be delivered in a variety of ways: paper-and-pencil questionnaire, face-to-face or telephone interview, or online survey. Name generators have a long tradition in social network research, and so are often associated with paper surveys. However, the concept of a name generator is quite independent of the method of delivery, and the data collection approaches in this chapter – unless mentioned otherwise – are not intended to be specific to online or offline delivery.

The point of using a name generator is to obtain information on network partners directly from the actor. A name generator will not be required when the relationships can be collected electronically from digital data, or captured by some other form of direct observation.

The name generator technique is applicable to both whole network and egonet studies. In this section I will discuss name generators for whole network studies, and later make some comments specific to egonet research.

First, let me mention an obvious point about a whole network study, but one that often gets passed over. For a tie census, you need to know who is sending and receiving the ties. So, all respondents in a whole network study need to be identified in some way. They can identify themselves on a survey, if that is how you are proceeding; or if the data is collected by interview, you need to record carefully who the interviewee is. Then you have data in the form of Figure 4.3 in Chapter 4 because you can identify the sender of the tie as well as those network partners they nominate. I will discuss the ethical implications of respondent identification in Chapter 7. For egocentric network designs, on the other hand, you do not necessarily have to know the precise identity of the participant, so they can be more anonymous.

In a whole network study, a name generator item prompts nominations of network partners either by recall or by recognition. You need to decide on the types of relational tie studied. Then you must draft name generators that elicit those types of relational ties from participants.

Suppose, in the top management team study, we are using a paper-and-pencil survey and wish to examine the advice network. Then a recall name generator might be as simple as this:

> In the space below, write the names of other members of the top management team from whom you regularly receive advice relating to your work. (Please note there is no right number of advice partners to nominate. Some people receive advice from many, and some from few. List those who are regular sources of work advice for you.)

The wording ('write the names') would of course be amended depending on alternative methods of data collection: computer entry, interview (face-to-face or telephone). A recognition version of the name generator might be worded as follows:

> Below is a list of the members of the top management team. Underline the names of those members from whom you regularly receive advice relating to your work. (Please note there is no right number of advice partners to nominate. Some people receive advice from many, and some from few. Nominate those who are regular sources of work advice for you.)

In Box 5.2, I make some comments about the particular wording of these name generator examples. Of course, there are many ways to format a survey – for instance, with columns for different name generators, where respondents might place a cross in the appropriate cell of the column – so 'underline' could be replaced by alternatives.

Sometimes, researchers limit the number of nominations a participant can make. They may ask, for instance, a question like: 'Write down three people in the top management team who provide you with advice?' In general, I do not favour restricting the number of nominations. For a start, the degree distribution is necessarily truncated, and it is possible that the fourth advisor is almost as important as the first three (see Box 5.1).

Even so, we do not necessarily want a large number of nominations, especially to minimize respondent fatigue. It is usually possible to limit the number of nominations by using stronger wording in your name generator: instead of 'list your friends', try 'list your closest friends, those whom you would rely on in difficult situations'. This version should produce a smaller number of nominations.

There is a balance here between pragmatics and not undermining the intent of the study. For instance, if your study is about weak ties, then asking for closest friend nominations is incorrect. Sometimes the issue may be specific to the research context or question. Merluzzi and Burt (2013) argued that when studying tie association with achievement in organizations, only five nominations may be sufficient for adequate data, so it may be possible to get away with a few nominations.

BOX 5.2

The wording of name generators

Let us consider the precise wording of the name generator 'other members of the top management team from whom you regularly receive advice relating to your work'.

- It requests partners who give advice to the respondent, not those to whom the respondent gives advice (and the two are likely to differ, at least for some actors). So, this data is going to be in the form of a directed network.

- It would be possible to include a second name generator, 'those to whom you provide regular advice', as a counterpart, if both advice giving and advice receiving were to be studied. These are different networks. They may agree in some dyads (i.e., actor *i* may nominate *j* as receiving advice, and *j* nominate *i* as giving advice), but the reality of social network data is that this does not always happen. Actors misperceive the social situation; they may wish to claim high status (and hence may exaggerate their advice giving and minimize their advice receiving); and they may genuinely regard occasional advice as unimportant while their partners do not. There are many reasons why giving and receiving advice are not mirror opposites.

- The name generator asks for regular, work advice. There are other possibilities, such as 'advice that is important for you to complete your work'. Instead of 'important', 'helpful' or 'crucial' could be used. Notice how wording such as 'crucial' as opposed to 'regular' will induce stronger ties and fewer network partners. We do not want participants to nominate everyone else, so do not use a weak name generator; and similarly, we do not want people to nominate hardly anyone, so we do not use a very strong name generator. It is a research decision as to the exact wording.

- If work advice is not specified, nominations may include alters who provide more general life advice (e.g., marital problems, good restaurants). If that is the research topic, the word 'work' should not be used, and respondents should be instructed that this question is about advice more generally.

- The name generator does not define 'advice'. Some researchers are quite definitive about the relational tie. Many, however, permit the respondent to decide who counts as a partner under a general descriptor, rather than being prescriptive with complex definitions.

Multiple name generators: Negative ties

If you have multiple types of tie in a multiplex study, you will have several name generators.

For some types of relational ties, especially those with emotional or affective content, participants may respond in socially desirable ways and even be cautious about nominating partners. If the network boundary defines a small group, respondents may feel uncomfortable discriminating among their colleagues. In small workplaces,

I have often found that people wish to say that they are friends with everyone (either to convince me, or themselves, or perhaps it is indeed so). I have sometimes found it useful to use a two-step name generator, first asking for 'friends' and then asking respondents to look over their list of friends to further select those they feel particularly close to. The first selection of friends usually suffices for respondents to exhibit their socially desirable responses; the second selection can then be used as data on 'close friends'.

In Chapters 2 and 3, I pointed to the possible value of including negative ties. Care needs to be taken with the definition and handling of negative ties in a survey or interview. It is usually not wise to ask respondents to nominate 'those they hate'. Even if 'hate' or even 'dislike' are the right relational tie for the research, respondents may not admit to much 'hating' or 'disliking'. Research review boards and ethics committees may take a dim view of overtly negative items. Clumsy wording may even lead to some respondents refusing to answer the question or withdrawing from the study.

In our top management team study, for instance, the goal is to study collaboration. There is probably no need to seek 'dislike' nominations. Participants may be happier to nominate those with whom they 'have difficulty collaborating'.

To elicit negative tie data, another two-step approach can be used. First, ask participants to identify those with whom they have to work to get their job done. Then, for each network partner, ask them to identify 'how easy' it is to work with them, perhaps on a five-point Likert scale with '5' signifying 'difficult'. Although the item is worded as 'easy' the goal is to obtain negative tie data. This method, of seeking additional information on the relationship after obtaining alters through a name generator, is known as a *name interpreter*.

These approaches to obtain negative tie data are not perfect, but they may be more effective than a blunt item that could disengage the respondents. Still, there are occasions when you need to be direct about a negative tie. If you are studying bullying in schools, it is difficult to avoid asking about bullying directly. Tolsma et al. (2013) adopted a whole network design with two recognition name generators: 'Whom do you bully?' and 'By whom are you bullied?' No definition of bullying was provided to the students. As children are readier to report victimization than bullying, the second of these name generators may be more fruitful (Huitsing et al., 2012b). A similar design was used by Faris and Ennett (2012) in studying adolescent aggression and social status.

Name interpreters

Once network partners have been identified through the name generator, further information on the relationship may be obtained from one or more *name interpreter* items. Name interpreters are applied to each nominated alter. In a paper-and-pencil survey, respondents are often asked to write the names of their alters into a separate table, permitting responses to name interpreters one by one. In an interview, the interviewer may do this rather than the respondent. A computer survey may be programmed to present the respondent with alters' names and name interpreters for completion.

The use and extent of name interpreters depends on the research topic. In our top management team study, we could ask respondents to report on their relationship with each advice-giving partner. For instance:

- Do you feel very close to this person?
- Do you socialize regularly with this person outside of working hours?
- Are you required by the organization to report to this person on important tasks?

The actual items depend entirely on the research question. Responses can be binary (yes/no), or in a Likert scale format:

How much support does this person provide you in your work?

1. A lot
2. Some
3. A little
4. None

The name interpreter items can be in any particular format as long as they obtain information about the respondent's perception of the nature of the dyadic relationship. In drafting these items, researchers should apply good practice in questionnaire design: no double-barrelled items, no vague wording and so on (see, for instance, Blair et al., 2014). There are no particular network-related considerations in the design of these items, apart from the fact that they pertain to relationships.

Nevertheless, be careful with the use of name interpreters. Some respondents may nominate many alters, and responding to the resulting name interpreters for each network partner can be time-consuming and tedious. So, in order to ensure that respondents continue to be engaged, it is usually sensible to limit name interpreters to those that are likely to be most crucial to the research question. In whole network studies, name interpreters can sometimes be replaced with additional name generator questions. For instance, instead of 'Do you socialize regularly with this person after work?', use an additional name generator – 'Nominate those top management team members with whom you socialize regularly outside working hours'.

In using name interpreters, thought needs to be given to the ordering, especially if there are many name generators. Name interpreters can be ordered by alter (in which case, all name interpreter items are asked of each alter one at a time, before proceeding to the next alter) or by item (in which case, each name interpreter in turn is asked of every alter, before moving to the next interpreter). Kogovšek et al. (2002) concluded that in terms of reliability it was probably preferable to order by alters rather than by interpreter items.

Other types of data collection for whole network studies

The name generator approach is clearly designed for interview or survey. Whole network data may also be derived from observation, from electronic traces and from archival records. I deal with these data collection methods in more detail in the next chapter, but let me make a few initial comments now.

Direct observation may of course require considerable time and resources, so is not all that common. In Chapter 1, I described the Hawthorne research program of the 1920s and 1930s. The Bank Wiring Room study involved an observer patiently sitting at a small desk making observations of the interaction patterns among the workers over lengthy periods. These observations were used to infer network structures for different types of relational tie.

Electronic data collection is obviously much more common nowadays. Patison et al. (2010) studied regularities in relationships within a herd of cattle by using electronic devices to record when cattle were in close proximity. Email data has been used to study network processes in organizations (Quintane et al., 2013). Facebook contacts can be used to study social capital and other network issues (Brooks et al., 2014). Electronically recorded interactions among characters in online gaming have been used to study different cooperative structures in small groups (Szell and Thurner, 2010).

Archival records can offer rich sources of data. Official records of company boards permit the construction of interlocking directorate bipartite networks (Kogut, 2012); the records of patient transfers between hospitals have been used to infer a hospital–hospital cooperation network (Lomi et al., 2014b); and records of ownership and supply chain relations have been used to study the networks of organizations in particular sectors (Lomi and Pattison, 2006; Powell et al., 2012).

In some of these cases the relational tie is natural and well defined: for instance, membership of a company board. But in other cases, a relational tie may be derived from the data, entailing decisions that may be of some consequence. The cattle herding, email and hospital cooperation studies are illustrations. If a researcher wishes to present and analyze the data in classic network form with nodes and edges (as distinct from, say, a relational event approach), then decisions need to be made about how many emails, how many cow interactions and how many patient exchanges matter in establishing a tie.

The original data is of event sequences across time. If the data is aggregated across time to produce weighted network edges, decisions need to be made about how long the time period should be. If the edges are further dichotomized, a cut-off point needs to be determined, below which an edge is deemed not to exist.

Obviously, creating a binary, cross-sectional network from such data – or even a series of networks for different time periods – may be problematic. These steps may simplify the analysis, but justification of the decisions will be necessary, and perhaps some form of sensitivity analysis undertaken to check whether different decisions lead to different conclusions. The alternative, of course, is to analyze with a relational events approach which does not aggregate the data.

Attribute and dyadic covariate data collection in whole network studies

Social network studies usually include actor attribute variables. Types of variables and related data structures were discussed in Chapter 4. There is not a lot about attribute data collection that is specific to network studies. Network researchers should consult the extensive social science literature on measuring individual-level variables to ensure they are engaging in best practice. Undoubtedly, good attribute measurement will enhance network studies; sadly, sometimes network researchers treat the attributes as something of an after-thought in terms of measurement.

As explained in Chapter 4, dyadic covariates may be derived from combinations of individual-level variables, and sometimes be dyadic data in their own right. In organizational network studies, for instance, a commonly used dyadic covariate is the formal structure or hierarchy of the organization. If this is not available, an additional name generator could be used, asking respondents to nominate their immediate boss.

Longitudinal panel data collection for whole network studies

The most common form of data collection for longitudinal social network studies is a panel design, where the entire network is measured at various points of time. Attributes and dyadic covariates may also be measured at the different time-points (depending on what these variables represent – obviously if the attribute is not going to change there is no need to remeasure). A co-evolution study, for instance, would collect data at several time-points, measuring both network ties and attributes, to analyze how the changes in ties and attributes affect each other across time.

In any form of social science, longitudinal panel data – unless it is collected automatically or electronically – is more costly and difficult to collect. Conceptually, however, the process is simply a repetition of cross-sectional data collection at various time-points. As explained in Chapter 4, care needs to be taken to record when an actor enters or leaves the network. In standard social science, the absence of a participant at a particular time-point can be handled in various ways. The simplest approach – but one that entails lower statistical power and so not always recommended – is to exclude from analysis any cases not present at every time-point. In network research, this is not usually to be recommended (see below on missing data), so careful tracking of the presence or absence of actors is desirable.

With the development of stochastic actor-oriented models for dynamic networks and the co-evolution of structure and behavior (Chapter 9), longitudinal data is increasingly popular in small social network studies. If you need to distinguish influence from selection processes, and if you have the resources and the energy, collect longitudinal data!

Name generators and egocentric methods

The name generator method was first developed by Laumann (1966) for egocentric studies. When applied to egonets rather than whole networks, there are some subtle differences in the use of name generators. First, there is no network boundary, so that the recall method, and not recognition, must be used. Second, respondents need not fully identify their network partners: researchers sometimes only ask for first names (perhaps with initial of second name, to distinguish alters with the same first name), or even nicknames.

A short name egocentric generator was first included in the 1985 US General Social Survey (Burt, 1984), and replicated in 2004 (McPherson et al., 2006). The name generators are described in Box 5.3.

Hogan et al. (2007) delineated two name generator types for egonets, originating from early work in the field:

- The 'Wellman approach' based on free recall but within a defined scope, such as 'Name those you are close to' (Wellman, 1979).
- The 'Fischer approach' where different questions are intended to elicit different supportive alters, such as 'Name someone who could lend you money' and 'Name someone who could babysit your children' (Fischer, 1982; McCallister and Fischer, 1978).

Marin and Hampton (2007) had a different categorization of name generators, based on the broad content of the ties and the intent of the data collection:

- *Role relations*: name generators principally concerned with role of ties within a specific social context, such as neighbors, friends or kin.
- *Interaction*: to identify alters with whom ego is in contact over a specific time period.
- *Affective*: to identify alters with whom ego has a relational tie of high emotional or affective content.
- *Exchange*: to identify alters with whom ego exchanges supportive or other content.

BOX 5.3

Egonet name generators from the 2005 US General Social Survey

McPherson et al. (2006: 355) reported the following interview instructions involving name generators for the 1984 and 2005 General Social Surveys:

'From time to time, most people discuss *important matters* with other people. Looking back over the last six months – who are the *people* with whom you discussed matters important to you? Just tell me their first names or initials. IF LESS THAN 5 NAMES MENTIONED, PROBE: Anyone else? Please think about the relations between the people you just mentioned. Some of them may be total strangers in the sense that they wouldn't recognize each other if they bumped into each other on the street. Others may be especially close, as close or closer to each other as they are to you. Are they especially close? PROBE: As close or closer to each other as they are to you?'

This was followed by a name interpreter item:

'Here is a list of some of the ways in which people are connected to each other. Some people can be connected to you in more than one way. For example, a man could be your brother and he may belong to your church and be your lawyer. When I read you a name, please tell me all of the ways that person is connected to you. How is (NAME) connected to you? PROBE: What other ways? (The options were presented on a card: Spouse, Parent, Sibling, Child, Other family, Co-worker, Member of group, Neighbor, Friend, Advisor, Other.)'

Alter–alter ties

Commonly, egonet studies ask participants (egos) to supply information about ties among their alters. This step is necessary to study the structure of the network around ego, for instance, to investigate structural holes. The standard approach is to ask the participant to report on relationships between every dyadic pair of alters in turn. This can be demanding: if ego has n alters, then there are $n(n - 1)/2$ possible ties. If the survey is computer-based, computer presentation of the dyadic pairs with a quick response is usually effective. The survey needs to be programmed such that the full list of alters is translated into a list of dyads.

In a paper-and-pencil survey or interview, the respondent or interviewer usually transcribes the list of names onto a matrix, with information about each relational tie entered into the relevant cell. In egonet studies that I have been involved in (e.g., Kalish and Robins, 2006), after completing a listing of alters through various name generators in another part of the questionnaire, respondents were asked to transcribe the nicknames or initials of the alters onto the margins of a matrix such as in Figure 5.1.

Nickname/ initials										
	1									
	2									
	3									
	4									
	5									
	6									
	7									
	8									
	9									
	10									
		1	2	3	4	5	6	7	8	9	10
Nickname/initials										

Figure 5.1 Alter–alter ties

Collecting data in paper-and-pencil surveys

In the figure, a maximum of 10 alters are requested, although this number could be increased. In my experience, a maximum above 15 or 20 makes the matrix too unwieldy for those with many alters. Respondents were instructed that they should only enter names drawn from their response to the name generator and should not add any additional names just to achieve the maximum.

If participants have more names listed than the maximum number of alters permitted in the matrix, then in an intermediary step respondents are asked to look through their complete alter list to identify those who are 'most important' up to the maximum (where 'importance' relates the relationship under study).

Once the names are entered into the matrix, respondents are asked to indicate in each cell (e.g., '1' or a cross) whether a relational tie exists between the relevant pair.

For participant-completed surveys, rather than interviews, instructions are important. Once they understand, respondents find this task manageable but it is easy enough to get confused at first. For the Kalish and Robins (2006) study, we gave participants written instructions along the lines of Box 5.4. It can also be valuable to give them a quick researcher demonstration if that is possible.

Of course, if the survey is delivered electronically or online, then it may be simpler to have each dyad presented via computer, with a quick response as to the presence or absence of a relational tie by the respondent. Software for egocentric data collection is discussed below.

BOX 5.4

Illustrative instructions for alter–alter data collection

The next task is to describe the strength of relations between the listed people. You do this by filling in codes in the matrix. This is a complex question, but it is essential to network measurement – and answering the question is a simple task when taken one column at a time.

You may find it easier to complete this task if you copy the names of your important people to the columns marked 'nickname/initials' (the first column on the left and the last row at the bottom).

Begin with the first person listed. Relations with the person are listed in the first column. Indicate his or her relationship with the person in each row in one of three ways:

Write **C** if there is an especially **CLOSE** relation between the row person and the first person.

Write **D** if the row person and the first person are **DISTANT** in the sense that they rarely spend time together in any social setting, or do not enjoy one another's company.

Write **NA** if the two people **don't know each other**.

Other egocentric methods and issues

As egonet data collection in survey form – especially alter–alter ties – is not especially straightforward, researchers need to take care in designing the survey/interview. There are plenty of trade-offs that are needed to make the survey manageable. Bidart and Charbonneau (2011: 269) put it well:

> Each researcher must choose between what is the most efficient (with a reduced number of name generators, of names generated or of secondary questions) and the most accurate representation of what the social actors actually experience (with a wider network, the maximum amount of information on its members and their relationships). Researchers seeking a more complete picture sometimes combine several generators with no overall logic – each of which have different objectives – laying the pieces of disparate networks. Keeping this in mind, the search for an exhaustive network is illusory, and we should probably abandon the idea of forming a complete picture of an individual's network. Indeed, the exercise generally involves working with a restricted subset, the construction of which is linked to the research question.

There are a number of extensions to the name generator approach that are worth considering:

- Bidart and Charbonneau (2011) proposed a two-step 'contextual' name generator. In the first step, participants are presented with a number of 'contexts' in which their social activities may occur (school, university, work, recreational activities, organizations, informal groups, social locations such as bars and nightclubs, neighborhoods, family, internet friends and so on). Respondents are asked to name those they interact with most in each context that is relevant to them. Using this list of names as a network boundary, the respondent is then presented with several name generator or name interpreter questions.

- Marin and Hampton (2007) found that a multiple name generator involving only two name generator items – 'Who are the people with whom you discuss matters important to you?' and 'Who are the people you really enjoy socializing with?' – performed quite well compared to multiple name generators that included exchange, social support and instrumental aid items. This result obviously depends on the research question, but it may be that a few particularly pertinent name generators can do the work of a larger set.
- A number of researchers have proposed visualization methods for data collection where respondents draw their own personal networks. These methods may involve physical (Hogan et al., 2007) or computer (McCarty et al., 2007b) aids. The Net-Map Toolbox (http://netmap.wordpress.com) relies on physical aids and can also be used for whole network studies where groups of people can work together to reconstruct the whole network.
- An older visualization data collection method going back to the 1980s is the *Social Convoy Questionnaire* (see English and Carstensen, 2014). Participants place alter names in three concentric circles, where the circles indicate degrees of closeness. Alter–alter ties are not collected. This has been used in psychological and other social science research but perhaps less so among egocentric network researchers.
- Software for personal network data collection includes:

  o Egonet, which can be downloaded from http://sourceforge.net/projects/egonet. It can be used to design computer-based interviews or surveys incorporating items about ego, name generators and interpreters, and alter–alter ties.
  o Vennmaker (www.vennmaker.com) draws on the Social Convoy approach, allowing participants to visualize and evaluate their own personal networks.

The big issue for egonet studies is how to balance good and relatively complete information against respondent fatigue. A decision depends on your research question, and whether you need alter–alter information and/or a large number of name interpreters. Too few alters certainly limits the amount of structural information that can be extracted from the data, but too many alters produces a large number of alter–alter pairs. McCarty et al. (2007a) examined these issues using sizeable datasets. They compared various methods, including asking for fewer alters; using a larger number of alters but randomly selecting a smaller number to investigate the alter–alter structure; and randomly selecting alter–alter pairs to investigate the structure. They concluded that for many network measures, 25 alters will capture the same structural patterns almost as well as 45, and that for some purposes the number of alters may be reduced to as few as ten randomly sampled from a larger list. But they did not recommend sampling alter–alter pairs.

Position and resource generators

The egonet approach has been adapted to identify sources of social capital, rather than individual alters. In the *position generator* approach pioneered by

Nan Lin (e.g., Lin, 1999; Lin and Dumin, 1986), a sample of *positions* with valued resources (e.g., certain professions and occupations) is provided to respondents who are asked whether they know someone who occupies that position. One advantage is that the occupations can be selected as relevant to social capital within a given research context (e.g., different occupations might be more important across different countries or cultures).

Van der Gaag et al. (2008) reported a social capital study with a position generator asking respondents whether they knew anyone who was a lawyer, a doctor, a policy-maker, and so on up to 30 occupations (see Box 5.5). They suggested that the position generator was helpful to understand social capital relevant to instrumental actions, such as finding a job or a house. It is perhaps less effective in measuring emotional or expressive support. As an alternative measure, van der Gaag et al. (see also van der Gaag and Snijders, 2005) proposed the *resource generator* where respondents were asked if they knew someone who had certain skills or who could assist them in certain ways (Box 5.5).

BOX 5.5

An example of network measurement using position and resource generators

Van der Gaag et al. (2008) described both position and resource generators to study social capital.

- They used 30 occupations in their version of the position generator, including: lawyer, doctor, policy-maker, engineer, information technologist, estate agent, mechanic, book-keeper, musician, cleaner, unskilled labourer, construction worker.

- These positions were sampled from a range of occupations of higher and lower social status. Respondents were asked whether they knew someone occupying that position, where 'know' meant that if they met accidentally on the street the respondent would know the person's name and could start a conversation.

- Van der Gaag's resource generator, on the other hand, asks respondents whether they know someone who can repair a car, play an instrument, owns a holiday home abroad, has knowledge about financial matters, can babysit their children, and so on.

In Box 5.6, I briefly describe the egonet survey used by Matous et al. (2013) to study agricultural innovation, geographical mobility and other factors among Ethiopian farmers. This is an interesting application of egonet methods to novel field studies in remote communities.

Reliability and validity of network measurement

In most areas of social science, the reliability and validity of measurement are big issues. *Reliability* is broadly conceived as the consistency of a measurement scale. This has several different interpretations. *Test–retest reliability* is the extent to which a scale continues to give the same result when it is applied more than once to the same person. *Internal reliability*, measured by Cronbach's alpha or the various Guttman coefficients (Sijtsma, 2009), shows the extent to which separate items in a scale are consistent in forming a continuous measure of the one construct.

For network studies, the internal reliability of a name generator is simply not a relevant concept. We are not attempting one measure on a continuous scale but rather to identify relational ties from one actor to others. But test–retest reliability is to the point: assuming a stable network, how sure can we be that network actors will nominate the same people if asked to do so on two separate occasions? A version of test–retest reliability occurs when two different measurement methods are applied: for instance, will actors nominate the same network partners if interviewed face-to-face or by telephone?

Validity is the extent to which the instrument measures the construct for which it is intended and not some other construct (or produces random noise). In network terms, this plays out as to whether the name generators capture the right network partners. For instance, if, in a management team study, respondents only select the most senior managers when asked 'with whom do you collaborate?', then that name generator may not be a valid measure of collaboration; but it may be a valid measure of the status of the most senior managers.

For some types of relational ties, the idea of validity seems uncertain. For instance, if I nominate George as a friend, who is to gainsay that (even if George himself would rather have nothing to do with me)? My choices of friends are a cognitive decision on my part. But of course there are types of network ties where validity is a precise notion because the response to the name generator can in principle be checked against other non-cognitive criteria. If I nominate someone as a person I meet daily, then that is a matter of fact that can be checked.

BOX 5.6

Egonet measurement in the field

Matous et al. (2013) used a variety of techniques in their egonet study of Ethiopian farmers in remote areas.

- They surveyed the farmers about demographics, agricultural knowledge and practices, and social preferences.

(Continued)

(Continued)

- They used a version of a resource generator, asking whether the farmer knew an agricultural expert, a researcher and so on.
- They used a name generator following McCarty et al.'s (1997) first name cue method, presenting respondents with a random selection from a large list of male and female Ethiopian names until the farmer identified 14 alters.
- Name interpreters were applied to each alter, especially frequency of contact and walking time to meet the person. (Given the remote context, encounters were typically made through walking.)
- Not all alter–alter ties were collected. Rather, a random sample of alter–alter ties were studied per ego in order to estimate the density of the egonet.

Informant accuracy

Validity and reliability relate to *informant accuracy* when actors respond to name generators. As Freeman et al. (1987) put it, the issue is the relationship between what people actually do and their recollections (or at least their reports) of those doings.

Informant accuracy in network studies was first examined in the 1970s and 1980s in a remarkable series of studies by anthropologists Russ Bernard and Lee Sailer, working with physicist Peter Killworth (Killworth and Bernard, 1976, 1979; Bernard and Killworth, 1977; Bernard et al., 1980, 1982 – much of this early work is reviewed in Bernard et al., 1984, and is known collectively as the BKS studies). The results of the five central papers are summarized in Box 5.7.

BOX 5.7

The BKS results

- *Paper I*: Informants' reports of their relational behaviors bear little relationship to their actual behaviors.
- *Paper II*: People do not know, with any accuracy, those with whom they communicate. Recall of past communication is not significantly more accurate than prediction of future behavior; the maintenance of personal logs does not improve accuracy; and informants do not know if they are accurate or not.
- *Paper III*: If reported (cognitive) and observed (behavioral) triads are compared, triad by triad, there is virtually no agreement between them.
- *Paper IV*: There was no useful relationship between the clique structures in observed communication network data and communication networks as reported by the actors. Cognitive data is useless for drawing any conclusions about behavioral social structure.
- *Paper V*: What people say about their communication bears no resemblance to their behaviors.

The conclusions from the BKS studies seem uniformly bleak. If we take them at face value, there seems little point in surveying or interviewing people about social network partners. But these studies all had a very precise design: they compared actual relational behaviors (e.g., communication) through observation on the one hand, with post hoc reports by the actors on the other.

In response, Freeman and Romney (1987) noted that network research typically related to social structure. They argued (somewhat archly) that if 'social structure' refers to anything at all, it is to regular, recurrent patterns of interaction, and not to specific behaviors at particular time-points. In short, they expected that if respondents did fail to recall accurately, the failure would be in the direction of longer-term patterns of interaction, which is indeed usually what we want to measure if we are dealing with social structure.

So, while name generators might be invalid and unreliable measures of specific relational behaviors at specific time-points, they may be valid and reliable in measuring more stable relational structures.

Following this line of argument, Freeman et al. (1987) showed empirically that informant responses about attendance at social events were incorrect about as often as they were correct. Respondents forgot some who were present and falsely recalled that some absentees were there. But the incorrect answers were strongly biased in the direction of long-term attendance at such social events. Name generators were a valid measure of long-term interaction patterns.

Short-term actions and long-term structure

I have spent some time on these early arguments because they exemplify important points extremely relevant today. Obviously, we need to think carefully and precisely about what our surveys are measuring. The BKS studies show that name generators are not especially valid measures of specific events or precise behavioral interactions; but the Freeman et al. (1987) work shows they can be valid measures of long-term regularities in interactions, that is, of *social network structure*.

The psychometric notion of validity is the relation of the measurement instrument to the theoretical construct. We have to understand the construct we wish to measure or observe, and then use the appropriate instrument or technique. In other words, the measurement process necessarily brings with it a fair dollop of theory, even if sometimes that theory is unseen. So, in your network research, are you measuring longer-term patterns – relationships – or a series of shorter-term events or transactions?

People coming to social network research for the first time, especially if they have a technical background, often assume that the 'real' data can be obtained through electronic means and that surveys are simply a proxy for this real data. Depending on the research question, this may be so. But electronic methods tend to produce data akin to the BKS behavioral observations, and if the study demands longer-term structure, then care needs to be exercised. In short, it is not always obvious how best to aggregate event-based observations into longer-term structure – or a series of dyadic time-stamped transactions into a relational tie that is indeterminate in time. This is not a technical issue (there are a variety of methods to aggregate event data, some more sophisticated than others). Rather, it is a theoretical question, and the theory is not well formulated at this stage.

So we should not assume that cognitive reports are a proxy for the 'real data', or that event observations are a fine-grained trace that can detail human cognitive responses. I have a friend who lives in another city and with whom I communicate seldom – but I can rely on him more than I can rely on some people with whom I deal 100 times a day. You can trace my behavior as much as you like, but you will not see this friendship as so strongly supportive from behavioral evidence, although I can tell you about its importance in a flash. In a crisis, he may be the person I turn to, not those with whom I exchange many emails. Again, we need to be clear about what we intend to measure and how we do that.

There are now mobile phone applications that can trace interactions between individuals, for instance, at a conference. By all means use this wonderful new technology, but think about what you are studying. If you want to study broad crowd movement, it is perfect. If you want to study the possible spread of influenza in the conference, it is excellent – and perhaps also for the spread of a rumour. But if you want to study important motivations or personal outcomes, it may not help that much: the five minutes I spend with a particular busy researcher may be the single most important thing I do at a five-day conference, because it fits in with long-term goals and collaborations impossible to measure by the app.

So my own preference is to think of observational or behavioral data, on the one hand, and so-called cognitive data, on the other, not as proxies for one another but as different types of measurement that validly measure somewhat different types of relational constructs. This is not to say there are not empirical relationships between these constructs. Since the early informant accuracy studies, various researchers (e.g., Quintane, 2013) have further studied the structural similarities and differences between them. Perhaps both types of measure can be usefully applied simultaneously in the one study, or kept apart for different types of studies. And perhaps we should analyze event data with an event-type model, and social structural data with other network methods, rather than conflating the two.

More recent work on reliability and validity

The study of network reliability and validity did not end with the early informant accuracy studies. Using a statistical modelling technique known as multitrait-multimethod, Kogovšek et al. (2002) investigated the reliability and validity of different name generator and interpreter methods: comparing face-to-face and telephone interviews and ordering by alters or by items. Name generators related to frequency of contact, feelings of closeness, and negative aspects in the relationships. The results had some surprises:

- In terms of validity, telephone interviews performed better than face-to-face. This was not expected. The researchers argued that people's relationships may be a sensitive matter and the relative anonymity of the telephone interview made it easier for respondents to talk about them.
- Nevertheless, frequency of contact was less reliably measured by telephone.
- Test–retest reliability was better when name interpreters were ordered by alters rather than by items.

The Kogovšek et al. (2002) paper is one of a series of studies into network measurement conducted by a leading network measurement group from the University of Ljubljana. Other interesting results from that research program include:

- When using the recognition method, reliability is worse if there is a binary response to a name generator (i.e., ego nominates or does not nominate a partner) as opposed to a five-point ordinal scale (e.g., ego categorizes the partner depending on the strength of the tie). This is not so for recall methods, when binary responses seem to perform equally well. The quality of measurement can be improved by giving respondents an informative example before the measure. Stronger ties exhibit greater test–retest reliability than weaker ties (Ferligoj and Hlebec, 1999).
- Respondent mood changes affect test–retest reliability in the number of network partners identified, particularly with recognition methods. Recall methods tend to produce strong ties and so are quite robust to mood effects on measurement (Hlebec and Ferligoj, 2001).
- Compared to face-to-face interviews, a telephone interview with by-alter name interpreters is the most reliable method, while a telephone interview with by-item interpreters is the least. Interview by telephone is more valid than face-to-face. So, telephone/by-alter appears the best choice. Respondents with smaller social networks have a higher validity of measurement. Older respondents have lower reliability and validity; tie characteristics are more validly measured among males. Behavioral questions, rather than emotionally-related questions, are more valid. Those who are more extraverted and more emotionally stable exhibit higher validity of measurement (Kogovšek and Ferligoj, 2005).

What are we to make of these various results? Recall methods seem preferable generally, but they tend to produce the strongest ties. Perhaps give respondents an example that epitomizes a name generator (but not necessarily a definition). Telephone/by-alter is a good choice if this option is available.

New methods of delivery for network surveys are now available. Mobile phone applications and tablet and computer delivery are with us and will become even more sophisticated. We need to study the effects of these methods, just as Kogovšek and Ferligoj (2005) compared face-to-face and telephone interviews. My advice for researchers wishing to use these technologies is to pilot everything, especially when surveying with a novel method. Do not assume that, because the technology is new or more advanced, it will produce better results with all populations. There is often an implicit assumption that new technologies will be particularly successful in obtaining data from the young digital natives of our world. I know of classroom data collection using the students' tablets where the digital natives rushed the question-naire so as to move on to more digitally interesting things. The resulting data was worse than a paper-and-pencil survey. Matzat and Snijders (2010) suggested that web respondents, compared to face-to-face respondents, tended to use more time-saving behaviors, reducing data quality. So it is not just a matter of availing yourself of the technology. Your respondents will implicitly or explicitly shape their responses depending on that technology and you need to understand how that might affect your measurement.

More research is needed on all these issues of network measurement.

Snowball sampling and respondent driven sampling

Snowball sampling

Methods for dealing with snowball sampled data are becoming increasingly sophis-ticated (Frank, 2011; Handcock and Gile, 2010; Pattison et al., 2013). In some cases, the sample is extracted from a very large electronic dataset in order to make the analysis tractable, in which case the snowball sample can be obtained simply by tak-ing waves through the existing dataset. In community and field contexts, however, the snowball sample has to be obtained through surveys, and that presents a number of difficult practical considerations.

Conceptually, the snowball sample procedure is straightforward enough: obtain a seed set of respondents, perhaps by a random sample from the community in the usual way; interview each of the seed set and obtain a list of their network partners; interview each person on the list of network partners; and so on, for as many waves as required. In practice, this process can be quite difficult. Respondents not only have to provide names of alters, but also contact details, presumably telephone or email so they can be easily reached. Some alters may not wish to respond, which disrupts part of the snowball. The analytic methods to date usually assume that the snowball is complete, so desirably the researcher wants most if not all alters to par-ticipate. To the extent that this is not possible, we must assume that the methods are robust to incomplete snowballs, but the methodological work to confirm this has not yet been done in sufficient detail.

Difficulties arise as the average degree in the sample increases, unless there is strong network closure. Suppose, unrealistically, there is no closure at all, so that the network has a tree-like structure. Let us suppose, again unrealistically, that every actor has exactly a low degree of (say) 5. Then for a seed set of n actors, there are $5n$ people in the first wave, $25n$ people in the second wave, and so on (i.e., wave

k has $n5^k$ people). After a few waves, this becomes a large number that may swamp the resources of the study. So, if possible, it is desirable to have a strong name generator that will constrain the maximum number of choices that the respondents are likely to make.

So, the number of waves in the snowball needs to be considered in relation to your resources to collect the data. As I noted in Chapter 3, there may be different goals for a snowball sample. If you use a snowball to find the boundary of the network, then you need to determine your criteria for a person to be added to the node set (e.g., nominated by a certain number of current participants), and proceed to enough waves to saturate the node set and thereby define the boundary (see Chapter 3). It is difficult to make general rules about how many waves will be needed: the decision is highly study-specific. If you are studying the structure and connectivity of a large community, then two or three waves may be sufficient, with an adequate seed set size. Daraganova et al. (2012) used a seed set of 58 for a community study of network and spatial processes.

Sometimes respondents do not know the email address or telephone number of a particular alter but can provide a name and approximate home location, albeit without sufficient detail for the researcher to contact the person to check. Another respondent may mention someone with a similar name and location, perhaps with more detail so that the researcher can interview this time. Under what criteria do we match these two cases – for instance, is 'George Smith' the same person as 'G Smith' or even 'J Smith'? So it is often desirable to have respondents report on demographics of alters (e.g., approximate age, home address, occupation). Then in a post hoc way the researcher can interrogate the data and engage in a *probabilistic matching* of cases: rules whereby two alters are deemed to correspond to the same person if their reported demographics are consistent across several categories.

What probabilistic matching can sometimes mean, however, is that a person you interviewed in wave 3 is in fact in wave 2 but was not well identified at the point of wave 2 data collection. So, post hoc adjustments of the wave of respondents may be needed. There is no definite consensus on criteria for probabilistic matches: the rules are best established on a study-by-study basis, perhaps by empirically checking the associations between the different demographic variables.

Of course, these cumbersome issues can be avoided by using a name generator that requires the respondent to know an alter well enough to have precise contact details. Maybe this will be fine for your research. But snowball samples are often valuable for hard-to-reach or *hidden* populations (e.g., drug user networks based on needle sharing; Rolls et al., 2013b). In such cases, the relevant activity may occur at places distinct from residences, so respondents may not always know their partners' precise contact details very well. The population may even be itinerant, moving from house to house frequently. One of the interesting capabilities of snowball sampled data is to estimate the size of such hidden populations (Frank and Snijders, 1994; Rolls et al., 2013b). But the practicalities of data collection can be difficult.

Respondent-driven sampling

In Chapter 3, I explained that respondent-driven sampling involves having respondents themselves recruit relevant network partners from the network population, so participants need to be motivated both to respond and to recruit. This is not always easy in a hard-to-reach population, so Heckathorn (1997) proposed a dual incentive system involving the following steps in data collection:

- All participants were offered a financial reward for completing the interview.
- Research staff recruited a 'handful' of participants as a seed set.
- All participants were offered an additional financial reward for recruiting network partners into the study; each participant was given recruitment coupons so that they were financially rewarded if the coupons were passed to peers from the population who then turned up for the interview.
- To ensure that no 'professional recruiters' emerged, each participant was given only three recruitment coupons to be passed to network partners.
- The trait defining membership in the population (e.g., drug use) had to be objectively verifiable, so that recruitment of non-population members was excluded.
- A participant database, recording personal and physical features, was carefully maintained to ensure that participants did not seek to duplicate participation under multiple identities.
- Extra bonuses could be used to recruit more of specific categories of people within the population, for instance, if some types of people were hard to reach or were rare.
- Sampling was ended when the targeted community was saturated or when a minimum target sample size was reached with stable levels of the traits of interest to the study.

An interesting feature of respondent-driven sampling is that, although a participant database needs to be kept rather carefully to prevent duplicate participants, apart from the original seeds (perhaps), no respondent needs to be identified to the researcher, thereby ensuring anonymity in the research (Chapter 7).

Missing network data: Non-respondents

Network measurement of whole networks is often confronted by missing data, where not all tie variables are observed. Missing data is common in empirical social science more generally, often arising when respondents fail to complete all of a survey, perhaps by omitting some survey items. This is known as *non-response*.

Huisman (2009) defined two forms of non-response in cross-sectional network data: *unit non-response*, where all outgoing ties and attribute scores of an actor within the network boundary are missing; and *item non-response*, where data on particular ties or attributes for an actor are missing.

When observations are independent in standard social science studies, a small amount of missing data may be imputed statistically under suitable assumptions

(Rubin, 1976); sometimes the missingness is ignored altogether (*available case analysis*). Usually we hope that the data is at least *missing at random* (Little and Rubin, 1987): given the observed data, the missingness is a random process. Then the missingness can be managed so that it does not affect the validity of our inferences.

The situation is not so benign for social network data because the presence or absence of even one tie can affect the network structure dramatically. A geodesic may be substantially shortened, two components may be linked, a structural hole may be bridged. In these cases, our understanding and interpretation of the network may change. It is for such reasons that, in whole network studies, researchers are encouraged to aim for a very high response rate from actors within the boundary, to obtain as complete a census of ties as possible. Of course, a response rate of 100% may be unusual – some people may choose not to participate at all, they may be away on the day of data collection, or they may choose not to respond to certain name generators.

For network data, some information may help with the missingness: even for unit non-response, there are still data on the ties from respondents to the non-respondents. Still, it is not uncommon in network studies simply to leave the non-respondent actors out of the study, a network form of available case analysis. Obviously the fewer non-respondents, the better this practice will be. From the respondents, you will have some indication whether the non-respondents are highly popular or not. If they seem rather peripheral, then perhaps your conclusions may not be greatly affected by omission. If, on the other hand, the non-respondents seem to be central, then any conclusions based on respondents alone will need to be made with caution.

Under certain assumptions, it is possible to fit network statistical models taking into account the missingness in the data, rather than pretending that it does not exist (Handcock and Gile, 2010; Koskinen et al., 2013). This is a more principled way to proceed than available case analysis, if the models address your research questions. I will say a little more on this in Chapter 9 on methods. It is also possible to impute missing tie data in various ways (Huisman, 2009).

Huisman (2009), in line with Kossinets (2006), showed that available case analysis can have large effects on network descriptive statistics, depending on the type of network. For undirected networks, he found that biases were larger for degrees and geodesics, whereas for directed network the biases were larger for reciprocity and closure. Encouragingly, he concluded that for low proportions of missing data, the bias in the descriptive statistics was not very large. Simple imputation procedures are not able to correct these biases all that well, although some do better than others. Smith and Moody (2013) showed that in-degree centrality and triangulation measures were quite robust to missing nodes but betweenness centrality was not: overall, the effect of missingness depended on the type of network and the question being asked of the data.

In Chapters 2 and 3, I noted various forms of structural equivalence and mentioned blockmodelling, an analytic procedure to simplify the network into positional *blocks* that can be more easily interpreted than the original network structure (I return to this in Chapter 9). Žnidaršič et al. (2012) studied how missing data can bias block-modelling. They concluded that structural equivalence procedures can be robust for a large proportion of missingness, but not regular and other forms of equivalence.

They have some excellent recommendations about reporting non-responses in your data collection:

- Report the percentage of non-respondents and the size of the network (i.e., the number of actors, including non-respondents, within the boundary).
- If you report a matrix of ties, report the missing ties by coding them as such by, fo example, NA ('not available').
- *Never* replace the missing ties with zeros. These are not zeros – and assuming then so is amongst the worst of imputation methods.

Tie non-response is not the only form of network missingness. Other forms of miss ingness include boundary misspecification and fixed choice of actors (Kossinets 2006). Koskinen et al. (2013) termed *fuzzy actors* as those whose ties are known bu whose attributes are not; *covert actors* where the researcher may not even know tha the actor exists (e.g., in criminal networks); and *network doppelgangers* where the on actor may appear as multiple nodes (e.g., as multiple email addresses). These can pre sent particularly difficult problems, but sophisticated methods are being develope to make some inference in these situations of complex incomplete data. The story c how to conceptualize and handle missing network data is just beginning.

Dealing properly with missing data is difficult; so work hard to get as high a respons rate in data collection as possible. In practice, few reviewers will complain if the amour of non-response is small and you conduct an available case analysis, but a large propor tion of missing data may require special treatment to get your work published. So, if all possible, it is best to tackle non-response at the data collection phase.

There are some good general social science practices that can optimize respons Ensure motivation among your actors: engage key players, encourage them as the value of the research and ask them to support it. This may require sensitivi to the politics involved in the research context. In some studies of organizations have obtained approval from management (of course) as well as the involvement staff unions. When union representatives gave a preliminary address supporting th study, the participation rate went up. Talk to the actors before the survey, introdu the goals and encourage them to participate. Keep the survey as simple and manag able as possible. Allow for follow-up with actors who could not be there on the d for whatever reason.

In conclusion: The key point

Social network observation and measurement is never simple – or, rather, if it simple (e.g., digital and automated), then perhaps the data cannot precisely addr your research question. Unfortunately, despite some serious individual efforts to the contrary, network measurement has not been given the same level of attention as in some other areas of social science. The remarkable advances over the last century in psychometrics, for instance, have not been matched by network measurement. Most network researchers, if they know of him at all, know Duncan Luce as a mathematician who helped introduced the graph term *clique* (Luce and Perry, 1949). Fewer know of him as the mathematical psychologist who co-authored (with Krantz, Suppes and Nobel Prize winner Tversky) the three-volume series on measurement in the social sciences, *The Foundations of Measurement* (Luce et al., 1990). I have argued in this chapter that measurement of social networks has some distinctive features, but to my knowledge no one is writing even a one-volume *Foundations of Social Network Measurement*. Too many network analysts are all too addicted to their analysis and not focused enough on their measurement. We do not have methods akin to a network factor analysis that can aggregate multiple name generators in a compelling way, let alone serious indices of validity and reliability apart from those obtainable from Kogovšek's multitrait-multimethod approach (and that type of analysis is not going to be applicable in most network studies).

I will write more on network data collection in specific contexts in the next chapter. In general, my advice at this point is to consider your measurement options carefully. A few name generator items, hastily thrown together without much thought, may simply not be good enough. Tie the measures to your theoretical arguments. Pilot, if possible. Be careful to motivate your participants to ensure good response rates. This is straightforward good practice in the social sciences. A network study – and subsequent fancy analysis – does not make that good practice go away.

BOX 5.8

Pulling back the curtain: What goes on in real network studies

In the sporting team study, as explained in previous chapters, the network boundary was well defined in terms of team members. We used several name generators with a recognition approach, providing a list of team members. The name generators covered professional relationships, including opinions on who were the best players; social-affective areas, including friendship, after-hours socializing, and trust; and negative ties in the form of aggressive behaviors towards others. Even though there were many name generators, the task was manageable for respondents because the teams were not large, and it was simple for respondents to tick off against a list of names.

We went to considerable effort to ensure high response rates. First, we approached the league administration, which agreed to support the study and recommend it to individual clubs. We then spoke to club administrators and coaches following introductions by the league, described the study and gained their support. Team members completed the survey at the club in a team meeting after a training session. Beforehand, we introduced the study, described the goals and explained how the name generator items worked. The coaches also spoke in support. We emphasized, however, that participation was entirely voluntary (Chapter 7). This is one advantage of a group session data collection in that these issues can be covered collectively. In the end, we had a very high response rate from the team members present. A few players were absent due to injury or other reasons, but we left surveys for them to complete later, so as to keep our response rate as high as possible.

The name generators in the environmental governance study were directed towards professional exchanges among the organizations: collaboration and flows of resources and information. We provided one name generator trying to elicit negative ties, asking for 'ease of collaboration' using a five-point Likert scale. We sought to ensure validity of measurement by a careful identification of the best informant within each organization, someone who could reasonably report on the organization's collaborations across the spectrum of activity. For organizations which were more heavily involved, we sought multiple informants. We interviewed each informant individually by telephone. The interviews included name generators, name interpreter and other survey items, as well as more open-ended qualitative items in a semi-structured interview format. We wanted not only good network data but also to match this to a rich qualitative understanding of how the participants understood the system of collaboration. The integration of these two approaches offered particular insights.

Unfortunately, after the interviews were completed, one organization withdrew from the study because of perceived legal and political issues. Sadly, this organization was rather central in the networks. Ethically (Chapter 7) we had no option but to withdraw the data provided by that organization. In our report to the contracting authority that had funded the study, we noted (without identification) that there had been an important non-respondent organization but we proceeded with centrality and other analyses using only respondents. While we are confident that the resulting conclusions are not seriously undermined by the missing data, we nevertheless offered our results with appropriate cautions.

Hot topics and further reading

In some areas of the social sciences, there is a hot debate between adherents of qualitative and quantitative research. To my way of thinking, it is a futile debate for network researchers: our distinction is surely more importantly between those who do networks and those who do not. Is a name generator a quantitative or qualitative observation method? There is no doubt that terms such as cliques, core/periphery and components relate to mathematical graph theory, so does that make them quantitative? If so, what are we to make of Elisa Bellotti's qualitative study of personal friendship networks, where she needs to invoke these terms to explain her results?

Bellotti, E. (2008) What are friends for? Elective communities of single people. *Social Networks*, 30, 318–329.

Peter Marsden has long been an important source of advice on network measurement, and his reviews are always worth reading.

Marsden, P. (2005) Recent developments in network measurement. In P. Carrington, J. Scott and S. Wasserman, (eds), *Models and Methods in Social Network Analysis* (pp. 8–30). Cambridge: Cambridge University Press.

Marsden, P. (2011) Survey methods for network data. In J. Scott and P. Carrington (eds), *The SAGE Handbook of Social Network Analysis* (pp. 370–388). London: Sage.

SIX

The empirical context of network data collection

Social network data collection always takes place in a specific context, whether it be a school, an organization, a large community, or a social media stream.

In the previous chapter, I discussed general data collection issues. But as social network research has a wide embrace across disciplines and domains of research, the specific context is crucial. Different types of research imply different data concerns, distinctive data types and particular data collection techniques. In this chapter, I first talk about some specific forms of data collection. Then I discuss a number of research contexts and the data considerations applicable to each.

Of course, you might want to try out your ideas on existing data. There are already plenty of network datasets available to researchers: classic older datasets, much analyzed over the years, and newer data, often collected digitally. For sure, these datasets may not be entirely suitable for your research question. But you can use them to experiment with some analytic techniques, and they may give you some ideas about the type of data that is possible. Box 6.1 lists some data repositories; more data sources are provided later in the chapter.

BOX 6.1

Some sources for existing network datasets

Plenty of datasets can be obtained from the web and elsewhere. Here are a few possibilities.

(Continued)

(Continued)

- The software network analysis packages *UCINET* and *Pajek* (see Chapter 9) come with some classic social network datasets.
- The UCI Network Data Repository (http://networkdata.ics.uci.edu) contains a number of classic and more recent datasets of different types.
- If you are interested in big networks derived from the web or other electronic forms of data, try the Stanford large network dataset collection (http://snap.stanford.edu/data). This repository includes the famous Enron email database.
- If you want *really* big, check out the Web Hyperlink graph (3.5 billion webpages, 128 billion hyperlinks) at http://webdatacommons.org/hyperlinkgraph. This is probably too much for most of us, but it is nice to know it exists! The website contains links to other large graph repositories.
- The *Gephi* website (see Chapter 8) has a number of interesting datasets itself, and a list of other data sources.
- The *Sonia* website at Stanford (see Chapter 8) includes longitudinal datasets (www.stanford.edu/group/sonia/dataSources).
- The *SocioPatterns* research group has data on human interactions collected by mobile technology (www.sociopatterns.org).

Forms of data collection

Online surveys

Before the digital world, social network data collection often involved a paper-and-pencil survey of individuals. Network surveys will not be going away, because they can be tailored to a research question, include measures of relevant constructs, and take into account a preferred research design. Automatically collected digital databases are typically assembled for other purposes, not for your research. Sometimes there is simply no alternative other than to ask people about their network connections and social behaviors.

I had much to say about surveys, name generators and name interpreters in Chapter 5. Here, let me make some further comments specific to online delivery of a survey, as opposed to the classic paper-and-pencil approach. Of course, surveys can also be delivered by mail and by computer-assisted telephone interview. I will comment on them further when I deal with data collection in larger communities below.

Online delivery of a network survey is now of course extremely popular. For whole network studies, online surveys have advantages. Depending on the numbers of actors within the network boundary, name generators and interpreters may place substantial demands on respondents. Paper-and-pencil surveys with long lists of names to be checked, and equally long lists of name interpreter items, may intimidate. A carefully designed online survey can present these lists in a more amenable way. Respondents can be asked to enter names that can then be checked electronically against stored lists. Name interpreter items can be presented for each alter, one at a time. If you have the computer skills to set up a good online survey, it is certainly worth considering, either for a whole network or an egonet study.

A big gain for you, the researcher, is that online delivery can be conducted remotely. You do not have to be present.

But it is not all so simple. With online surveys you have to consider survey design carefully. Poorly designed web instruments affect the representativeness of samples and lead to biases and poor response rates, whereas if the web instrument is well constructed it can give results comparable to traditional surveys (Reips, 2012). If you are interested in general issues of online delivery, the Web Survey Methodology site is a great resource (www.websm.org).

Motivation

Think especially about how to motivate your respondents. With face-to-face data collection, participants personally see you, the researcher, delivering your network survey. They see someone who is enthusiastic about the research, someone who addresses any queries and concerns immediately. If they like you and are reassured by you, they will provide better data. So, even if you are going down the online track, consider whether you can set up preliminary group sessions where you explain the research and deal with any issues before introducing your participants to the website. If face-to-face sessions are not feasible, think of other strategies to engage your participants.

Piloting your survey

Whether online or offline, piloting a survey is almost always a wise step. My suggestion is to pilot your instrument carefully on a set of generous volunteers who are happy to test out your initial survey. Decide whether you are getting the quality of data you need. If not, think carefully about additional strategies to improve the survey.

How do you know if your pilot data is of sufficient quality? Check the pilot data for the amount of missing data, measure how long the survey takes respondents to complete, check that they are not just nominating one or two alters on average, and at the same time that they are not nominating everyone (too many is as bad as too few – you want discriminating choices). Do a quick analysis of your attribute variables, to check that you have good variance across the pilot sample (again, if participants all respond in the same way, the results will be useless). Check that you have some correlations in the pilot data, including apparent associations between network and attribute data, and associations between different types of network tie (if that is what you are expecting).

Importantly, get feedback from the pilot respondents as to what was interesting, difficult and tedious in the survey, using post-survey interviews or a focus group. If and when there are issues, some may be fixed by revised survey layout, others by redrafting the wording of items, and perhaps some items should be dropped.

As you can see, there is potentially quite a bit of work in a good pilot (and in fact you might even want to pilot more than once), but it is better to know the weak points of your survey before rather than after the final data is in.

Interviews and qualitative data collection

A survey is sometimes completed through face-to-face or telephone interview. The researcher records the responses, rather than having the respondent complete a paper-and-pencil or web instrument. There are several advantages: the interviewer can prompt for additional alters when using a name generator, can check back that all parts of the questionnaire are answered well, and can answer any queries on the spot. If you have a good interviewing style, the interviewee may feel flattered that you are so carefully eliciting his or her responses, and make an effort to provide better and fuller data. Yet, interviews can be expensive in terms of time and other resources (e.g., travel costs if face-to-face), even though they do enable a richer data collection.

And that richer data may include qualitative data. A qualitative approach adds to the resource costs but can be valuable in understanding the social processes you are studying and the motivations of your participants. Qualitative data is often collected through a semi-structured interview, where the researcher follows a predetermined interview protocol but one that has the flexibility to enable interviewees to respond widely. Usually the interview will be audio-recorded, and later transcribed into a text to be coded and analyzed. There is plenty of work here – and the extraction of relational information from the transcript to create a network datafile may not be simple. Careful decisions are required about how to code the relational information in consistent and meaningful ways. Sometimes several coders are used to check the results against one another for consistency.

There are a variety of qualitative methodologies for data collection and analysis; and a variety of theoretical stances within qualitative research. If you are new to this area or a die-hard quantitative methodologist, do not think that qualitative research is simple or easy just because it does not focus on numbers or statistics. Texts such as Denzin and Lincoln (2011) provide an introduction to qualitative methods more generally.

The growing group of qualitative network researchers generally advocate a mixed methods approach, whereby qualitative information is combined with quantitative network data and analysis (Hollstein, 2011). So if you are a qualitative researcher newly starting with networks, do not think you can avoid the graph theory concepts of Chapter 2, or ignore some knowledge of the methods I will describe in Chapter 9. Your peers in the network research world will know these ideas and will use them to enhance and explain their qualitative analysis.

Bidart and Cacciuttolo (2013) argued that for a really rich understanding of a social system or of a person's social world, qualitative and quantitative approaches should not just be used in a disjointed and sequential way but should be fully integrated into mixed methods research. Their research design was of longitudinal egonets, where participants were interviewed four times across a period of nearly ten years. Data collection included name generators and standardized questionnaires, as well as interviews that typically lasted several hours and sought fine detail of the network relationships. A mixed methods approach was applied for both data collection and analysis.

The growing importance of qualitative and mixed methods in social network research is emphasized by the appearance of new texts that give good guidance to the area (Bellotti, 2015; Dominguez and Hollstein, 2014). The very best of social network analysis often includes a qualitative understanding alongside quantitative analysis. If you have a chance to collect some qualitative information in addition to a network survey, do so.

Observation

In Chapter 1, I described the Bank Wiring Room study from the Hawthorne research program. The social network datasets were constructed by the researchers after two years of painstaking observation of worker interactions. In fact, if you look at Roethlisberger and Dickson's (1939) figure of the layout of the Bank Wiring Room, you will even see where the researchers' desk was located in relation to the work-benches.

Direct observation of interactions is a time-consuming and resource-intensive process. It is perhaps most common in anthropological research, where researchers often spend long periods of field work in a community. Some of the giants of early social network research followed this procedure. Bruce Kapferer (1972) spent nearly ten months in an African factory, observing the social interactions of the workers. John Barnes (1954) described the intersecting relationships of a small Norwegian community after being in the field for over 12 months. In this important article, Barnes was the first to coin the term *social network* in a scientific context.

Direct observation also occurs in research into organizational behavior. For instance, David Gibson (2005) observed some 100 hours of meetings of managerial groups and recorded when the discussion shifted from one person to another, comparing the pattern of conversation shifts with network data collected by more traditional name generators.

Gibson's work highlights the distinction between relational interactions, on the one hand, and network ties, on the other. If researchers wish to use direct observations of interactions to infer network ties, then decisions need to be made about how best to do this. There may also be potentially difficult decisions – depending on the research context – as to how to define and code an interaction itself. Of course it is now possible to video a small group such as a managerial meeting quite cheaply, so the researcher no longer needs to be physically present, but the issues of coding and of tie inference remain. New algorithms and software to assist through automation are being developed (e.g., Mathur et al., 2012).

The presence of a researcher (or of a video recorder) has the potential to alter social behavior, so researchers need to consider their own effect on the observations. Such issues were acute for the early network anthropologists: Kapferer (1972) has some interesting comments about habituating participants to the researcher, how researcher actions will be observed in turn by the participants (so that observation applies both ways), and how to minimize bias in the observations.

Public databases, archival sources and texts

Network data are often extracted from public databases containing relational information: for instance, trade flows between countries, co-authorships of academic articles, and company board memberships. If your research topic requires only such data you are in the lucky situation of not having to collect it yourself. All you need do is to get access to the database and extract the relational and attribute information in the most efficient way. (Of course, this may not be that easy!)

Sadly, the data may not be recorded in an overtly network way, so you may have additional work to extract the information you need. Regrettably, not all archives and databases have been set up with the network analyst in mind. The 'database' may not even be in a nice digital format. Historical network research is exemplified by John Padgett who has worked for years in the Florentine archives on records from medieval and Renaissance Florence, detailing links between major Florentine families through trade, financial, marriage and other data. Padgett and Ansell (1993) is a classic network study of this period of Florentine history.

Sometimes, a text is a source of information about the existence of a network tie. The researcher may predetermine a rule about what constitutes evidence for a relationship. The full network data may then be built up from one or only a few larger texts, or from a series of smaller singular items (e.g., social media messages, newspaper articles, or a series of situation reports). It is beyond the scope of this book to discuss the many and growing sophisticated algorithms for text mining. While there have been recent advances (e.g., Tambayong and Carley, 2012), difficulties remain (Butts et al., 2012) and it is still the case that more research is needed on the automatic extraction of relational data from text. This is a very active space for methodological research, so stay tuned to what is happening if it is relevant to your work.

Contact diaries

The researcher may ask each participant to keep a diary listing the people he or she met during each day of the study. Of course, decisions need to be made about what counts as a contact and how to handle occasions where the numbers of contacts might be large or even overwhelming (e.g., larger meetings, shopping centres). Contact diaries have been used in disease transmission studies (e.g., influenza) to understand the contact structure of humans in their daily lives. The nature of the disease transmission process from person to person needs to be considered in the definition of contact. Close proximity might count as a contact if a disease can be spread by airborne means (e.g., coughing). But a broad definition like proximity accentuates difficulties of recording many anonymous individuals such as in a shopping mall. There is a trade-off here between a definition that is true enough to the contagion mechanism and problems in adequately recording the contacts. Participants are not going to be able to (let alone want to) record huge numbers of contacts, especially if many of them are not personally known. So even the most conscientious respondents are likely to take shortcuts that could undermine the data.

Fu (2007: 211) described the contact diary as 'one of the most tedious and difficult means for collecting information about ego-centred networks', but at the same time argued that it was 'one of the most comprehensive research instruments for measuring personal networks'.

Rather than identify specific individuals as contacts, an alternative method is to specify places the individual has visited during the day. This is often a more manageable task for the participant and can still give information about the possibility of disease transmission. This procedure collects information on the daily bipartite egonet of participants in a person-to-place bipartite graph (Bolton et al., 2012; McCaw et al., 2010).

Do not lose sight of the fact that in using contact diaries you are observing just that – contacts. These are not necessarily social network relationships, and it is not obvious how best one can aggregate contacts in a simple way to define a strong relationship.

Digital data collection, including mobile electronic techniques

The advent of mobile technology makes the automatic collection of data about daily activities much more feasible. Participants' mobile devices, or some other form of wireless device, may automatically record those others who come into (and go out of) close proximity at a particular time-point. For a whole network study, of course, this needs to be conducted within a well-defined boundary where everyone uses the relevant device. For instance, Barrat et al. (2013) described the use of radio frequency sensors in an academic conference, a hospital ward, and a museum exhibition. For a similar study of contact structures during a typical school day, see Salathe et al. (2010).

When the network boundaries are not well defined – for instance, as people wander through shopping malls – these automatic methods still have limited applicability unless a large enough proportion of people entering the target location agree to participate in the study and to use the mobile device or app. In some subpopulations, enthusiasm for such a type of data collection might be quite high but perhaps not quite yet for the general population.

There is nevertheless a growing use of purpose-designed mobile phone apps to record volunteers' mood states or activities at random time-points in the day as they go about their activities, the 'study of daily life' (Mehl and Conner, 2012). This requires very short-form responses from participants at the sampled time-points. This approach may be applicable to the collection of egonet data akin to a contact diary, but it is not obvious how easily participants can respond to an 'instantaneous' egonet query (McCaw et al., 2010). Again, this is a fast-moving area, so keep an eye on developments if it is relevant to your research.

Automated electronic data collection of course also includes the massive data now available through website links, emails, social media and so on, much of which is relational. I shall comment on such data later in this chapter.

Longitudinal and relational event data

Much longitudinal social network data is collected in panel form: a network relationship among a set of actors is measured at a distinct time-point. The collection of panel data is obviously more resource-intensive than cross-sectional data, and additional steps are needed to manage the dataset. Researchers need to ensure that participant responses at one time-point can be matched with responses from the same participant at the next time-point. This may seem blindingly obvious, but I have known of studies where inexperienced research assistants forgot to do this!

With network data, it is also important that alters be consistently identified across time-points. This may be simple enough for a whole network study with a well-identified boundary, through the use of a common name list from which respondents can choose. It may not be so simple with an egonet study, where respondents may forget the name or other identifier of an individual they nominated at the last time-point (for instance, at one time-point they might use a nickname, and at another a real name, for the same person). It may be necessary to provide the previous list of alters to respondents to check whether the same people have been included this time.

Node change

A longitudinal network study may face important changes in the node set. Any longitudinal data collection risks high drop-out or churn rates. Participants may decide to leave the study, or come in and out of the study at different time-points.

New actors may join the network between measurement points. For instance, in a longitudinal study of a network of businesses in a given industrial sector, new businesses might form, companies might merge, and some may go out of business.

It is, of course, simplest if your node set does not change across time. It is tempting to create the dataset using only those nodes present at all time-points. When there are relatively few changes only relating to nodes on the periphery of the network, perhaps such an approach does not matter that much. Otherwise, it can be risky: if a highly central node at the first time-point has gone at the next, it is doubtful that the first network panel is a good representation of the real social system if you leave out that node. So, it is worthwhile checking the centrality (both degree and betweenness) of your changing nodes if you are contemplating excluding them.

Of course, sometimes node changes might be the essence of the study – the mergers, bankruptcies and start-ups in the industrial sector could well be the topic of investigation – in which case you will not want to exclude nodes at all. In that case, you want methods of analysis that can handle changing node compositions. More methodological work still needs to be done, but longitudinal stochastic actor-oriented models (see Chapter 9) can handle changes to the node set across time, as long as the changes are not too extreme. However, methods to model the joining of two nodes (e.g., a company merger) are not yet well established.

The amount of change

More generally, the amount of change in the data needs to be related to the time period between measurement points. Whether it be change in the node set, change in the network ties, or change in the attribute measures, if you have too much variation between adjacent panels, it is impossible to infer processes from one measurement point to another. On the other hand, if you have too little change, there is nothing to observe. It is difficult to make general rules about this. If the period between measurements is badly wrong, there will be little to be said longitudinally about your data. So be careful in selecting a measurement period – take advice from experts about the likely amount of change, be sensitive to external events that might create a shock to the system, and where possible look back at previous or historical data about how this type of social system has evolved in the past.

Relational event data

Event-based data are not as vulnerable to the issue of changing node sets. In recent event-based statistical models (Chapter 9), the composition of the node set at a particular time-point determines the opportunity set (the actors with whom a given node has the opportunity to make a relational exchange), and so changing composition is naturally accommodated in the model. As relational event data are nowadays typically collected electronically (e.g., through email records, social media streams, or data loggers of various sorts), and are automatically time-stamped, some of the panel data issues discussed above do not apply.

Research contexts

Let me turn to some empirical contexts in which social network data have been collected. I want to give a sense of the type of data and some of the issues distinctive to each area. My goal here is to provide a starting point for researchers interested in particular topics. What this all-too-short summary does, however, is to illustrate the wide variety of social science domains in which empirical social network research has been conducted. And the list below is not complete, nor is it primarily discipline-based. For instance, I do not have headings for sociology, communication or physics, areas in which a lot of network research is always being undertaken. But the list covers many of the data collection contexts in which empirical sociological and communication research is being conducted, resulting in data amenable to the network techniques being developed in physics.

Inter-organizational studies

There are several different types of studies of networks among organizations.

- Studies of 'organizational fields', such as industry sectors, often focus on a variety of economic network ties, including ownership, contractual and supply relationships. Lomi and Pattison (2006) studied a network of organizations involved in the manufacture of transportation components; and Powell et al. (2012) a network of biotechnology companies. Data often derive from company and other records, sometimes supplemented by other sources such as interviews.
- Inter-organizational communication and collaboration data may be extracted from organizational records, but are often collected from respondents who are expert informants about their organizations. These are usually senior organizational executives or managers with coordinating responsibilities. These informants may be asked to identify other organizations which are collaborators with their own organizations (or competitors, information sources, resource suppliers and so on): in short, a name generator survey but applicable to organizations, not persons. Collecting such data requires some careful decisions. Who are the right informants with the right knowledge and expertise within each organization? Should there be one or more informants from each organization, perhaps separate informants for different divisions in a particularly large organization? If so, should the separate divisions be treated as separate nodes in the network, or the informants' responses aggregated to apply to one actor? These are not always easy questions, and the answers may require a mixture of theoretical argument and local knowledge.
- Inter-organizational communication and collaboration data can cover a range of different research interests, such as disaster management and network governance, discussed below.
- Interlocking directorate studies – of companies and their board of directors – are also inter-organizational studies. The data are usually extracted from company records and then examined as a bipartite network (Chapters 4 and 9). Kogut (2012) illustrated the type of data that can be collected in this way.

Intra-organizational networks

There is a very long tradition in network research in organizations, going right back to the Bank Wiring Room of the Hawthorne studies. Organizational network research continues to grow. The wide-ranging reviews by Borgatti and Foster (2003) and Brass et al. (2004), although now written some time ago, are still excellent sources to gain a feel for the type of research conducted within organizations, together with the type of data that is collected.

- Intra-organizational network data are often survey-based. More recently, electronic traces (e.g., email exchanges) have been used, although these cannot always address the research question. For instance, if your research is on the topic of organizational trust, patterns of email exchanges alone are unlikely to be sufficient to understand who trusts whom. Nevertheless, email exchanges can be just the right data if the goal is to understand the rhythm of organizational activity (Quintane et al., 2013).
- Given that organizational boundaries are often clearly delineated, whole network studies are common. Multiple types of tie (e.g., advice, collaboration, trust, friendship) are frequently measured, as well as the formal structure of the organization (e.g., who is the supervisor of whom), so these are quite often multiplex studies. Data may be collected at various levels: within smaller workgroups, within organizational divisions, or across the entire organization. The research may focus on the top management team, management more generally (i.e., both senior and junior managers), or the wider workforce including lower-level employees. Several attribute variables are usually measured to control for individual factors; and if the study includes multiple levels akin to a multilevel network, then attributes for higher level groupings, such as workgroups or divisions, may also be collected. We can expect more multilevel network studies of organizations into the future, as methods and theory develop.
- Because of the difficulty of getting access to many organizations, much organizational network research tends to be case studies, or at best comparisons across a small number of organizations. I will say more about case studies in Chapter 10.
- There are many business consultants claiming to have social network expertise, and able to advise changes to organizational structures and behaviors to improve performance and efficiency. I have to say that some are more experienced and knowledgeable than others. By the time you have read this book, you will be able to assess whether they do indeed have expertise or are just using network jargon rather superficially. If you want examples of some of the best, Valdis Krebs (www.orgnet.com) and Rob Cross (www.robcross.org) are two consultants who also have strong research reputations in organizational networks.

Small-group research

Much organizational network research could be considered small-group research when it relates to workgroups or other smaller organizational units. Nevertheless, there is a considerable body of small-group research that sits outside the formal organizational literature.

- Laboratory experiments have a long tradition in network research. Participants are brought into the laboratory and 'networked', with the outcomes compared across different network structures. An early example, the famous Leavitt (1951) experiments, compared the effect of different structures of communication networks on group performance. Noah Friedkin and Gene Johnsen have long used experiments on group dynamics to develop their Social Influence Network Theory (Friedkin and Johnsen, 2011). Laboratory experiments are well established in psychology, sociology, economics and elsewhere. You should follow the standard practices for good experimental data collection from these disciplines.

- The distinctive feature of network-based laboratory studies is that participants are situated in a network according to the experimental design. In early experiments, participants were set up in separate cubicles and exchanges between cubicles controlled according to the network structure imposed by the experimenter. Nowadays, of course, the communication is typically managed by computer, with constraints applied consistent with the imposed network.
- Studies of power and exchange networks have a long history both in experimentation and in theoretical and mathematical argument. The position of an actor in a small-group structure is considered against the pay-offs available when they can (or cannot) play one exchange partner against the other. Cook and Emerson (1978) made foundational arguments for a networked view of exchange processes, rather than a dyadic perspective, and described some early experiments. For a recent review of work in this tradition, see Cook et al. (2013).
- Of course, small-group studies can also be conducted in the field by careful observation and measurement of group network structures and processes either cross-sectionally or across time. One of my favourite examples is Jeff Johnson's study of changing roles in an Antarctic field station during a southern winter (Johnson et al., 2003). The study illustrates detailed data collection across a period of months for a real small group.
- Nosh Contractor and his colleagues have undertaken a novel combination of small-group research and electronic data collection by studying the dynamics of team collaboration in massively multiplayer online games that require group formation – the so-called *Virtual Worlds Exploratorium* (Williams et al., 2011). Because these are real groups of individuals cooperating towards certain gaming objectives, albeit operating within a virtual environment, and yet at the same time large amounts of electronic data are digitally recorded, the fine temporal dynamics of individual and group decisions and outcomes can be examined in a way that is impossible in a laboratory context.
- For another example of network research into massive multiplayer online games, see Szell and Thurner (2010) who have compiled a dataset of actions of 300,000 players over a period of three years. These virtual world studies are small-group research using Big Data!

Schools

Surveys in schools have been a long-standing source of whole network data (see Box 6.2, which lists some past and present projects relating to schools – there are many others). The research focus can range from bullying to diffusion of health behaviors (uptake of smoking and drinking) to social aspects of teenage delinquency. Research is often multiplex, and because school membership is well defined, whole network studies, rather than egonet studies, tend to be the norm.

- There are important issues of level: is the right network boundary within classes, within year level, or within the entire school? A decision depends in part on theoretical considerations, but also on practical issues. Depending on school size, a whole school study may be unwieldy. As most student relationships are likely to be within class or within year level, these may be sensible categories on which to base a network boundary.
- In contrast to organizational research, the tendency in school-based network research is towards comparisons across many networks, rather than case studies of a few. It is not unusual to have access to multiple schools in which to collect data, and once a researcher has access to a school it is not usually difficult to study multiple classes. The design then becomes overtly multilevel, with networks nested within classrooms and possibly within schools. I introduce methods for making inferences across a number of classrooms in Chapter 9.
- Collecting data in schools requires care. I discuss some of the ethical issues in Chapter 7. Be aware that you are likely to have students who will not have parental consent (so decisions will need to be made about how to handle such missing data). But it is not just a question of ethics: do your best to ensure participant motivation even for those students with consent. I suggest a rather hands-on approach to data collection – not a sole reliance on teachers, or on online collection – unless and until you know you can rely on these sources to provide quality data. Do not assume that because students are 'digital natives' you will get good data from a perfunctory tablet-based survey: digital natives are good at switching away from your survey to other digital tasks.

BOX 6.2

Some network datasets relating to schools

Schools have long been a favourite environment for collecting network data. If this is for you, then check out the design and instruments used in previous studies. Here are some examples of past and present projects.

- The well-known National Longitudinal Study of Adolescent Health, known as Add Health. This is a longitudinal study of a representative sample of adolescents in US schools in the mid-1990s (www.cpc.unc.edu/projects/addhealth).
- The Children of Immigrants Longitudinal Survey in Four European Countries (CILS4EU). The project website (www.cils4.eu) sets out the study design clearly. There are both classroom and egonet network data.
- John Light's Adolescent Peer Social Network Dynamics and Problem Behavior, a three-year study of middle schools in western USA (Light et al., 2013).
- Some historical datasets are still available to researchers under certain conditions. For instance, the 1953 Danish Male Birth Cohort study included name generator ('sociometric') items among several other school-related variables. See Osler et al. (2006).
- I have already mentioned the Salathe et al. (2010) dataset. It records contact structures for a typical school day using wireless technology. The dataset is available through the Supplementary Information accompanying the article.

Larger communities[1]

For larger communities where a whole network study is impossible because of the size of the population, there are several different methods for collecting survey data: face-to-face interviews, mail-out surveys, telephone interviews, and online surveys. Traditional approaches may need to be adapted to collect network data.

- In standard social science, a random sample, perhaps stratified in various ways, would be the usual way to proceed. Of course, obtaining a fully random sample is never easy, and in practice some compromises may be necessary. Random samples may be fine for egonet studies, but some network studies may require snowball or respondent-driven sampling where the sample is not random (although the seed set may be).
- Face-to-face interviews can be very expensive, especially if the community is geographically dispersed, so that travel time and costs begin to feature. Telephone interviews, depending on the time taken, can also be costly, but have the advantage that many commercial firms will undertake this work for you if you have the resources to pay their fees. Mail-out surveys are cheaper. The easiest of all to apply is probably a web-based survey, but there are issues of response rates and representativeness of the sample with web surveys.
- It is still the case that response rates for large online surveys are typically lower than for mail surveys, even among internet-literate communities (see Millar and Dillman, 2011, who argued that a combination of mail and internet approaches was most effective). If you need your sample to be representative of the general population, Szolnoki and Hoffman (2013) argued that face-to-face interviews with a well-selected sample were optimal, although telephone interviews may be fine with a somewhat larger sample. But they pointed out that with snowball sampling, we should probably forget about obtaining a representative sample. So trade-offs occur between ease of delivery, the nature of the sample, and the quality of the responses.
- With egonet research, the network sampling issues are not as sharp. Participants can be sampled in a standard way and asked to provide egonet data as part of the survey. This is illustrated by the 2005 US General Social Survey described in Chapter 5 (see Box 5.3). One of pioneers of community-level personal network research is Barry Wellman, whose East York egonet studies were conducted in the 1960s. Wellman (1993) provided an entertaining account of the origins of these studies and details of their design, as well as historical antecedents.
- An egonet approach can be implemented in a web, telephone or mail survey, although the risk with the web and mail survey is that if the instructions are not very clear the participant may become confused by the unusual nature of the network items, especially alter–alter ties (Chapter 5). With a telephone interview, a well-trained interviewer can guide the participant through any confusion.
- However, if you are interested in connectivity across a community (e.g., in studying diffusion processes), egonet studies may not suffice and snowball sampling may be necessary. This adds another layer of complexity, as participants need to name (at least some of) their alters and provide contact details. Analogous difficulties arise with respondent-driven sampling. In these complex cases, I much prefer face-to-face or telephone interviews, than mail or web surveys.

---

[1]Here I am not talking about 'community structure' but real human communities, such as cities, suburbs, towns, larger rural areas and so on.

- With snowball sampling, even with good piloting, you can never be entirely sure how good your response rate will be and how many alters will take up the opportunity to participate in a snowball sample. Design your research so that if these factors do not work out well, you can fall back on a solid egonet study with the data you have collected along the way.
- And think about other larger-scale factors that may come into play for whole communities. For instance, if geospatial distance is likely to be important then you may need to measure the location (e.g., home address) of your respondents (adams et al., 2012).
- Computer-assisted telephone interviews have the advantage that the instructions can be programmed for the interviewer so that the computer will proceed to the item that follows naturally from a given interviewee response. This is ideal for name generators and interpreters, in that once the names are given, the interviewer can then ask about the name interpreters in a consistent and regular way.
- Some words of caution are in order if you are using a commercial polling company for telephone interviews. These companies are not always familiar with network research, the complexities of name generators and so on. They may not be well prepared for a snowball sample. Make sure that the company is fully aware of what you require. My advice is to check the instructions to be given to the interviewers, down to the detail of the flow charts that will be implemented through the computer screens the interviewers use. Make sure that the interviewers are given full training so that they understand what is intended from the survey. *Never* leave the company to cut corners based on their 'past experience' without your approval.
- These are words of caution, not of despair. Good network research can be done with snowball sampled data obtained through telephone interviews (e.g., Daraganova et al., 2012; Kashima et al., 2013). One of the earliest studies of network connectivity across a large community was Milgram's original small-world research (see Chapter 2). There was no web, no telephone interviews, only the US postal service. But even given this famous historical antecedent, it is still a challenge to investigate large-community network connectivity from sampled data.

Individual social capital, well-being and social support

Individual social capital is often studied using egonet methods, sampled across larger communities.

- In Chapter 5, I described Nan Lin's position generator and van der Gaag's resource generator which can readily be used in a large community survey. As an example of this type of research, Bian and Huang (2009) described a large-scale study on job mobility across five Chinese cities, based on a multistage probability sampling design, with a number of network-related and social capital-based items in their survey. Often the outcome measure for these types of studies is the social or subjective well-being of the individual: that is, how satisfied an individual is with their life or their current economic and personal situation.
- Social support is a related construct sometimes studied with egonet approaches (Song et al., 2011). Social support is the physical or emotional support that a participant receives from his or her social network partners, or from the social environment more generally. Social support has been widely studied in the

health and psychological literatures and so data is often collected within health or related contexts. This is a complex area of research in part because of a distinction between perceived and received social support: a person may perceive that social support is available from others without ever having received it, and different types of support may have different outcomes. There are many measures of social support available, some of which are more explicitly network-oriented than others. For an example of a recent study of networks and social support among homeless men, see Green et al. (2013).

Health behaviors

There has been considerable interest in the diffusion of health behaviors across social networks (Valente, 2010). In the past, these studies often focused on smoking or alcohol abuse, particularly among school or adolescent populations; recently there has been a trend to collect longitudinal data in an effort to disentangle selection and influence effects (e.g., Mercken et al., 2011; see Chapter 9 for some details on these longitudinal models). With the appearance of Christakis and Fowler's (2007) study on the diffusion of obesity across friendship networks, attention has also turned to eating-related behaviors (e.g., de la Haye et al., 2013). I shall say more on Christakis and Fowler's work in Chapter 10.

If your interest is in social networks and public health, you will want to look at the recent special issue of *Health Education and Behavior* on systems science applications in health promotion and public health (Mabry et al., 2013).

Epidemiology

The AIDS epidemic in the 1980s provided the impetus for modern network epidemiology.

- Klovdahl (1985) argued that infectious diseases should be studied as a network phenomenon. The famous Colorado Springs study commenced in 1987, with the collection of sexual network data involving prostitute women to understand the magnitude of the HIV epidemic in heterosexual populations (Klovdahl et al., 1994).
- The network epidemiologists necessarily have a focus on connectivity across larger communities and contributed to the development of respondent-driven sampling, contact diary and automated data collection.
- For general issues around data collection for network epidemiology, the edited volume by Morris (2004) is still a good place to start, not only for disease transmission but also for collecting network data in larger communities more generally.
- Data collection is never easy in network epidemiology. For instance, the Burnet Institute's study of the transmission of hepatitis C through needle-sharing in drug user networks (www.burnet.edu.au/projects/42_hepatitis_c_and_injecting_networks) involved placing data collection vans at certain well-known street drug sites to interview possible participants and to collect blood samples.

Anthropology, demography and geography

I mentioned above the crucial early work of anthropologists in setting the foundations for social network research. This type of fieldwork continues today and can focus on a range of topics including demographic, environmental and geographical factors (Johnston and Pattie, 2011). Here are some examples:

- For a good example of how original anthropological fieldwork can be translated into a novel network formulation, look at how the anthropological data described by Tengö et al. (2007) provided relational information from which to extract a network-based social-ecological system (Bodin and Tengö, 2012). I will say more about this work below under network governance and environmental systems.
- The Nang Rong projects in Thailand encompass 12 studies of a farming district over 20 years, covering changes in social networks, migration, agricultural practices, land use and land cover, and population–environment interactions (www.cpc.unc.edu/projects/nangrong). Faust et al. (1999) described a specific network study from this program, with an interesting discussion of how geospatial factors relate to social and economic networks.
- In Chapter 5, I noted the interesting work by Matous et al. (2013) among Ethiopian farmers, studying a range of network, economic, agricultural and geographic factors.
- Kinship networks are a field of study in their own right and were important in social network analysis for the development of algebraic and blockmodelling approaches (Chapter 9). Peter Bearman's (1997) classic article on generalized exchange in complex kinship structures illustrates how kinship data, in this case from indigenous communities, can be analyzed from a network perspective to produce novel conclusions. White (2012) reviewed recent work in the field of kinship networks.

Economic networks

Economic-related networks are a fast-growing area of empirical research. Schweitzer et al. (2009) argued that the global financial crisis emphasized the need for a more fundamental understanding of economic networks.

- Jackson (2011) and Goyal (2011) provided recent reviews of social network research in economics. David Knoke's (2012) book examined economic networks at a variety of levels, from individuals to the world economy. Readers with specific interests in economic networks will also want to read the text by Matt Jackson (2010), one of the leaders in this field.
- Of course, the study of economic networks in the form of labor markets goes back at least to Granovetter's (1973) work on strong and weak ties, because his empirical example involved job search. An example of more recent work on labor markets is provided by Toomet et al. (2013); other recent empirical examples of economic network research include the examination of trade flows (Ward et al., 2013). The work on embeddedness (Chapter 2) is relevant to economic networks.
- As noted above, there is a long tradition of research into *exchange networks* to understand economic resource distributions across certain network structures (Cook and Emerson, 1978).

Illicit networks and defence issues

Criminal, terrorist and other illicit networks are often referred to as *dark networks*. They present some interesting challenges for data collection because of course one aim of a criminal organization is not to be observed – and yet at the same time, the organization needs to intersect with the non-criminal world at various points in order to achieve its goals. The trade-off for criminal actors is between security and non-visibility, on the one hand, and activity and results on the other. So data is difficult to obtain, network boundaries are not clear and there will usually be uncertainty as to the identity of all the relevant actors. Information may be obtained piecemeal, and it will not always be obvious whether it is relevant or not. Data may be obtained from several different sources, including biographical information, police phone taps, court transcripts, and even interviews of criminals serving a prison sentence. Readers interested in illicit networks will want to check out some of the following research.

- Valdis Krebs (2002) was the first researcher to use a network analysis to examine the 9/11 terrorist attacks. Marc Sageman is prominent in research on terrorist networks, well known for his network data of suspected Al-Qaeda associates (Sageman, 2004). Sean Everton (2012) has a recent text on dark networks, with some illustrative data on the website associated with the book.
- David Knoke (2013) described how social network analysis was introduced into US military thinking as part of counter-insurgency strategy in the Iraq and Afghanistan wars. Social network analysis reportedly contributed to the capture of Saddam Hussein and the death of Osama bin Laden.
- The CASOS group at Carnegie Mellon, under the leadership of Kathleen Carley, studies complex socio-technical systems, including covert networks (www.casos. cs.cmu.edu).
- Carlo Morselli is a leading researcher in criminal networks. Morselli (2009) described a variety of methods for collecting criminal network data and included a number of datasets. He has edited a recent collection of papers that illustrates the current state of research well (Morselli, 2014).
- Carrington (2011) and van der Hulst (2011) provided good overviews of network research on criminal and terrorist networks, respectively.

Networks and psychology

In the mid-twentieth century, considerable empirical social network research was undertaken by such notable social psychologists as Festinger (1949), Milgram (1967) and Sherif et al. (1961). Unfortunately this interest died down with growth in the study of individualized social cognition (Robins and Kashima, 2008), even though there are intermittent signs of renewed engagement (e.g., Burt et al., 2013; Mason et al., 2007; Pattison, 1994).

- Only recently has long-standing psychological interest in social influence processes tended to move beyond dyadic-based research to more of a network perspective

(Mason et al., 2007). Similarly, psychological theories of social relationships have a long empirical tradition (e.g., Byrne, 1971; Fiske, 1991, 1992) but are essentially dyadic-based and have not been extended to a network conceptualization. Network research has seldom drawn on this fine-grained empirical detail about interactions, and – for the most part – psychologists have not picked up the systemic elements of a network perspective. The gaps remain.

- Individuals with different personality profiles may prefer different network environments, that is, have differently structured personal networks (Kalish and Robins, 2006; Selfhout et al., 2010). The research focus is often on the personality profiles of network brokers, people with a tendency to occupy structural holes (e.g., Kalish, 2008). *Self-monitoring* – the extent to which individuals tailor their behaviors to their immediate social environments – is a personality trait that has been shown to be associated with network brokerage, especially in organizational contexts (Mehra et al., 2001; Oh and Kilduff, 2008).
- Social network research in psychology is often egonet-based. For instance, English and Carstensen (2014) used the Social Convoy Questionnaire (Chapter 5) to study social network characteristics among older participants. Egonet size decreases as people age, although the number of close alters remains fairly constant.
- Psychology, networks and big data are intertwined in such projects as myPersonality (mypersonality.org/wiki/doku.php) at the Cambridge University Psychometrics Laboratory. This large dataset (participants number in the millions) includes several psychometrically well-established psychological scales – mainly of personality traits – as well as Facebook relational data from which various network indices have been extracted.

Political networks

In contrast to the somewhat intermittent nature of network research in psychology, interest in political network analysis is growing quickly.

- Fowler et al. (2011) noted well-established associations between political networks and political behavior, across a range of empirical areas such as public opinion, voting behavior, interest group coalitions and influence, party factions, and institutional development.
- Readers interested in political networks will want to read the recent special issue of *Social Networks* covering a wide range of political topics, from international sanctions to political power, and illustrating different data collection and analytic options (McClurg and Lazer, 2014). See also the special issue of *American Politics Research* on social networks and American politics (Heaney and McClurg, 2009).
- For those interested in an example of visualizations of political networks, I recommend the depiction of US Senate voting behavior across time by Moody and Mucha (2013).
- Social movement research has had a natural focus on social network ideas: for recent work, see the special issue of *Social Movement Studies* (Krinsky and Crossley, 2014) and the review by Diani (2011). Mische (2008), in her study of Brazilian youth activist networks, showed how the combination of excellent fieldwork and archival sources can lead to rich data and fascinating conclusions. Her comments about the pragmatics (and, indeed, sensitivity) of data collection are worth reading for those who are planning empirical work in highly charged political contexts.

Policy networks, network governance and environmental systems

Rhodes (2006) defined policy networks as linkages between governmental and other bodies involved in public policy-making and implementation. This idea is similar to the concept of a network governance system, which is usually construed as collaborations among a set of organizations to manage ('govern') some form of collective resource, often in the absence of a centralizing authority. Lewis (2011) and Knoke (2011) overviewed this rather broad field.

- Much of the earlier research on policy and governance networks was of a conceptual nature. The idea of a network was used somewhat descriptively or metaphorically, rather than as an object of empirical study. Some of this literature tended to consider a networked system of governance as generally good, whereas empirically, we network analysts know that a network can both facilitate and impede, and it is necessarily an empirical question, requiring careful data collection, whether a given system is working as intended. In a welcome step, recent research in the policy network domain has taken a more overtly empirical network orientation, often with the use of sophisticated network analytic methods (e.g., Lubell et al., 2012).
- Much attention has been paid to the governance of environmental resources, particularly influenced by the ground-breaking work of Nobel Prize winner, Elinor Ostrom. Towards the end of her career, she gave special attention to social-ecological systems, which integrated both a social system (governance structure) and environmental dependencies (Ostrom et al., 2007; Ostrom, 2009). An innovative, network-oriented conceptualization of social-ecological systems was developed by Bodin and Tengö (2012), who envisaged the system as a two-level network, with both a social and an ecological level, and with network ties among nodes within and between levels.
- Network governance of environmental resources highlights the relevance of 'network effectiveness': we want the governance structure to be effective in sustaining the environmental system. There have been several theoretical proposals for effective governance structure (e.g., Berardo and Scholz, 2010; Carlsson and Sandstrom, 2008; deLeon and Varda, 2009; Jones et al., 1997; Kenis and Provan, 2009; Robins et al., 2011) but to date without a lot of empirical support. Lubell (2013) argued that a richer understanding of governance structures requires a bipartite network conceptualization with both organizations and higher-level institutions.
- It is a complex business to collect data in this area. I discussed some of the issues above when describing inter-organizational data. Given that there are new bipartite and multilevel conceptualizations, it is not even certain what data is best to collect. For his organization/institutions bipartite network data, Mark Lubell uses a novel 'hybrid' name generator, asking organizations which institutions they are involved in, and then which organizations they principally deal with in each of these institutions. Örjan Bodin, for his social-ecological network, draws on expert advice about ecological dependencies to represent the ecological network.
- If we are studying network effectiveness, we also need a good measure of system outcomes and at present there is no consensus about this. Research in this field tends to build one case study at a time, whereas well-based empirical conclusions about effectiveness require data across several cases. These are difficult but fascinating issues that will be subject to future work, so watch this space. I return to some of these matters in Chapter 10.

- Readers with specific interest in network governance of environmental resources will want to read the book by Bodin and Prell (2011), with its strong network orientation and discussion of theoretical, empirical and network analytic issues.

Disaster management

Disaster response is a new area of interest for empirical social network research. The basic idea is that organizations of various types come together in response to natural or human-made disasters, resulting in a network of collaboration or cooperation (sometimes, non-cooperation – it is an empirical question, whether the coordination of agencies works!).

- To date, network connections have often been derived post hoc from archival reports of the disaster management. For instance, Carter Butts et al. (2012) described the use of archival sources to reconstruct the dynamic network of over 1500 organizations involved in the response to Hurricane Katrina (the dataset is available with the online publication). This article is worth reading not just for the description of the data, but for an interesting discussion of the role of source organizations, the use of situation reports as opposed to media accounts, and the challenges to automated coding of organizational network information from these sources.
- Even though data has been collected from archival sources, there is no conceptual impediment to a more dynamic data collection, when an event has recently occurred or even as it is unfolding. For instance, Butts (2008a) developed the relational events model (Chapter 9) in part to analyze early radio communications in response to the World Trade Center disaster, although again in this case the data was based on post hoc analysis of the records.
- The World Trade Center attacks have been an important stimulus for network reconstruction about disaster response. Schweinberger et al. (2014) described a large-scale inter-organizational dataset collected during the first 12 days after 11 September 2001, and proposed novel methods for its analysis.

Historical network analysis

I mentioned above the influential work of John Padgett. Historical network analysis has a small but growing group of practitioners using texts and archives to extract and analyze network data, to draw conclusions about historical events.

- As an example, check out the (slightly extended) egonet of Julius Caesar, derived from the works of Seutonius, produced by the University of Groningen (http://bluenetworks.weebly.com/sna-in-ancient-history-julius-caesar.html).
- Historical network researchers have formed their own scholarly group, with regular conferences and workshops (www.historicalnetworkresearch.org).

Internet studies and social media

These are very hot topics in network science more generally, often driven by computer science and data mining disciplines, and involving Big Data, digitally collected.

- In internet studies, the focus is on hyperlinks between a given set of sites or between sites involved in a common theme or activity. Software to do this includes *Webometric Analyst* (http://lexiurl.wlv.ac.uk) which produces network visualizations of links between a set of websites or blogs; and *VOSON* (http://voson.anu.edu.au) which incorporates web mining, data visualization, and social network analysis. But other software suites are available, and more become available all the time, so do a web search to find the package that is right for your research. Ackland (2013) provides an introduction to data and methods in web social science. Gruzd and Haythornthwaite (2011) review common internet data sources in the context of automated discovery of social networks. Of course, big data methods (see Box 6.1 for big web data examples) and visualizations (see the hot topics section of Chapter 8) are particularly relevant in this area.
- There is major interest in social media from a network perspective, much of it in the computer science community. One of the attractions of social media is the hope that it can be analyzed to predict future major societal events. The use of mobile phone messages was widely seen as instrumental in the London riots of 2013, and social media was reported to have contributed to the street demonstrations in the Iranian 'Green Movement' of 2009. (Both of these events should give pause to those who see social media overwhelming more traditional political networks. In both cases, government authorities quite successfully countered by utilizing institutional structures and other political and governmental resources.) Other political events facilitated by social media include the Arab Spring and the Occupy Wall Street movement.
- Less political goals for social media analysis include early notice of disease outbreaks (e.g., bird flu) or of the need for disaster response. The research to date has often concentrated on the structure of and processes within social media data, as a forerunner to actual successful prediction. There is still a lot of work to be done in the area of actual prediction (Lazer et al., 2014).
- Different data collection tools may be required specific to the type of social media studied. There are a variety of online tools for importing Facebook data into other programs: for instance, Social Network Importer (http://socialnetimporter.codeplex.com) will import Facebook data into NodeXL, an Excel-based network package (Chapter 8; see Hansen et al., 2010); and CollegeConnect (www.oii.ox.ac.uk/research/projects/?id=116), developed by Bernie Hogan from the Oxford Internet Institute, visualizes Facebook social networks, particularly for college students. Hogan's *NameGenWeb* software (http://namegen.oii.ox.ac.uk/fb) will also produce a Facebook egonet. Examples of network research with Facebook data have included personality profiles (see the section on psychology above) and social capital (Brooks et al., 2014).
- Kumar et al.'s (2014) book on Twitter data analytics provides an introduction to the collection and storage of Twitter data and some simple approaches to network analysis of Twitter feed. In network terms, follower links on Twitter may not provide a lot of information, and of course the Twitter stream constitutes a sequence of events and probably should be analyzed as such, rather than as a static network (Chapter 9). Nevertheless, Harrigan et al. (2012) showed there is sufficient information in the structure of user exchanges to draw novel conclusions about the social diffusion of information through tweets.
- Data collection for social media, however, is necessarily sampled, but not enough attention has been given to the extent to which it might be biased. González-Bailón et al. (2014) showed the extent of bias that can occur in social media data collection, even in large samples, and called for a more careful account of data quality and the creation of standards to facilitate the comparability of findings across research studies.
- Mobile phones have also been used to collect network information. Eagle et al. (2009) used mobile phones of participants to obtain location information and so

to record whether two participants were physically proximate. They compared the mobile phone data with self-reports and found that it was possible to infer 95% of friendships from the phone data, given distinctive temporal and spatial patterns for friends. There are interesting variations on this type of research: for instance, Sun et al. (2013) used travel smartcard data to infer the structure of physical encounters across a whole metropolitan area.

Co-authorship and citation networks

Co-authorship and citation networks provide a new approach to bibliometrics and to the scientific study of an academic disciplinary field or research area (*scientometrics*). White (2011) reviews recent work on scientific and scholarly networks. Co-authorship networks have authors of academic articles as nodes with an edge between them if they co-author an article; citation networks, on the other hand, have academic outputs (e.g., articles) as nodes with a tie from one to another when the first cites the second. Co-authorship networks have undirected ties, whereas citation networks are directed. Co-authorship networks reflect the actual collaboration among authors, whereas citation networks, of course, can have links even when the authors have no direct social relationship. In this sense, the two are quite different and subject to different processes.

- The data for both these types of networks come from bibliographic sources that are now available digitally. As the data is much more accessible than previously, the study of co-authorship and citation networks is growing rapidly.
- Networks of very large size can be extracted from the databases and studied. Radicchi et al. (2012) and Mali et al. (2012) provided recent reviews of co-authorship and citation networks, respectively.
- Loet Leydesdorff (www.leydesdorff.net) and Katy Börner (http://info.slis.indiana. edu/~katy/) are prominent researchers in scientometrics with plenty of interesting information on their websites.

Education and learning analytics

Learning management systems in universities and elsewhere require that students access websites for course information and materials, be involved in discussion lists, submit work digitally, and so on. These digital traces of student engagement with a subject can be analyzed to assess when students are at risk of poor performance, and to understand the patterns of effective learning.

- The appearance of massively open online courses (MOOCs) has dramatically increased the amount of data available for such research.
- Although learning analytics often focuses on individual learning, the role of social interactions in effective learning behaviors is attracting new attention (Haythornthwaite and Andrews, 2011). Shum and Ferguson (2012) used the term *social learning analytics* to encompass socially situated learning.

- With social learning analytics, we have data that might be both unipartite (students responding to students on discussion lists) and bipartite (students accessing subject material) and is in event-type format. Big data is once again available from these large digital resources. For recent work in this area, see the special issue of *American Behavioral Scientist* (Haythornthwaite et al., 2013).

Animal networks

Of course, humans are not the only social beings, and the study of animal social organization is particularly interesting. In what ways are animal social networks similar to or different from human networks?

- In her review of animal social network research, Katie Faust (2011) pointed to some of the hurdles in collecting animal social network data: the need to identify individuals, to catalogue their characteristic forms of social behavior, and to systematically record interactions and associations over time.
- Of course the definition of a social network tie among animals is not always clear, and sometimes there are issues around whether animal relationships are dyadic or more collective (e.g., herd-based).
- Dominance hierarchies have been studied among different species. To study more affiliative ties, often prolonged or regular proximity is taken as an indicator of a relationship. Data has been collected by observation but now commonly through various forms of wireless technology, with individual animals carrying electronic devices that record when close pairwise contact occurs (e.g., Boyland et al., 2013; Patison et al., 2010).
- Croft et al. (2011) provided an overview of animal networks research and some good methodological advice.

In conclusion: The key point

Do not just think about network data collection in general. Think about the context of your research and what will be required to get good data that will address your research question in that context.

BOX 6.3

Pulling back the curtain: What goes on in real network studies

For the sporting team study, data was collected by paper-and-pencil survey in a group setting, at the club after regular training activities. The researchers described the survey and answered any queries, and then asked the athletes to complete it. As we had the coach's endorsement of the survey, the athletes were generally interested and cooperative, and we had a good response rate. We collected the surveys as they were completed. The whole process took about 30 minutes.

In the environmental organization study, the survey was conducted by telephone interview of key informants. We faced some tricky decisions about what counted as a node. Some of our data related to government agencies which were notionally part of the one organization but in fact had quite different patterns of collaboration due to their different responsibilities. We needed multiple respondents from these larger organizations to get the detail of these network ties. For most of these agencies, we decided that they would be better represented as multiple nodes in the network, rather than the one organizational actor with many links. But this step required us to go carefully through the list of organizations and the data, to consider the nature of each organization, each agency, and their responsibilities, in order to make a decision about a final set of nodes that did justice to the actual collaboration system, rather than to the formal organizational affiliations.

Hot topics and further reading

There are so many hot topics here it is hard to know where to start. Every research context has its own set. Some of these issues I will pick up in Chapter 10. But let me suggest two hot topics to think about now:

Network data collection advice in articles and books tends to be general, along the lines of Chapter 5. Indeed, there are issues that generally apply; but there are also data collection demands specific to individual disciplines, contexts and topics. So, in another sense, social network data collection is fragmented, rather than general, with practices in one domain not always applied in others. How do we find the right balance between the specific and the general, and how do we learn from the data collection experience across the entire field, rather than from our own little sector?

And the hottest topic for you: in your own research, how will you best collect your network data?

Further reading

- For another overview of different contexts for empirical social network research, I recommend the Scott and Carrington (2011) volume, with its chapter-by-chapter description of research areas, with more detail than I can provide here.

Scott, J. and Carrington, P. (eds) (2011) *The SAGE Handbook of Social Network Analysis*. London: Sage.

SEVEN
Ethical issues for social network research

Distinctive ethical issues arise in network data collection and in reporting network results. Ethical issues may be less acute when the data are already publicly available through digital or archival sources, but even so do not entirely disappear.

Needless to say, social network research is not exempt from standard ethical practices that apply to other social science research. Participants recruited into studies should be able to give proper, informed consent; they should be assured of appropriate anonymity or confidentiality; they should be free to withdraw any unprocessed data; and they should be entitled to knowledge of the outcomes of the research. Practices vary slightly from country to country, and even between universities and research institutions within a country, but the general broad principles are well recognized. (For an introduction to ethical practice in social science research, see Israel and Hay, 2006.)

Empirical social science research normally requires ethical review. Review boards and ethics committees often have limited experience in dealing with social network studies, so it is important that the ethical controls intended for your research be explained clearly. Issues often arise about anonymity and confidentiality.

Because social network data is typically based on connections between people, often data cannot be collected in anonymous form, unlike many social science surveys. So additional protection may be required to ensure confidentiality. In reporting results, there may be interest in network participants who occupy certain network positions. Care must again be taken to ensure confidentiality.

For the most part, I use the terms *participants* and *respondents* interchangeably. But sometimes there is a difference – for instance, if your network constitutes links between organizations, then the organizations are the participants (the actors in the network), but the respondents may be the organizational experts who provide you with the information about the inter-organizational links. In such cases, there may be different levels at which to apply anonymity or confidentiality: at both the organizational and the personal levels.

Good ethical practice will help reassure and motivate your respondents to engage with the study. The ethical constraints will help you collect better data. In Chapter 5, I noted the importance of obtaining good response rates. Convince participants that their confidentiality will be properly protected and their personal interests appropriately taken into account. This issue may be especially acute in certain studies. In workplaces, for instance, employees may be concerned that management will use information about their network positions to assess their performance. Unless you reassure employees that this will not be the case, they may be reluctant to give accurate responses and may even try to 'game' the survey. If so, you will simply get bad data. Whenever possible, make a point of reassuring your participants that you are very conscious of the ethical issues, that the study has been approved by an independent body to assess its ethical standing, that their confidentiality will be respected, and that they can respond openly without repercussions.

Ethical issues for egocentric designs

Egocentric designs are the easiest for us to deal with in this chapter because in important ways they resemble standard research designs and so there are few distinctive ethical issues. Participants are typically selected under a sampling frame and do not know each other. The only novel feature is that the participant will nominate alters. Usually the researcher does not need to know the identity of these alters: what is required is that the alters be distinguishable from each other. So it typically suffices for the participant to provide a list of alters using first name, first name and initial of last name, or even a nickname. In this case, anonymity of the alters is assured. Moreover, there is usually no need for the participant to be identified on the survey instrument. Then the study is completely anonymous and should present no special ethical issues beyond those normally applying to social science research.

Ethical issues for whole network and other designs

Whole network studies using name generators in survey or interview format, on the other hand, do present some particular ethical issues. Ethics review committees will often be unfamiliar with such studies, so explain your research design and measures carefully. Some standard issues seen as central by these committees are not always applicable in network terms, but the committee is unlikely to understand that (see Box 7.1 for an example.)

BOX 7.1

Ethics review boards and statistical power

Especially in health and medical sciences, ethics review often includes issues of statistical power. The statistical power of a study is its ability to detect a significant effect. This depends on a number of factors, but ethics committees usually focus on sample size. The ethical implication is that it is inappropriate for the study to proceed unless there is a solid chance that it will uncover relevant effects.

If you have an egonet study, then you can conduct a power analysis in the standard way based on the number of egos proposed for your sample. However, if you are studying one or several small networks, you may be quizzed about whether you have enough participants to provide sufficient power.

Strictly speaking, power analysis as developed by Cohen (1988) and others is part of the paraphernalia of null hypothesis significance testing (NHST). The application of standard NHST to network studies is dubious given the network dependencies in the data. So a standard power analysis is quite simply inapplicable to a whole network study.

Do not rely on this argument in your ethics application! Ethics committees are unlikely to be sympathetic. It is fine to point out that power analysis has not been fully developed for network studies, but go further. Often we are interested in network structure, so I usually note that the number of observations of network ties is $n(n-1)$, not n, which is what the committee members are used to. They are usually sufficiently impressed when I tell them that my study of 100 participants will result in nearly 10,000 observations.

Anonymity and confidentiality

The most distinctive aspect for ethics review is that participants need to be identified as senders of the relational tie (Chapter 5); their nominated partners similarly need to be identified as the receivers of the tie.

So, complete anonymity is very difficult in a whole network study. At the least, the researcher needs to be able to match senders and receivers of ties in order to enter data in the form of Figures 4.1–4.3 in Chapter 4. The simplest procedure is for the researcher to guarantee participants that the data once entered will be completely de-identified. Each participant is coded with an ID number and that is what is entered into the dataset. If necessary, the lists of participant names with associated ID codes can be destroyed once the data are entered, after which there is no documentary means to link the identities of the participants and the data. In my experience, such procedures are often sufficient to reassure participants and ethics committees. You, the researcher, however, need to establish your credentials and integrity with participants. It may be important to assure participants that feedback and reports of the research will also be completely de-identified. I make some further comments on feedback and reporting below.

Methods to ensure anonymity in special cases

Sometimes there are special reasons why you want to maintain complete anonymity for the participants. For instance, in sensitive studies, perhaps involving children, ethical review committees might insist that de-identification is not sufficient. I have conducted network survey research in special classrooms with a two-step procedure. The teacher was asked to compile a list of all students in the class (the network boundary) and to number the students consecutively on the list. The list was given to the students along with the survey, but as a separate document. In name generator items, the students were asked to enter the numbers of their nominated network partners but not their names. Respondents were asked to enter their own numbers in a special box at the beginning of the survey. After the survey, the teacher collected the name lists and the researcher the surveys. So it was impossible for the teacher to know the responses of the students, and it was impossible for the researcher to identify the students. Anonymity was preserved.

This more elaborate procedure is a little cumbersome but quite manageable. It is worth keeping as an option if ethical review committees are not comfortable about the absence of complete anonymity. On one occasion, however, I had the pleasant surprise of an ethics committee itself proposing that this more complex procedure was not necessary and that the simpler confidentiality approach would be fine.

Non-respondents

Of course, you will be a lucky researcher if every actor within your network boundary agrees to participate. There is an interesting ethical issue for whole network research about the treatment of those who choose not to participate. As I noted in Chapter 5, it is usually not optimal to pretend that such nodes do not exist. Certainly, non-participants have a right to have their data and their identities not included in the study. Does this mean that if they are nominated by another actor that nomination should be withdrawn from the data?

I suggest not. Certainly, non-participants have the right not to be identified in any way; but other participants' nomination of them is not their data, so they do not have the automatic right to have that data withdrawn (Borgatti and Molina, 2005). Non-network studies often involve non-participants in analogous ways: for instance, in social support studies, participants may be asked about whether their close family members are strong sources of support. It is not considered ethically necessary to ask the permission of the family members whether they agree to the participant responding to this item. In network studies, with non-participants not identified, but with participants' nominations of non-participants retained, in effect the data contains the following information. Participant *i* and participant *j* agree (or do not) about the nominations of others outside the network boundary defined by participation. The data is blind as to who these others are, and any information specifically about them is not part of the data. The important point is the extent to which *i* and *j* have links through third parties, to determine the network connectivity between them. This is a property of *i* and *j*, and hence constitutes part of their data, and is not a property of any third-party non-participant.

Informed consent

These particular network issues emphasize the importance of properly informed consent. Depending on the research context, there may be several levels to consent. For instance, if the study is conducted in an organization, the permission of the organization at an appropriately senior level will be required, and then perhaps at intermediate levels, before informed consent is sought from individual participants (see Box 7.3).

Consent means that the participants indicate through their *free* actions that the data they provide can be used for the purposes of the study. In some cases, completion of (part of) the survey counts as consent, but if so this should be stated clearly and prominently to participants before they begin. In other cases, a separate consent form needs to be signed, indicating that the participant understands the purpose and the tasks of the study. *Informed* consent means that there is sufficient information available to participants to make a sensible, personal decision before commencing the study.

For network studies, participants should be given general information explaining that they will be asked to nominate network partners in various ways. It is helpful to give brief general background to network studies, and to your study in particular, to indicate the purpose of this type of data collection. For instance: 'Network studies in organizations enable us to draw conclusions about the circumstances under which people collaborate effectively with one another.' You want the information to be succinct, otherwise people will not read it properly, but at the same time do not ignore this opportunity to motivate respondents to provide good data. It is particularly important to reassure them about the controls you have in place to ensure confidentiality and/or anonymity.

Sometimes, with vulnerable or special populations, informed consent requires more than just the consent of the participant. For instance, research on children typically requires the consent of parents or guardians. Network research is no different in this respect from other types of social science research.

An important consideration is that participants be able to make a *free* decision about consent without undue pressure. It is best that the researcher is independent of the research context and that there is no coercion for participation. This is not always a simple matter. If you have a contract to do network research in an organization, senior managers may insist that all relevant employees participate. Convince them that you will get better data if their employees freely agree, rather than perfunctorily comply with a top-down directive. Borgatti and Molina (2005) proposed a signed agreement between management and the researcher about how the data will be handled, an agreement that can be included in the consent documents for participants. Ideally, management should not see any data that has not been anonymized and aggregated to group level.

Duty of care

We have a duty of care to our respondents, to ensure that completion of the survey, interview or other data collection task does not lead to serious distress or discomfort. For the vast majority of network surveys, distress is a very unlikely occurrence and the risks to respondents are no greater than the risks that they are exposed to in normal life, which is a good criterion for safe social science research. Of course, sometimes the risks are a little greater, often depending on the vulnerability of the population. These are good reasons why you should phrase name generators relating to negative ties, and even sometimes positive ties, with care. If you are studying bullying networks among children, for instance, you need to do so with sensitivity. It is hard to give general advice here, but check out the ethical standards and norms that apply in your field of research. If they have not been used in network research before, they can usually be readily adapted.

If the risks are greater, you should have in place contingency plans if data collection results in some participants seeking further support and assistance. Whatever the level of risk, participants should be able to contact the researcher with any comments or questions. These practices should be standard in social science studies, and again social network research is no different.

Other network designs

These general principles obviously apply to any network designs that use surveys, interviews or related forms of data collection, whether they be longitudinal, snowball sampling, cognitive social structure designs and so on. Each design brings its own features with possible ethical implications. For instance, snowball sampling requires more information about network partners in order for the researcher to be able to contact them. This implies that issues of confidentiality and de-identification need to be even more strongly enforced.

In Chapter 6, I briefly described network laboratory experiments where small groups of individuals are brought together, with their responses networked in some way (perhaps through computers) to study the effects of social interaction under various conditions. Such experiments are increasingly popular in social psychological, behavioral economics and other research traditions. There are well-established norms and ethical protocols for conducting behavioral experiments in these areas, and best practice should be applied. There are no special implications here because of the network basis of the experiment.

Feedback to participants

It is good ethical practice for participants to have feedback on the results of the research.

Individual debriefing

It is not uncommon in individual data collection to provide a short debriefing session on the study, immediately after the data collection session. This can be achieved most simply by a short handout, or perhaps access to a webpage, that provides a statement of goals, some background on the research, the specific research questions and perhaps some references. Details on how to obtain the eventual results of the research might be included.

Reports, websites and publications

Participants should be able to get at least a short report on the results of the research. Often participants are given contact information for the researcher and can apply to have such a report emailed to them. Sometimes researchers set up a website containing summary results and conclusions. If you are doing longitudinal research, consider this option. It is one way of maintaining participant motivation and minimizing drop-out rates between measurement points.

In reports and academic publications, you need to think carefully about the maintenance of confidentiality. Although there can be different standards for different studies depending on the topic and its sensitivity, I feel uncomfortable if I have to break any of the rules in Box 7.2.

BOX 7.2

Good practices in reporting social network results

These do not have to be applied universally, but if you do not follow these rules, make sure you have a good reason to do so – one that you can defend if your participants later complain!

- Do not identify the particular sites of the research (e.g., do not name organizations, schools and so on – provide a general description of the sites instead).
- Do not identify respondents – even if the study is about organizations and you feel you can note a particularly important organization in a report without serious consequences, do not identify the respondent(s) from that organization who provided the data.

(Continued)

(Continued)

- Do not identify isolates or very low-degree nodes: in fact, my preference is not to identify nodes at all, but isolated nodes may be particularly problematic because 'isolation' tends to be regarded as negative.
- In network visualizations:
  - o Do not label the nodes with actual identities.
  - o If you represent continuous node-level variables by size, vary the scale so that node size cannot be used to identify nodes; note in the publication that you have done this, so that node size in the figure is only an approximation.
  - o Check the visualization to make sure that a combination of degree, node colors (if any), and node size cannot be used by knowledgeable observers to guess correctly the identity of prominent or peripheral nodes; otherwise, adjust the layout so that it is not so transparent.
- Be particularly careful about visualizations. If you present visualizations to individuals or groups of people who believe they know specific details about the context, the first thing they will do is try to guess which node is which. They may ask you. Firmly, tell them that you will not identify the nodes. Tell them that the visualization has been slightly adjusted so that – while it is still a faithful representation of the network system – it is not possible to use it to identify nodes definitely. Appeal to the integrity of your research ethics. In the long run, you will win more kudos this way than by slyly suggesting whether their guesses are right or wrong.

Group feedback

Sometimes it is valuable to provide results and interim conclusions to your participants collectively in seminar format. This works well when you have studies of organizations who can send along representatives (perhaps the respondents, perhaps others). There are several striking advantages:

- You can advertise this seminar before collecting the original data. This will provide motivation for organizations to participate in the study and offer good data.
- The seminar fulfils the obligation to provide good feedback to participants.
- You can use the seminar as a focus group to discuss whether the results make sense, and, if so, how best to interpret them. The seminar then becomes an extension of the research.
- It may be possible to collect further data during the seminar to cover issues that have emerged from the results but were not handled well in the original survey.

Electronic and digital data

The profusion of electronic and digital data nowadays does not alleviate ethical concerns, and adds some complications. I have noted above that participants have the right to withdraw their own unprocessed data from studies. With many electronic datasets, the question often arises as to who owns the data. For instance, an organization may have an extensive dataset on email exchanges among employees. We often feel that our emails are our property, for we created them. However, if we use a company email system, arguably the emails are the property of the company. In that case, the organization may have the right by ownership to pass the email data to a researcher for analysis, and the individuals may not have the right to withdraw emails.

Sometimes these are grey areas which have not been fully tested legally. In any event, it is still sensible to engage in good ethical practice, to the extent of de-identifying the email data, so that there is confidentiality for individual senders and receivers of emails.

One potential grey area is what counts as a public space in a digital world. It has been generally accepted that in public spaces, such as town squares or shopping centres, a researcher can observe individual behavior without seeking consent. For instance, transport research might count the numbers of people who use a certain train station at different times of the day. It would be absurd to suggest that consent should be sought from every person counted, or that an individual could choose not to be counted.

Internet websites seem to be accepted as public spaces, so for some time now web-crawlers have been trawling through the World Wide Web without seeking anyone's permission. This makes good and obvious sense. If you put up a website with hyperlinks for everyone to see, then it is reasonable that researcher might study those hyper-links without contacting you. Wilkinson and Thelwall (2011) pointed to a distinction between individuals and documents as research objects. Public documents can often be used without ethical issues and consent may not be necessary. Because many web-based objects are in effect electronic public documents, Wilkinson and Thelwall argued there may not be the need for ethical review. They do, however, distinguish between privacy and consent, and recommend that anonymity be considered carefully, although in public documents obviously anonymity cannot be a universal principle.

Social media are less clear. To what extent is a Facebook page a public space or a private domain? Who owns the page? (Is it yours? Is Facebook the owner?). Our new digital, interconnected society is still working through these issues and it is too early to be definitive. In this world, definitions of privacy and ownership seem to be changing, and it is conceivable that norms of ethical research will change with them. Nissenbaum (2004) argued that privacy should be regarded as context-based: different contexts have different norms. Proper consideration of privacy will respect 'contextual integrity'. She noted that personal information revealed in one context is still 'tagged with that context and is never "up for grabs"' (p. 143). In short, researchers are not ethically able to utilize any information about individuals just because it is on a website that they can access. Proper privacy concerns require that the norms applicable to the original context of the provision of the information be respected.

Contextual integrity constitutes an important ethical and privacy issue if researchers wish to combine datasets. Even if the data are publicly available, individuals may have a reasonable expectation that the information in one dataset not be linked with the information in another. In short, if the context of providing one set of information is that it should not be associated with the other, then contextual integrity requires that the two datasets not be combined. An obvious example is that of identity theft, where various distinct pieces of information may be aggregated to 'steal' a digital identity. Researchers need to be careful if they are combining datasets, and, even for public data, perhaps formal ethical review is a desirable step.

If you are studying social media, it may be that people have already agreed to conditions that provide clarity. It is worthwhile examining the formal conditions under which people agree to use the service. Currently with regard to Twitter, for instance, each user agrees (before use) that Twitter may make public, reproduce, and disseminate tweets to anyone, and that Twitter data may be processed in any way. So if you, the researcher, obtain data from Twitter under established protocols whereby Twitter provides samples of tweets for research purposes, and you use no parallel questionnaires, surveys or other methods to obtain data from individuals, the data can be regarded as freely available in the public domain. In a situation where information is freely available publicly and individuals are not identified or identifiable, depending on local practice human ethics approval may not be required.

Nevertheless, care is still necessary. Lewis et al. (2008) published a dataset derived from Facebook accounts for a cohort of students over several years at a US college, the 'Tastes, Ties, and Time' data. The researchers did not release the name of the college and replaced the names of students with unique ID numbers. Even so, other information available in the dataset enabled very quick identification of the college and there were sufficient demographic variables so that some students could be identified. According to Zimmer (2010), the argument that 'the data is already public' was not sufficient: 'consent, privacy and anonymity do not disappear simply because subjects participate in online social networks; rather, they become even more important' (p. 324). The dataset was withdrawn from use, and at the time of writing remains unavailable.

An example of a rich network-based dataset that is available to other researchers, but only under appropriate protections, is the National Longitudinal Study of Adolescent Health (Add Health). This is a longitudinal study of a representative sample of adolescents in United States schools in the mid-1990s (www.cpc.unc.edu/projects/addhealth).

Archival, public sources and secondary data analysis

The topic of electronic data neatly slides into consideration of archival sources, most of which are now digitally available. Questions of ownership of the data, whether it is in the public domain, and the extent to which confidentiality should be applied, remain the main issues. If the data arises from public sources – for instance, if networks are derived from textual analysis of newspaper articles (see Chapter 6) – ethical issues seem minimal, again because these are public documents.

It is rather a tradition in social network research for new methods to be tested out on old, publicly available datasets, akin to a form of secondary data analysis. Informed consent implies that participants be properly informed about the purpose of the study, and that if the purpose of the study changes, the consent no longer applies. Depending on local standards, ethical review boards may now require that, if the original consent is not sufficiently broad, then new consent be obtained for secondary data analysis. This may be impossible if participants cannot be contacted. If you think that your data may be reanalyzed for somewhat different purposes in the future, then my advice is that you ensure the original consent form is drafted specifically to the purposes of the immediate study but also more broadly. For instance, you may wish to include words like: 'The de-identified data (without your name or any identifying details) will be analyzed to draw general conclusions about the overall network structure, and it may be passed to expert methodological analysts to assist with this goal.'

In conclusion: The key point

Do not avoid or ignore the ethical requirements. Treat them as a means to establish your credentials and integrity with your participants and hence obtain better data.

BOX 7.3

Pulling back the curtain: What goes on in real network studies

The sporting team study provides a good case in point of the levels of consent that may be necessary and desirable. I have already mentioned this point in Chapter 5. First, we obtained agreement from the overall league, then of the individual club and obtained the support of the coaches, before we obtained individual informed consent from the players just prior to data collection. Our ethics application included letters from the league and the club, together with the proposed consent form and study information to be given to the players.

In the environmental governance study, we conducted a post-study seminar with representatives of the participating organizations. We not only presented the results of the study, including network visualizations, but also asked the representatives for their interpretation of the results and conducted further data collection on the type of organizational structures that would be desirable for effective management of the resource. Naturally, we obtained additional ethical clearance for the data collection aspects of the seminar.

Hot topics and further reading

For those conducting social media and other digital studies, I think it is important to look at the problems that arose with the 'Tastes, Ties, and Time' data, and arguments advanced against its ethical provisions.

Lewis, K., Kaufman, J., Gonzalez, M., Wimmer, A. and Christakis, N. (2008) Tastes, ties, and time: A new social network dataset using Facebook.com. *Social Networks*, 30, 330–342.

Zimmer, M. (2010) 'But the data is already public': On the ethics of research in Facebook. *Ethics of Information Technology*, 12, 313–325.

For ethical issues in other types of social network research, I suggest you read the articles in the special issue on ethical dilemmas in social network research in the journal *Social Networks* in 2005. The issue considers various hot topics still relevant today: Breiger's (2005) overview of ethical issues for social network research, Goolsby's (2005) paper on the ethical risks involved in defence research, Borgatti and Molina (2005) on ethical network research in organizations, Klovdal (2005) on infectious disease control, and Kadushin (2005) on who benefits. However, given the pace of change in the digital world, and given that network research has a new focus in that area, it would be good to have an updated discussion on these and other areas.

Breiger, R. (2005) Introduction to special issue: Ethical dilemmas in social networks research. *Social Networks*, 27, 89–93.

Goolsby, R. (2005) Ethics and defense agency funding: Some considerations. *Social Networks*, 27, 95–106.

Borgatti, S. and Molina, J. (2005) Toward ethical guidelines for network research in organizations. *Social Networks*, 27, 107–117.

Klovdahl, A. (2005) Social network research and human subjects protection: Towards more effective infectious disease control. *Social Networks*, 27, 119–137.

Kadushin, C. (2005) Who benefits from network analysis: Ethics of social network research. *Social Networks*, 27, 139–153.

For a more recent discussion of ethical issues relating to digital data, see Hoser and Nitschke (2010).

Hoser, B. and Nitschke, T. (2010) Questions on ethics for research in the virtually connected world. *Social Networks*, 32, 180–186.

EIGHT

Network visualization:
What it can and cannot do

Once the data is collected, there are decisions to be made about how to understand the network structure and network effects. Network visualization is a commonly used aid. In this chapter, I discuss how to use network visualization to gain some understanding of a network structure, how to use visualizations in presenting results, and the limits to visualization as an analytical tool.

Graph-drawing methods and advanced algorithms for effective presentation of graph structure are active fields of research, especially in information technology and software development (Tamassia, 2013). Freeman (2009) noted, however, that visual images of social networks, especially kinship and genealogical trees, go back at least to the ninth century. According to Freeman, the first non-kinship network visualization was of South African interlocking corporate directors produced by Hobson (1894) – although the visualization seems to appear only in later editions of his book, after Hobson returned from working as a journalist covering the Boer War. Moreno and Jennings (1938), whom I noted as early network researchers in Chapter 1, produced what they termed *sociograms*, visualizations of unipartite social networks. For the Bank Wiring Room study (Chapter 1), Roethlisberger and Dickson (1939) produced a number of network visualizations of different relational ties among the workers. Brandes et al. (2013a) provide several other historical examples.

From the distance of the twenty-first century, it is worthwhile looking back at these early hand-drawn efforts – as well as noting that these researchers also had to draw more standard charts by hand – and to reflect how modern computing and statistical technology have made our lives so much easier. If we were still using hand-drawn figures, network visualization would be a much lesser aspect of our network research lives. The great strides that have been achieved in modern graph visualization can be seen by the many examples displayed on the internet (see the hot topics and further reading section at the end of this chapter). These are depictions of graphs and social networks of ingenuity and often great beauty.

My goal in this chapter, however, is not to traverse the entirety of graph visualization, and I do not intend to give step-by-step instructions on using the many programs available (all of the programs have manuals or publications that will help you with that – see Box 8.1). Rather, I will cover some general issues and principles, including introductory tips for those who are coming to network visualization for the first time.

If you want more and are particularly interested in this rich field, including the algorithmic details, you may wish to check out recent edited collections such as Tamassia (2013), or the annual International Symposium on Graph Drawing, the results of which are typically published in the Springer Lecture Notes on Computer Science series. Krempel (2011) provides a helpful summary of some network visualization techniques.

Most social network researchers have rather modest aims for their visualizations. They wish to produce an effective visualization that will:

- help explore the network data;
- provide some insight or assist with interpretation of analytic results; or
- help to present the research effectively, in seminar or conference presentations and in publications.

Even if it is much easier for us than our early forebears to draw a graph given our access to modern software, that does not mean that a network visualization will provide us with everything we need. A good visualization of social network data can aid interpretation and provide insight; it is visualization *plus* analysis that gives us strong grounds for inference and/or conclusions. Visualization alone should be seen as a network exploratory method or a presentational device.

Software for network visualization

Batagelj (2009) traversed the recent history of sophisticated network drawing algorithms for complex networks and described some software options for researchers. Software commonly used by social network researchers is listed in Box 8.1.

Social science researchers do not need to know the details of the algorithms that are implemented by these programs. Nevertheless, they usually share common principles. Let me give a simplified sense of what a good graph drawing program will attempt to do for a unipartite binary network. The data is entered as a matrix or an edge list, with the precise format dependent on the program. The program places the nodes in an initial position in a two-dimensional display. The initial position may possibly be entirely random or some variant (e.g., randomly placed on a large circle). The program may also allow an initial position to be specified by the researcher (or from an earlier iteration of the algorithm). Lines are drawn between nodes to represent edges. The important step is next. The program rearranges the nodes depending on the particular algorithm used, and there are several such algorithms that can be tried. Standard objectives for the display include the following:

1. Nodes should be distinguished from one another (i.e. not on top of one another).
2. Nodes with a line between them should tend to be close together.

There are other possible criteria, but not all algorithms seek to optimize them. For instance, Brandes et al. (2013a) noted the avoidance of meaningless line crossings as a desirable goal for readability. The overall aim is to maximize human visual perception of the network.

Of course, criteria may be contradictory – placing linked nodes together tends to increase the number of crossing lines. So usually there is no one solution that is the 'best'. Different algorithms attempt optimization in different ways. For instance, some are better at separating out components than others. That is why you should try different algorithms within your preferred program, and select the one that best illuminates the points you wish to make. Indeed, most programs allow users to move nodes manually as well.

Sometimes it is also useful to experiment with different programs. For instance, the examples in this chapter generated by Pajek and Netdraw use straight lines, but other programs (e.g., Gephi) also permit curved lines to give a different effect.

BOX 8.1

Some visualization programs used in social network research

There are several software packages readily available for the drawing of graphs. You should investigate to see which program is best for you. Here I list some that are commonly used for social networks, although these are by no means the only options:

- *Netdraw*: A program which comes with the popular network analysis package *UCINET* (www.analytictech.com). Borgatti et al. (2013) includes a chapter on how to use the software.
- *Pajek*: Software developed at the University of Ljubljana in Slovenia, under the leadership of Vlad Batagelj (http://pajek.imfm.si/doku.php?id=pajek). The word 'pajek' is Slovenian for 'spider'. Use of the software, which also includes analytic capacities, is described in de Nooy et al. (2011).

(Continued)

(Continued)

- *Visone*: This is the result of a long-term research project originating at the University of Konstanz to develop algorithms for the analysis and visualization of social networks. The Visone website (http://visone.info) includes a manual to guide new users. The Visone group includes Ulrik Brandes, a leader in graph visualization methods.
- While the above three programs are perhaps the most commonly used by social network researchers to date, Brandes et al. (2013a) noted a number of other options that are worth checking out.
  - ○ *Gephi*: Open source software for visualizing networks (http://gephi.org).
  - ○ *NodeXL*: This can be used with edge lists entered into Microsoft Excel (http://nodexl. codeplex.com). It is especially designed for the importation of social media data.
  - ○ *ORA*: This package has been developed by Kathleen Carley's software research group at Carnegie Mellon, and contains a network visualization routine (http://www.casos.cs.cmu.edu/projects/ora).
  - ○ *Tulip*: Developed by French researchers, designed to support visualization of any form of relational data (http://tulip.labri.fr/TulipDrupal).
- Those interested in visualization of longitudinal network data, including event data, should check out *Sonia* (http://sourceforge.net/apps/mediawiki/sonia; see also www.stanford.edu/group/sonia).
- Huisman and van Duijn (2011) reviewed a number of network visualization programs.

Different layouts for the one network

In Figure 8.1, I use *Pajek* to draw a 20-node undirected friendship network in four different ways. *Pajek* has several different available 'layouts'. In Figure 8.1(a), I have used the *circular* layout; Figure 8.1(b) uses an algorithm known as *Kamada–Kawai* (KK) after its creators; Figure 8.1(c) uses *Fruchterman–Reingold* (FR; there is an arrow in (c) that I will explain below); and Figure 8.1(d) is derived from Fruchterman–Reingold but with some manual adjustment.

KK and FR are energy minimization methods, also known as *spring embedders*. As Batagelj (2009) explained, these methods set up repulsive forces between the nodes (akin to particles) while the lines attract or repel the nodes if they are too far apart or too close (akin to springs between the particles). The algorithms then place the nodes in a way that minimizes the energy of the system. These methods are not too different from multi dimensional scaling that will be familiar to many social science researchers. One alternative is to use algebraically based singular value decomposition methods (Freeman, 2009).

Looking at the visualizations in Figure 8.1, we can see that the circular layout in (a) is not very revealing. Notice that the network visualizations in (b)–(d) reveal some important network brokerage (i.e., the two groups of nodes at the left and right of the displays are connected by a handful of bridging ties), but this is not so easy to see in the circular layout.

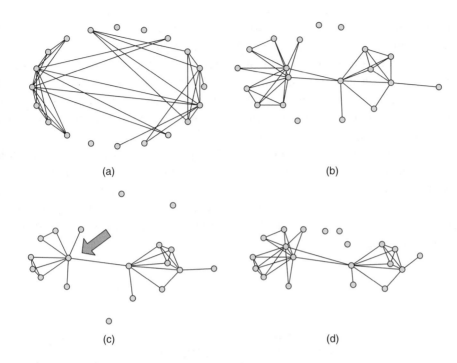

Figure 8.1 Four different visualizations of the one network

(a) circular layout; (b) using the Kamada–Kawai algorithm; (c) using the Fruchterman–Reingold algorthm; (d) using Fruchterman–Reingold but with manual adjustment

Compare the KK and FR algorithms in Figure 8.1(b) and (c). In this case, the FR algorithm does not do a good job of differentiating the nodes (principle 1 above), and in (c) the arrow points to what seems to be one node but is in fact two nodes placed in the same position. This happens because, as is clear from (b), the two nodes are structurally equivalent: they have connections to exactly the same other nodes. And (b) is not perfect either: some of the triangles in the denser regions are not well spaced. Similarly to the other programs, *Pajek* permits me to 'drag' the nodes into positions that I prefer. So in (d) I dragged one of the structural equivalent nodes apart from the other, spaced the triangles a little better, brought the isolated nodes together (just because I rather like that), and made some other small adjustments.

The phrase 'because I rather like that' is entirely apposite. The different parts of Figure 8.1 are all visualizations of the one network – they are a complete representation of the data. In that sense, there is no 'objective' data-based reason to prefer one to the other. You choose the one that makes the most compelling impression. The reasons for a choice can include aesthetic considerations. This emphasizes an important point: the placement in these visualizations is not fixed to any external axis (as is in the case in standard charts), and the individual position of any node by itself is meaningless. This is not always the case. If there were geographical data on the actors, we could place the nodes in a fixed position on a map, for instance, in which case we would not use spring embedders to optimize placement.

The arrow in (c) illustrates that the algorithm may not give a good result. But do not think that FR is always misleading or performs worse than KK, just because of this example. Always try a couple of different algorithms, experiment with moving the nodes, and do not trust the visualization until you are confident that it is not inadvertently hiding important features.

With a directed network, the programs will represent the direction of a tie with an arrow. Depending on the program, a reciprocated dyad is often represented as a double-headed arrow. If the network ties are weighted, then the values of the edges may be represented as thicker lines. In this case, the weights on the edges may be taken into account in a spring embedder algorithm, aiming for nodes with stronger ties to be closer together.

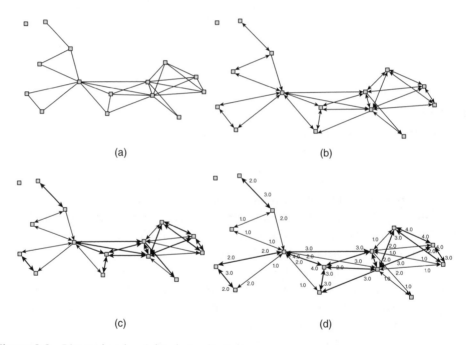

Figure 8.2 Directed and weighted visualizations

In Figure 8.2, I have drawn a small friendship network of 15 nodes, using *Netdraw*. The data is directed and weighted, with a tie indicating whether actor *i* provides support to actor *j*, with support measured on a scale from 1 to 4. In (a) I have simply drawn all the lines ignoring weights and arrows. In (b) the arrows are included. In (c) and (d) the tie strengths have been added. In (c) the thickness of the lines indicates the maximum strength of the tie in the dyad, whereas (d) additionally indicates, by small labels near each node, the strength of the tie sent from that node.

Visualization of directed, weighted graphs is not simple. Actor *i* may send a tie of strength *s* to actor *j*, while actor *j* may reciprocate with a tie of strength *t*. The thickness of the line – an elegant way to depict tie strength – needs to be weighted by either *s* or *t*, or some combination of the two, and any rule for that decision is rather arbitrary. Alternatively, the program needs to depict two arcs within each tied dyad, which can soon clutter the visualization. Labelling the edges with weights as in (d) is not an ideal solution; nor is the option of using different size arrowheads.

The world of visualization has a real aesthetic; but a visualization is neither unique, nor perfect. You will need to make choices and compromises.

Some simple issues for the novice graph drawer

Let me cover a few, perhaps rather obvious, points:

1. Larger networks (i.e., with many nodes) are much more difficult to draw well. It is very hard to distinguish any patterns visually. Figure 8.3(a) shows a 400-node network with density 0.05. Notice that even with a low density, the visualization is cluttered (there are nearly 4000 edges to squeeze into the diagram). It is very hard to draw any interesting conclusions from this visualization. This type of picture is sometimes colloquially called a 'fuzzball' by network researchers.
2. Even smaller networks with high density are difficult to draw well. Figure 8.3(b) shows a 40-node network with density 0.4. Again it is difficult to discern patterns.
3. It is pointless including a visualization of a particularly simple graph with hardly any structure. Perhaps it is obvious that there is no advantage in visualizing a complete graph or an empty graph (but, then again, perhaps not so obvious – see Koschade, 2005).
4. All programs permit user decisions about the size of nodes and the thickness of lines (and arrows for directed networks), as demonstrated in Figure 8.2. Do not necessarily use the default settings. Too large sizes for nodes, and too much thickness for lines and arrows, can cloud the visualization.
5. The more information you attempt to include in a visualization, the more confusing it may become (unless you are very skilled). The line weights in Figure 8.2(d) complete the data representation – everything in the dataset is included here – but they have no visual impact and add neither meaning nor understanding.
6. Think about your visualization in relation to the size of the figure you have available. If I projected a very large image in a conference presentation, you might be able to read the data weights in Figure 8.2(d) well enough (but would my conference audience scan through all that information and make sense of it?). In the version in the figure here, you will need either extremely good eyesight or even better glasses. It is a rather pointless inclusion in this case.

Lest you think I am a paragon of visualization techniques, let me assure you that I have broken these rules sometimes. But it is best to have a good reason to do so.

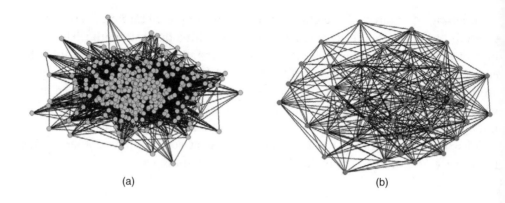

Figure 8.3 Unrevealing visualizations

(a) 400-node network with density 0.05; (b) 40-node network with density 0.4

Attributes in visualizations

Visualizations with attributes on the nodes can be especially helpful. As explained in Chapter 4, attribute data usually takes one of three forms: binary, categorical or continuous. Most graph-drawing programs will provide some straightforward options:

- Binary attributes can be represented by two 'colors' on the nodes: for instance, black and white as in Figure 8.4(a).
- Categorical attributes can be represented by multiple colors on the nodes, one for each category: for instance, black, grey and white as in Figure 8.4(b).
- Continuous attributes can be represented by different size nodes, where the size is scaled to the measurement scale of the variable: for instance, the different sized nodes in Figure 8.4(c).

Figure 8.4 presents the same data as in Figure 8.2, ignoring directions and weights on the ties. The two colors on the nodes in Figure 8.4(a) represent the sex of each actor; the three colors in (b) represent the country of origin of each actor; and the size of node in (c) represents the age of each actor.

Notice that I have drawn these figures separately. It is possible to draw a number of attributes together in the one visualization. Figure 8.5 presents a visualization for the data in Figure 8.4 with age and country both included.

It is possible to have two categorical (binary) attributes included in the one visualization. There are a few simple options for two such attributes: for instance, half of each node might be colored by one attribute and the other half by the second attribute. Sometimes, different categories of nodes might be represented by different shapes (e.g., square and circles, rather than just circles as in Figures 8.4 and 8.5). To

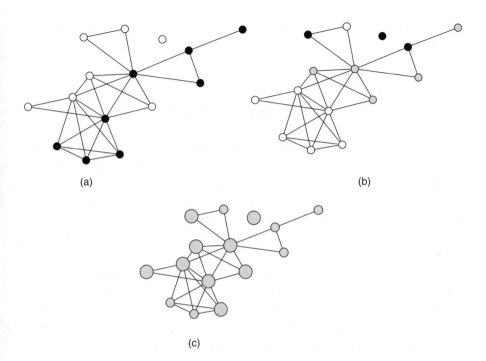

(a)

(b)

(c)

Figure 8.4 Visualizations with attributes

(a) binary; (b) categorical; (c) continuous

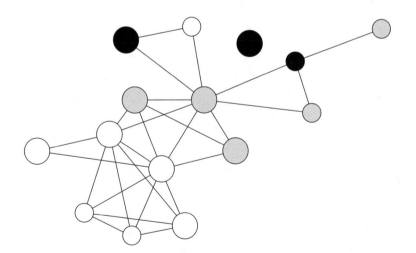

Figure 8.5 A visualization with multiple attributes

my mind, however, these more complicated visualizations do not always work that well for the eye, so adopt them with some care, unless you are an expert and can find more sophisticated solutions. It is necessary to find the balance between the visual insight that can be obtained by simplicity and the need to preserve complexity in the visualization.

Multiplex networks

Let me make a few remarks about visualizing a multiplex network, with several different types of tie among the same set of nodes. A simple way to depict such a graph is to draw different types of lines with different colors. Sometimes this can work well, but again the risk is that the visualization soon becomes cluttered and the eye cannot readily discern important patterns in the data. With your own data, check out the result of this approach and if you find you have sacrificed clarity for visual complexity, think again.

It is not a bad idea to present the different types of tie in separate visualizations but with the nodes in the same position. All programs will enable you to specify a fixed position for your nodes that you can apply from one set of ties to another. When I do this, I experiment with suitable layouts using spring embedders and other algorithms, together with a bit of manual adjustment, and, once satisfied, I apply the final positions to visualizations of the different types of ties. This is how I have drawn Figure 8.6. These nodes represent 60 managers in a government organization and the ties among them: reporting relations in (a), frequent interaction in (b), and crucial collaboration in (c) (Robins and Pattison, 2006).

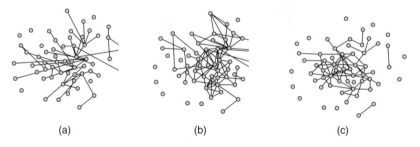

(a) (b) (c)

Figure 8.6 Visualization of a multiplex network

One issue is that the position of the nodes may be optimal for one type of tie but not for others. For instance, the reporting relationship in Figure 8.6(a) is more hierarchical and tree-like than is observable from this visualization. Again, there are decisions to be made and no right answer. I find that if I wish to emphasize the multiplex network aspect (i.e., that these are different relational ties all on the one set of nodes), then it is helpful to fix the nodes in the same positions as I have done in Figure 8.6. If, on the other hand, I wish to emphasize that these are different types of ties, I might prefer to optimize the visualization for each type of tie separately.

Visualization and analysis

To my mind, visualization can be particularly helpful when it is combined with separate analyses of the data. Sometimes it provides insight into why the analysis produces the results it does. Sometimes it can emphasize the results of the analysis.

Some time ago, I conducted a simulation study of a particular network statistical model. At an early stage, I was intrigued by some of the statistics resulting from the simulation but could not quite understand them (or rather, I misinterpreted them). But once I inspected a visualization of one of my simulated graphs, the structural outcomes from this model became immediately apparent. Then I could think through what it was in the simulation rules that produced these results. This led to the introduction of an additional parameter in the simulation model and a substantially better study (Robins et al., 2005).

In the organizational network data depicted in Figure 8.6, we conducted an analysis based on structural equivalence (Chapter 2), seeking to find classes of structurally equivalent nodes. This type of analysis will be summarized in the next chapter. The data suggested three classes of nodes, so it made sense to regroup the nodes based on these classes in a way that would emphasize that result. I created an attribute file based on the class membership for the nodes and then used the program to help me redesign the visualizations. The result is in Figure 8.7, with the three structural equivalence classes of nodes circled consistently across the three visualizations.

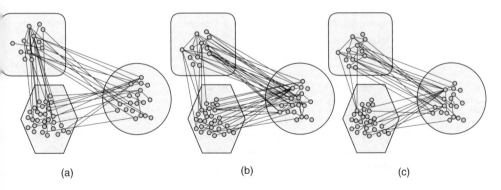

(a)   (b)   (c)

Figure 8.7 Visualization of a multiplex network with three structural equivalence classes

Again, the visualization does not show everything: for instance, the densities within and between the three classes of nodes need to be presented in a separate table. Nevertheless, such a figure is a prelude to a *blockmodel* (see Chapters 2 and 9).

In conclusion: The key point

Good visualization can help your network study, but it is at its most powerful when combined with good analysis.

BOX 8.2

Pulling back the curtain: What goes on in real network studies

For the sporting team study, we used visualizations in a number of ways. We provided a visualization, suitably anonymized so that no athlete was identifiable, as part of our report back to the club. We used visualizations in conference presentations and some publications, where they have had good impact in emphasizing certain points we wanted to make. The purpose of visualization in this study was primarily to assist with these presentations of results. Our analysis used techniques described in the next chapter, but we did not use visualizations for analytical or exploratory purposes.

In contrast, visualizations were used explicitly as exploratory mechanisms in the environmental governance study. We particularly wanted to see whether we could obtain good blockmodels, and we wanted to understand those blockmodels in part by visualizing the data in ways akin to Figure 8.7. This was overtly exploratory because we had no obvious theory to guide us as to expectations. It is always possible to produce blockmodels, but whether they are good representations of the data is another issue. The blockmodels for Figure 8.7 did capture important tendencies in the data, but we found in the governance study that this was not so. This was a pity because a good blockmodel can simplify the structure of a complex multiplex network. The visualizations from the blockmodels did not provide much insight into important features in the data, and we had to turn to other methods of analysis in the end.

We did use visualizations in our reports on the study, however, to illustrate the connections among the organizations. A fundamental result was apparent from the visualizations. Originally, the study envisaged two separate (albeit geographically adjacent) regions. What was apparent from the network visualizations was that organizations in the two regions were so intertwined that we were dealing with one network here, and it would have been artificial to analyze it in two separate segments. Anyone who disputed this result was immediately silenced once presented with the visualization.

As I noted in the previous chapter, we used visualizations, suitably anonymized, in our workshop presentations to responding organizations. They were helpful in generating good discussion about how the system operated.

Hot topics and further reading

Check out some of the creative network visualizations that are available on the internet:

The Gallery of Large Graphs from the University of Florida (http://yifanhu.net/GALLERY/GRAPHS/index1.html).

The Journal of Social Structure's Visualization Seminar 2010 (www.cmu.edu/joss/content/issues/vizsymposium.html).

The Visual Complexity site (www.visualcomplexity.com/vc).

Cytoscape is a visualization and analytic tool for complex networks. Its website (http://www.cytoscape.org) provides some examples of elegant visualizations produced using the software.

The NodeXL Graph Gallery (http://www.nodexlgraphgallery.org/Pages/Default.aspx).

NINE

A review of social network analytic methods

There is a wealth of methods for the analysis of social network data. Sometimes the entire field is described as 'social network analysis', with the acronym SNA. That is a pity. As I argued in earlier chapters, social network research is much more than just analysis. Still, statisticians and methodologists are often fascinated by the complexity of network data, with a focus on new, sophisticated methods. So it is not so hard to understand why social network research has been conflated into social network analysis.

Do not be fooled. As always in social science, ingenious methods will not rescue poorly planned research. Optimally, you want a strong theoretical base, a well-designed study, and good measurement or observational techniques. Then fancy methods can have their impact.

In this chapter, I review social network analysis without getting into all the fine detail. This is a book on network research design, not principally on SNA. My goal in this chapter is to give an overview of some commonly used classes of methods, and so to build intuition about what they do and how they can be applied in actual research (hence, I note research examples). If you want to use a method, this chapter will provide guidance about where to go for further information.

So the chapter is not intended as exhaustive. For instance, my principal focus will be on the analysis of binary networks, for which analytic techniques are most established. I have chosen classes of methods because they are commonly discussed in the literature, or are those I have found useful in my own research. If another network expert tells you of other possibilities, listen. The methodological field is growing rapidly, so you have more options than I can mention here.

A variety of books and articles have extensive reviews on SNA. The now classic text is by Wasserman and Faust (1994), and even though some of its later chapters are now out of date, its summary of basic SNA is still extremely useful. The Scott and Carrington (2011) handbook covers a very wide range of recent methodological (and theoretical) advances. I have listed these and other important texts in the further reading section at the end of this chapter.

Software for social network analysis

You have a wide choice of SNA software packages. Some offer a variety of standard techniques; others are specific to a particular analysis. Many are free but some require a small licence payment. Beware of network software that seems expensive. It will be commercial: other cheaper, and perhaps better, options are likely to be available.

In Box 9.1, I have noted a few of the more commonly used software packages in the social network literature. Huisman and van Duijn (2011) reviewed SNA software and have an accompanying website (www.gmw.rug.nl/~huisman/sna/software.html) that describes the different packages with helpful links. If your interest goes beyond social networks to other types of complex networks, then the field of available software is even wider.

BOX 9.1

Selected social network analysis software

- *UCINET*: A comprehensive package for the analysis of social network data, including the network visualization software *Netdraw* (Chapter 8). It is not focused on statistical methods, which often require specialized software, but covers other fundamental techniques very well indeed. You can find UCINET via the Analytic Technologies website (www.analytictech.com). Borgatti et al. (2013) provide good advice on how to use the software.

- Most of the *Visualization software* packages mentioned in Chapter 8 also have SNA routines. *Pajek, Visone, ORA, NodeXL* and *Gephi* all have analytic capabilities. The precise methods implemented vary from package to package, so check out the software against your particular needs.

- *Statnet:* For users of R. R is a major, flexible statistical computing platform, not just for network analysis. The R Project website is www.r-project.org where you will find a page on recent books, including introductory texts if you need to learn R (there can be a bit of a learning curve, depending on your enthusiasm, but it is a powerful platform to use).

o A number of network routines have been written for *R*, one advantage being that there can then be a rather seamless transition from the output of the network analysis into other statistical routines.

o Many network analytic routines are grouped in the *sna* package in *R*, developed under the leadership of prominent methodologist Carter Butts (see Butts, 2008b, and the package documentation at http://cran.r-project.org/web/packages/sna/sna.pdf).

o These have more recently been subsumed into the package *statnet* (http://cran.r-project.org/web/packages/statnet/index.html), designed originally for the estimation of exponential random graph models (see below) principally under direction of network statistician Mark Handcock (Handcock et al., 2008). Relational event models can also be fitted using this package.

- *Siena*: For the analysis of network evolution, including the co-evolution of networks and behavior, using stochastic actor-oriented models, developed by network statistician Tom Snijders, and discussed later in this chapter. There is an older version of the software available for Windows users but more up-to-date versions are again written in *R*. The siena webpage has plenty of support materials and references (www.stats.ox.ac.uk/~snijders/siena).

- *PNet, MPNet*: To estimate exponential random graph models for Windows users (http://sna.unimelb.edu.au).

- *Egonet*: (Already mentioned in Chapter 5) for the collection and analysis of egocentric network data (http://sourceforge.net/projects/egonet).

Basic network descriptives

It is standard in social science to report basic descriptive statistics of a sample: for instance, sample size, demographics and other relevant characteristics. Often means and standard deviations of major variables are reported, and perhaps bivariate correlations. But what should you report about your network data?

For a network study, be clear whether the data is directed or undirected. Report the number of actors in a whole network. With a multiple network study (e.g., networks of a number of school classrooms), report the mean and standard deviation across networks of the number of nodes. With an egonet study, even a qualitative study, report the mean and standard deviation of the number of alters across egos.

Report descriptive statistics of major attribute variables in ways consistent with the standards applied in your research area. Often this will include means and standard deviations for continuous attributes, or frequencies under different categories for categorical or binary attributes. For egonet studies, where you have collected alter data, report means and standard deviations across egos of important alter attributes.

Report network density. An alternative is to report average degree: perhaps use average degree rather than density when your study focuses principally on the number of ties for each actor. With multiple networks, report the mean and standard deviation of density and perhaps also the range (i.e., the highest and lowest density). For egonet studies with alter–alter ties, report the density among alters in the same way. With a multiplex network study, report the densities for each relational tie and perhaps record the amount of overlap between different types of tie.

Sometimes, researchers report the degree distribution in more detail, the types of network configurations present in the network, and provide a visualization of the network.

Research example: Gondal and McLean (2013) studied financial networks in fifteenth-century Florence. As descriptives, they reported the number of nodes, the density, degree distributions, various network configurations, and important features related to attributes including associations between degrees and attribute categories.

Dyad and triad census

As explained in Chapter 2 (Box 2.1), a *dyad* is a pair of nodes and the state of the relational ties between them. In an undirected network, there are only two types of dyad – tied or untied – but in a directed network, there are three possibilities, depicted in Figure 9.1: *mutual* (*M*) where there are reciprocated arcs between the nodes, *asymmetric* (*A*) with only one arc between the nodes, and *null* (*N*) with no arcs present. This terminology was introduced by Holland and Leinhardt (1976), who proposed that an empirical social network could be described through the counts of small subgraphs, such as dyads. A count of the *M*, *A* and *N* dyads in the graph is known as the *dyad census*.

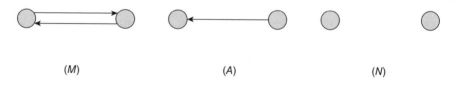

(M)   (A)   (N)

Figure 9.1   Mutual, asymmetric and null dyads

Holland and Leinhardt (1970) also proposed a triad census based on different types of triad. For an undirected graph there are four types of triad, depicted in Figure 9.2; and for a directed graph, the 16 possible types of triangle are presented in Figure 9.3.

In Figure 9.2, compare the complete triad in (a) with the 2-star in (b). These two types of triad contrast network closure against a non-closed 2-path (or 2-star). The presence of a 2-path is a precondition for network closure into a complete triad (or *triangle*): without a 2-star (b), you obviously cannot add an extra edge to create a triangle (a). So, if the graph has many non-closed 2-paths (b) but few complete triads (a), then we might infer that closure (sometimes called *clustering* – see Chapter 2) is not a strong process in this social network.

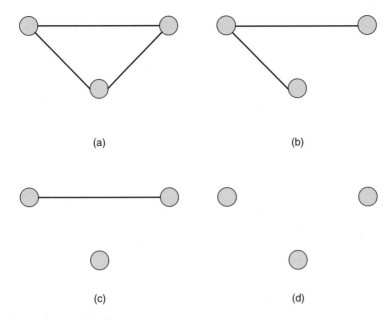

(a)

(b)

(c)

(d)

Figure 9.2 Undirected triads

(a) complete triad or triangle; (b) 2-star; (c) single edge; (d) empty triad

For directed graphs, the complicated labelling convention in Figure 9.3 was introduced by Holland and Leinhardt (1970), the details of which need not particularly concern us. I want to draw your attention, however, to some important triadic configurations here – I have extracted them for convenience into Figure 9.4. To keep it simple, I have ignored triads with reciprocated ties, although the arguments can be extended to include mutuality.

In Figure 9.4 there are two closed triads: 030T, a *transitive triad*, and 030C, a *cyclic triad*. Notice the difference between the two: the transitive triad is more hierarchical in that one node is selected by the two other nodes (i.e., is popular), and one node is not selected by any others. In the cyclic triad, all nodes are equivalent in selecting one partner and being selected by another. So counts of these configurations may indicate levels of local hierarchy in social networks. Notice also that the non-closed triads (021D, 021U, and 021C) are 2-paths and 2-semipaths (see Chapter 2 – these are all directed 2-stars of various forms). Each is a precursor to transitive network closure (030T) if an additional arc is formed in the right direction; but only the 2-path (021C) is a precursor to cyclic closure. So the relative counts of these 2-path configurations compared to the closed triads gives an indication of the strength of hierarchical and non-hierarchical closure in the network.

So we can see why these dyadic and triadic counts give information about structural processes in the network. The basic idea that a complex network can be described in terms of its small subgraphs was reinvented by Milo et al. (2002), seemingly unaware of the Holland and Leinhardt articles 40 years earlier. Milo et al. called the small subgraphs *network motifs*; an alternative terminology is *network configuration*, drawing

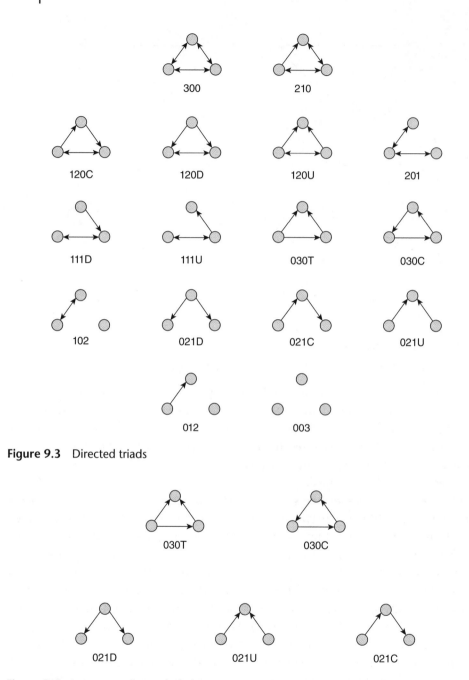

Figure 9.3 Directed triads

Figure 9.4 Important directed triads

on the early work by Moreno and Jennings (1938). I prefer *configuration*, given its long antecedent.

The full triad census is not often spelled out nowadays as a method of analysis. But the triad census contains important ideas that are picked up in more sophisticated methods, particularly statistical models, described below:

- Networks can be thought of as being built up by small local structures.
- Different types of configurations indicate different structural processes that could have generated the network (reciprocity, closure).
- There are different types of closure, indicating local hierarchies in the network.

Research examples: Uddin and Hossain (2013) used a dyad and triad census to analyze a crisis communication network. You will see Milo's network motif idea in plenty of applications in network science more generally, especially biological networks.

Degree distributions

I gave examples of degree distributions in Chapter 2 (Figures 2.2 and 2.3). I pointed to the important theoretical idea of preferential attachment, where popular nodes attracted more popularity ('the rich get richer'), leading to *scale-free* degree distributions. In a network governed by preferential attachment, there will be hubs in the degree distribution: a few extremely high-degree nodes. Even if a particular degree distribution is not so extreme, it is often skewed with some highly popular or active nodes.

Formally, *scale-free degree distributions* are characterized as follows. If K is the degree of a *randomly chosen person* in the network, then a statistical model for the degree distribution is $P(K = k) = f(k)$, where $f(k)$ is a probability distribution. For a scale-free degree distribution, $f(k) = Ak^{-\rho}$, for some constant A and a scaling parameter $\rho > 1$. Because of this formula, these degree distributions are also called (*inverse*) *power law* degree distributions, with the degree taken to the power $-\rho$.

If we take the logarithm of both sides, we get $\log P(K = k) = \log A - \rho \log k$, linear on a log–log scale. So a simple-minded way to test a scale-free degree distribution is to fit a regression line to the log–log scaled degree distribution. This procedure was strongly criticized by Jones and Handcock (2003), so if you want to know whether your network is scale-free, either use the methods they recommend, or if you must plot on a log–log scale, then understand that this procedure is rough-and-ready at best.

Why, empirically, does a social scientist need to know whether the degree distribution is scale-free? A scale-free degree distribution is evidence that a preferential attachment-type process could be operating in the network. An interesting feature of scale-free networks is that they can be vulnerable to 'attack' in the sense that removal of high-degree nodes easily fragments the system. At the same time, in disease transmission networks, for instance, the hubs can be all too effective in spreading the disease. In organizational networks, high-degree hubs may indicate bottlenecks in organizational functioning. So a scale-free distribution may have implications for processes on the network, depending on context.

Nevertheless, much empirical social network analysis does not require a precise specification of the degree distribution $f(k)$, whether it be scale-free or otherwise. It often suffices to know qualitatively that you have some hubs or high-degree nodes in the network, or that the degree distribution is otherwise skewed. It would be good practice to report the average degree (or density), standard deviation and skew of our degree distributions, but typically only the first is reported, sometimes with a chart of the degree distribution as in Figure 2.2.

Research examples: Gondal and McLean (2013), in their study of Florentine financial networks, discussed the in- and out-degree distributions, with a focus on the presence of some high-degree nodes. Shore et al. (2013) examined power law degree distributions for 'flow' networks (e.g., networks of financial resources or ecological networks). They showed that these networks need not depend on a rich-get-richer process but are nevertheless highly skewed and vulnerable to turbulence and sudden collapse.

Node importance: Centrality

The degree distribution is a feature of the network as a whole, but it is a simple step then to ask which nodes have high degrees, and thereby to identify the most *central* nodes in the network. In Chapter 2, I explained that *degree centrality* was only one form of centrality. The software in Box 9.1 will calculate major centrality measures.

In Box 9.2, I provide more precise mathematical definitions of centrality indices available in *UCINET* (Chapter 10 of Borgatti et al., 2013). If mathematics is not for you, then ignore the formulae, but it is helpful to understand the different concepts behind them. Each centrality index measures a slightly different property, and as it is popular to invent new indices, those in Box 9.2 are not the only ones available. In my own research, I tend to use degree and betweenness, but there are circumstances when the other indices come into play, so think about the theoretical interpretation that you need before you settle on a final centrality measure. Often researchers report multiple indices.

Sometimes researchers calculate centrality scores for each node and then enter them as variables into a regression analysis to predict an individual outcome. I do not want to be too dogmatic, but researchers should realize that the regression assumes nodes are independent of each other once centralities are taken into account – in other words, that the network is entirely decomposable into a set of nodal centralities. This is quite a dubious assumption and ignores, for instance, closure effects in human social networks. So if you go down this analytic track, you should understand this is a rough-and-ready procedure and the results should be treated with caution. Some researchers adjust the standard errors to compensate statistically for any remaining dependence amongst nodes. This is a case of trying to fit existing standard techniques into an analytic world for which they were not originally intended. There are network statistical models that are designed to handle network dependence explicitly and so provide more principled inference. Generally, it is better to try them first before reverting to half-way-house analysis.

BOX 9.2

Different types of centrality

These centrality definitions apply to undirected graphs. For precise details of directed versions, consult Borgatti et al. (2013).

- *Degree centrality* of node i can be interpreted as the activity/popularity of the node. It is simply the degree of i and equals $\sum_j x_{ij}$. Directed versions comprise *in-* and *out-degree centralities*.

- *Betweenness centrality* for node i measures the importance of i in connecting the network through short paths (Figure 2.6). In effect, it is a measure of how frequently i sits on geodesics between all other pairs of nodes and is calculated as $\sum_{j<k}\left(g_{jik}/g_{jk}\right)$ where g_{jik} is the number of geodesic paths between j and k that include i, and g_{jk} is the total number of geodesic paths between j and k (the ratio is taken to be 0 if node j and k are not reachable, i.e., there is no finite geodesic between them). Betweenness can be interpreted as a measure of network brokerage for the node, the 'control' the node has in flows of (say) communication through the network (Freeman, 1979). Directed versions of betweenness follow automatically, with the geodesics defined as the shortest path (not semipath), so that the direction of the arcs are consistent.

- *Closeness centrality* of node i is the sum of all geodesic distances from i to all others: $\sum_j d_{ij}$ where d_{ij} is the geodesic distance between nodes i and j. Large values of closeness under this definition indicate a less central node, but there are normalized versions whereby a higher value indicates greater centrality. While closeness centrality has a nice interpretation in terms of rapid diffusion of flow through the networks, it is really only applicable for connected networks where geodesic distances are all finite. This can limit its usefulness.

- *Eigenvector centrality* for node i indicates how central are i's network partners. A node with high eigenvector centrality is connected to well-connected nodes. The mathematical concepts of eigenvector and eigenvalue come from matrix algebra. The eigenvector for i is $\lambda\sum_j x_{ij}e_j$ where e_j is the eigenvector centrality of node j and λ is the eigenvalue. For directed networks, there are left and right eigenvector centralities analogous to in- and out-degree. Borgatti et al. discuss some issues for eigenvector centrality when networks are disconnected, or when the first eigenvalue is not large.

- *Beta centrality* is a measure of the total number of ways of getting from node i to all other nodes (i.e., *walks* from i to j) with longer walks downweighted by a power of a parameter $\beta < 1$. The precise mathematical definition is given in Borgatti et al. Beta centrality is often thought of as a measure of power or influence. One issue is how to choose a good value for β.

An examination of the degree distribution differs from an analysis of degree centrality rather subtly. The degree distribution is a property of the network as a whole, whereas the centrality analysis differentiates nodes from each other, casting attention on those nodes with many network partners. This shift in focus from a whole network property to a node-level property is a feature of network analysis. Your emphasis – node level or whole network – will depend on your research question.

Research examples: Check out Valdis Krebs's (2002) study of the network of World Trade Center bombers, where he compares degree, betweenness and closeness centralities.

Structural holes

Burt (1992) proposed a number of conceptually similar indices to measure the extent of structural holes in an egonet. The most prominent are *network constraint*, which measures how much the egonet is 'constrained' by ego's ties concentrated on a densely connected set of alters; and *effective size*, a measure of how much redundancy there is in the egonet in the sense that ties are to connected alters (see also Borgatti, 1997; Borgatti et al., 1998). These indices can be calculated from either an egonet study or by extracting egonets from a whole network by taking the subgraph of each node and its adjacent nodes. *UCINET* will calculate the indices for each node. Often, the results are then correlated with other node-level variables to see whether a variable is related to the presence of network brokerage.

There are alternatives. For instance, the density of alter–alter ties in the egonet is an indication of the presence of structural holes.

Of course, the use of egonets is a little problematic because 'holes' in the egonet could be bridged by paths that do not intersect with the egonet at all. So in whole network studies researchers sometimes use betweenness centrality to indicate brokerage, rather than the specific structural hole measures. If in doubt, use both betweenness and constraint, to see whether your conclusions are consistent.

Research examples: Check out Ron Burt's (2004) analysis, using network constraint, leading to his conclusion that occupying a structural hole is associated with having good ideas.

Connectivity and cohesive subsets of nodes

In Chapter 2, I introduced a cohesive subset of nodes as having an induced subgraph with higher density or connectivity. The basic idea is that of a *clique*. A *clique* is a complete induced subgraph: a subset of nodes with all possible ties present. This idea is important in graph and network theory, but as cliques often overlap, analysis using this approach is not always easy or revealing. Borgatti et al. (2013) showed some practical methods to analyze the overlap.

The notion of a clique is sometimes seen as too restrictive. (What about subsets that are otherwise cliques but missing one or two ties? Should they not be regarded as 'cohesive'?) So, extensions of the clique idea have been proposed, based on either density or connectivity. Relaxation of the criteria for a clique in different ways results in other notions of a cohesive subset of nodes: *n-clique*, *k-plex* and *k-cores*, for instance.

- In a *2-clique*, each pair of nodes is connected by a path of length 2 or less.
- In a *2-core*, each node is connected to at least two other nodes.
- In a *2-plex* of *m* nodes, every node is connected to at least *m* − 2 nodes.

You will occasionally see empirical analyses involving these concepts, perhaps less so for 2-cliques and 2-plexes. For those interested in more details and further extensions, consult the texts listed at the end of this chapter. Most network software packages can extract these subsets of nodes from whole network data.

As can be seen from this list, the use of density as a defining feature for cohesion transmutes into notions of connectivity. Notions of connectivity, including importantly the concept of a *geodesic*, often come into play in the analysis of networks. Trade-offs between density in the form of network closure and connectivity in the form of short average geodesics are important in determining whether a network is a small world (Chapter 2).

It used to be common to investigate whether an empirical network was a 'small-world network'. This trend has faded, given that many empirical social networks (but not all) exhibit small-world properties. If you want to go down the small-world analytical track, read Schnettler (2009b) for advice on best practice.

Research examples: For a deep analysis of how connectivity and cohesion come together in understanding the structuring of social groups, read Moody and White (2003).

Network closure

Network closure is such an important and prevalent effect in many human social networks that it is important to consider whether it is present in your own data. Closure is sometimes referred to as *network clustering* (in the sense that the network nodes cluster into triangles). For an undirected graph, there are a couple of clustering coefficients that are often reported:

- The *global clustering coefficient*: calculated as $3T/S_2$ where T is the number of triangles in the network and S_2 the number of 2-paths (or 2-stars), whether they are closed into triangles or not. Look at Figure 9.2(a): you can see that each triangle contains three 2-stars (one centred on each node). Hence the ratio $3T/S_2$ ranges between 0 and 1 and indicates the proportion of 2-stars that are closed into triangles.
- The *local clustering coefficient*: Consider the egonet for each node in the network (the node, its alters, and the ties among the alters). As each alter is connected to the node, an alter–alter tie by definition completes a triangle. The density of the alter–alter ties then indicates the extent of closure around that node. The local clustering coefficient is that local density averaged across all nodes.

Research examples: For a discussion of clustering coefficients for valued networks, see Phan et al. (2013).

Network position and subgroups of nodes: Equivalence, community structure, and blockmodels

Methods that partition nodes into subgroups based on network position are often an effective way to analyze a social network. Apart from the convenience of non-overlapping subsets of nodes, the idea of grouping actors based on the notion of a structural or network position is appealing. Once the nodes are partitioned into separate subgroups, it is possible to examine whether the subgroups are associated with other variables. For instance, in a study of organizational advice, suppose there is a subgroup of popular nodes in the advice network, which perhaps might be interpreted as an emergent leadership group. An interesting question is whether this group is largely the same as the formal, recognized leadership of the organization. What are the properties of individuals associated with this group (perhaps intelligence, knowledge, long tenure, political skills?) that on average can distinguish this group of actors from other groups?

As explained in Chapter 2, there are two broad approaches to network position: equivalence and community structure.

Structural equivalence

Two nodes are *structurally equivalent* if connected to the same other nodes. A *structural position* or *social role* is a set of structurally equivalent actors. Whether you think of structural equivalence sets as positions or roles depends on the framing of your research (here I use the terms interchangeably). There are other versions of equivalence, including *regular equivalence*, where pairs of nodes do not have to be connected to the same other nodes but rather to other nodes that are regularly equivalent. I will concentrate on structurally equivalent nodes here: those wishing to investigate regular equivalence further should consult the texts listed at the end of the chapter.

So, how to find network positions, that is, sets of structurally equivalent nodes? First, let me stress that in real data there are usually few pairs of nodes exactly structurally equivalent. So, the question becomes how to find sets of nodes that are approximately structurally equivalent. In short, we want to find nodes that in a binary network have similar patterns of 1s and 0s in their rows and columns of the adjacency matrix.

A simple way to do this is to use one of the standard clustering algorithms, familiar to many social scientists. (If you are not familiar with clustering algorithms, do not confuse them with the network clustering coefficient. Standard clustering groups respondents into categories based on scores on multiple variables.) With a standard clustering approach, we create a distance measure between pairs of nodes, treating their rows in the adjacency matrix as two vectors and taking (say) the Euclidean distance between the vectors. The usual hierarchical clustering techniques can then be applied to the resulting distance matrix among all nodes. If the network is directed, this procedure only takes into account out-degrees (rows) but we also want to include the columns. So for directed graphs a vector of length $2n$ is created for each node, using both the row and the column, hence clustering on both out- and in-degrees. In fact, this procedure need not be confined to one adjacency matrix, and multiplex networks can be handled by ever larger vectors, using the rows and the columns of the matrices in turn.

If you are not familiar with clustering, and do not quite follow the previous paragraph, it need not matter. The bottom line is that there are algorithms that can group nodes based on the similarity of their profiles in out- and in-degrees, including across multiplex networks simultaneously. The software packages will do all the work for you. The resulting groups can then be taken as approximately structurally equivalent subsets of nodes. One issue is that the researcher often has to decide on how many groups to use. This is not always an easy choice, but a small number is desirable for simple interpretability. I often try four to six groups to see whether these make good interpretative sense.

I have described clustering in the previous paragraph because many social scientists will be familiar with it. But there are alternatives. One of the original methods for producing structural equivalence groups was CONCOR (Breiger et al., 1975), slightly different from hierarchical clustering, and still available in UCINET. Other UCINET options, and a lengthier demonstration of the technique, are described in Borgatti et al. (2013).

Blockmodels

Once you have a small number of structurally equivalent groups, then it is possible to abstract the network structure into what is called a *blockmodel*.

Figure 9.5(a) depicts a small advice network among 16 actors. I ran CONCOR in UCINET on this data and asked for a partition of four subsets of nodes. The output provides me with information on which nodes are grouped together (not shown here), as well as a density matrix (Figure 9.5(b)), with the densities within and between the subsets of nodes. (Notice that the diagonals are now non-zero, because the nodes within a subset can have ties with each other.)

If we think of each subset as a position or role in the network, then we can see that, based on the densities (Figure 9.5(b)), the strongest effects in this network are for nodes in position 2 to choose nodes in position 1, and for position 4 to choose position 3. In Figure 9.5(c), these densities are presented in a visualization of the relationships among the four positions, which are now depicted as nodes. (There are loops on the nodes to indicate the within-role densities.) The overall density of the network is 0.125, so if we

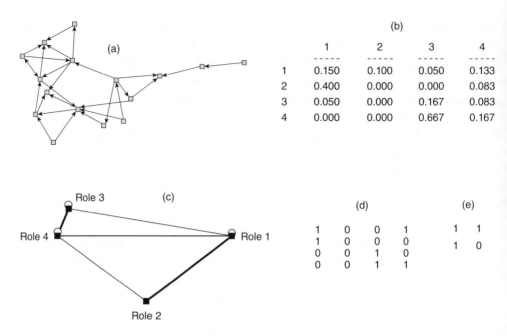

Figure 9.5 Blockmodelling

(a) small advice network; (b) density matrix for a blockmodel; (c) strongest effects; (d) image matrix; (e) image matrix for a core–periphery structure

consider a tie between positions to be present when there is a density greater than this value, then we reach what is called the *image matrix* in Figure 9.5(d). This is a simplified abstraction of the network. We have given up a lot of information to reach this point, but we have a relatively simple structure that provides an understanding of some main effects in the network.

This result is called a *blockmodel*, where a block is the set of ties within positions and between pairs of positions.

A particularly important example of a blockmodel with two positions is a *core–periphery* structure (Borgatti and Everett, 2000), with a dense core based on central nodes and a periphery of nodes connected to the centre but not to each other. Figure 9.5(e) contains the image matrix for a core–periphery structure.

Doreian et al. (2005) and Ferligoj et al. (2011) provide further advice on blockmodeling.

Community structure

Social networks often exhibit denser regions of the network that can be construed as *communities*, so that identifying these regions enables the network to be simplified in terms of its *community structure*. Newman and Park (2003) introduced the idea of community structure, and Girvan and Newman (2002) developed a well-known algorithm to partition nodes into communities from empirical data. Since then a large number of other algorithms have been proposed as extensions.

The Girvan–Newman algorithm is based on finding the edges that keep the network connected. *Edge betweenness* is a counterpart of betweenness centrality, where edges have higher betweenness scores if they sit on more geodesics. Edges with low betweenness are those likely to exist within communities. The algorithm simply deletes the edges with the highest betweenness score in an iterative fashion until a desired number of communities is produced.

Notice one important difference between community structures and structural equivalence. By definition, the subsets of nodes in a community structure must have high within-group density. This is not a requirement for an equivalence blockmodel, where the nodes can be in the one position but do not have to be linked to one another.

Stochastic blockmodels

Statistical methods for blockmodelling have also been developed. The positions are taken to be latent classes for the nodes, and the distribution of dyads is assumed to be independent conditional on the node class (Holland et al., 1981; Nowicki and Snijders, 2001; Airoldi et al., 2008). These elegant models are not so commonly used empirically, but if you have a statistical bent and need to do blockmodelling, you will want to check them out. There is a lot of current work in statistics on stochastic blockmodels (e.g., Rohe et al., 2011), an interesting development because over the last decade attention in the physics literature seemed focused more on community structure. Before long, this renewed statistical attention to blockmodels may feed back into sophisticated methods for empirical network data – so watch this space!

Research examples: The original papers on blockmodelling by Harrison White and his colleagues are now social network classics and are still worth reading today. Try White et al. (1976). It is also worth reading the Newman and Park (2003) article, where they suggest it is community structure that differentiates social networks from other types of networks.

Network algebras

It is not often realized that network structure can be expressed in terms of formal mathematical algebras. *Relation algebras* were first used in the analysis of kinship systems (Boyd, 1969; White, 1963), with algebraic structure representing the strict familial rules in complex kinship structures. Relation algebras were then used to summarize regularities in networks more generally, including algebraic structures for blockmodels and role systems (Boorman and White, 1976; Pattison, 1993, 2011). More recent examples include algebraic systems for dynamic network transactions and events (Kontoleon et al., 2013).

These approaches attracted a lot of attention when they were first introduced but are not so common nowadays as statistical approaches to network analysis have become more prevalent. Nevertheless, if you have a mathematical background, check them out. If you are an anthropologist studying kinship structures from a network perspective, they are certainly worth investigating.

Research examples: If you are interested in the detail of this area, the standard text is still Pattison (1993).

Quadratic assignment procedure

I now move on to some statistical approaches to social network analysis.

The *quadratic assignment procedure* (QAP) is a statistical method to compare pairs of multiplex networks, taking into account the dependencies inevitable in network data. The QAP was originally designed for comparing data matrices more generally, so the extension to networks was quite natural (Krackhardt, 1987a). In an organizational study, for instance, you may wish to check whether the formal hierarchy (who is the boss of whom) matches the trust network. In short, do the employees trust their bosses (and vice versa)?

To answer this, you might correlate the cells of one matrix with the cells in the other (i.e., treat the respective cells of the two matrices as cases on two variables). If the correlation is positive then that is evidence that trust mirrors the hierarchy (at least to some extent). But, unlike standard statistical approaches, you cannot test whether the statistic (in this case, a correlation, but there are many other possibilities) is significantly different from 0. The standard methods rely on independent observations, whereas you have network data and dependence.

The QAP produces a bootstrapped null distribution against which to test the null hypothesis that the true value of the correlation is 0. A permutation is applied to the node labels of one of the two matrices and the statistic recalculated. In terms of our examples, let us shuffle randomly the identities of the actors in the formal hierarchy (that is what a permutation is in this case). Even if trust and hierarchy are associated in the original data, we do not expect that to be the case any longer, once we have shuffled the actors for one of the relational ties. Yet the overall structures of the two networks have not changed. Let us do this many times and calculate the correlation each time. This produces a distribution of correlation statistics where we do not expect there to be any association, but the network structure is the same. Is our observed statistic (the original correlation) very large compared to most values in the distribution (e.g., 95% of them)? If so, then we have evidence that the original correlation is significantly different from purely random values, so the data is suggesting some association between the two types of tie.

Correlations and regressions are closely linked, so the QAP has been extended to a version of multiple network regression (MRQAP). Multiple matrices are used to predict another network (Krackhardt, 1988). The regression coefficients are estimated in standard ways using the matrix cells as data points, but the significance of the coefficients are determined using the QAP. This is a very useful method, and much preferred to doing a standard regression. So, if you must regress (see my comments about centrality above), use the QAP to test significance. Yet the QAP regression (not the correlation) remains a little controversial. Dekker et al. (2007) developed new permutation procedures to improve the MRQAP, but concluded that further work was needed for binary data. In other words, proceed with the MRQAP if you wish but be a little cautious in your conclusions when using binary networks (as we so often do).

Research examples: There are plenty of examples. Zagenczyk et al. (in press) used the MRQAP in an organizational study to examine aspects of leader–member exchange theory.

Conditional uniform graph distributions

Similarly, other bootstrapping methods can be used to create null distributions against which to test the significance of network statistics. Consider the triad census described above. It is simple enough to calculate the number of complete triads (Figure 9.2(a)) in a graph. Even if the number seems quite large, that is not enough to be confident about a tendency for network closure. If the graph is dense enough, plenty of triangles will be present just by chance. So, we need a null distribution that encapsulates the phrase 'just by chance' given the density. Then we can see whether the number of triangles in the data generally exceeds chance expectations.

Suppose we examine all graphs having the same density as our observed network, and we find that our data have many more triangles than most of them. Then that constitutes evidence that our network has more triangles than expected by chance given the density.

A conditional uniform graph distribution on a fixed number of nodes n assumes that, conditional on some network property, all graphs with the property are equally probable and graphs without that property have probability 0. To test the triad census, we might take the property as density, a given number of edges L for the number of nodes n. This is the so-called $U|L$ distribution, the uniform graph distribution conditional on a fixed number of edges or arcs L.

So, every graph with L edges is considered in this distribution, and those without that level of density are left out. From all of those graphs (or rather, let us simulate a sample of them – perhaps 1000), we calculate the number of triangles in each of them. This then gives us a distribution of triangles expected from $U|L$: this is what we expect to see if the only property driving the graph formation is density. If our observed data has more triangles than most graphs in the distribution (say more than 950 of the 1000 in the sample at a 5% significance level), then this is evidence for processes of triangulation/closure in the network over and above simple density effects.

A number of different conditional uniform graph distributions have been proposed, going way back to Katz and Powell (1957). The general approach has been used in social network analysis continuously since then (see Robins, 2013, for a little of the history) and described in a number of prominent texts including Wasserman and Faust (1994). When Milo et al. (2002) introduced their idea of *network motifs* (see above), they rediscovered the method.

Research examples: With a novel application of multilevel networks to social ecological systems, Bodin and Tengö (2012) used a conditional uniform graph distribution to examine network configurations relating to sustainability of tribal forest management in Madagascar.

Simple statistical models for network structure

The QAP and conditional uniform graph distributions are statistical methods for testing hypotheses about certain features of the observed network. However, they are not statistical models *of* the network structure. I now turn to some important models of network structure and network processes (e.g., social influence), beginning with early simpler versions.

Erdős–Rényi graphs

The *simple random graph model* of Erdős and Rényi (1959; see also Rapoport, 1953) is the simplest model for network structure. It is often referred to as the Erdős–Rényi graph or the Bernoulli graph distribution (Frank and Nowicki, 1993). It is similar to the null model produced by the $U|L$ conditional graph distribution.

In this model, for a fixed node size n, network ties occur independently and with probability p. Empirically, p is easily estimated as the density. The model has been extensively examined, but as it is based on independent ties, it is not a good representation of empirical social networks. With independent ties, there is no expectation that there will be any patterning in the network (no reciprocity, no closure): in short, no endogenous network processes. For this reason it is useful as a null model against which to compare more complex effects, as with the $U|L$ distribution.

The p_1 and p_2 models

Holland and Leinhardt (1981) proposed the p_1 model, an extension of simple random graphs, postulating independence between dyads (not arcs) in directed networks. The model parameterizes effects for reciprocity, activity and popularity. It is seldom used nowadays but is an important forerunner of exponential random graph models (below). The more recent p_2 model still assumes dyadic independence, but conditional on random node-level effects (van Duijn et al., 2004), so that it can be used to investigate random attribute effects (see also van Duijn and Huisman, 2011)

Research examples: Sainio et al. (2011) used the p_2 model to study relationships of victimized children who were bullied in schools.

Exponential random graph models

In empirical social network research, exponential random graph models (ERGMs) have become one of the most popular methods to analyze cross-sectional network structure. These are statistical models for the presence or absence of a network tie that explicitly take into account complex dependencies among the ties. They assume that the network is built up of small configurations of network ties, akin to the dyadic census and triadic census discussed earlier in this chapter. However, the range of configurations is not at all limited to the dyad and triad census. Model specifications can include more complicated structures such as the k-star, k-triangle and k-two-path configurations depicted in Figure 9.6 (where I have set $k = 4$).

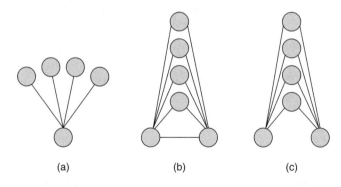

(a)	(b)	(c)

Figure 9.6   ERGM configurations

(a) 4-stars; (b) 4-triangles; (c) 4-two-paths

The star configurations help model the degree distribution, whereas the k-triangle configurations represent network closure, but closure that occurs in denser regions of the network, akin to community structure (that is why the four triangles in Figure 9.6(b) are 'stacked' on one another). The two-path configurations represent short-range connectivity in the network. In Figure 9.6(c), the two nodes at the bottom are connected to the same nodes, akin to structural equivalence, so that this configuration can be interpreted as representing the presence of structurally equivalent classes of nodes in the network.

Of course, such configurations are available for all possible *k* in the network, but the practice is to combine all the different star, triangle and 2-path configurations into a single parameter for each, respectively, with a geometric weighting that stops the larger configurations from dominating the statistic. These steps keep the overall model manageable (Snijders et al., 2006). The single triangle and 2-path parameters are also called the *geometrically weighted edgewise shared partner* and *dyadwise shared partner* in *statnet* (Box 9.1).

Models that only include a single rather than the 'stacked' effects (e.g., a single triangle configuration as opposed to the *k*-triangles in Figure 9.6(b)) do not usually fit real social network data well (Snijders et al., 2006). These are known as Markov graph models, and often converged parameter estimates are unobtainable.

ERGMs have been developed for directed, bipartite, multiplex, longitudinal and multilevel network data. Attributes can be included into ERGMs to test for the presence of homophily and other attribute effects. Dyadic covariates such as the geospatial distance between actors can be included. The advantage of an ERGM is that these various effects can be modelled together and so tested one against the other, rather like a regression. In contrast, the uniform random graph distribution approach looks for the presence of configurations, but has to do this one configuration at a time. In a loose way, ERGMs can be compared to a logistic regression, predicting the presence or absence of a tie from other network structures. But because ERGMs explicitly take into account network dependencies, they should not be fitted as a standard logistic regression and require specialized software that uses complex simulation techniques to obtain estimates (Box 9.1). These techniques can be computationally demanding, and are not normally applied to large networks (although see some new innovations in sampling below).

For further advice on ERGMs, consult an introductory text such as Lusher et al. (2013).

Research examples: Huitsing et al. (2012a) used ERGMs to study liking, disliking and bullying networks among school children. Lomi et al. (2014a) used ERGMs to study organizational structure and boundary crossing in a multinational corporation.

Models for network influence

ERGMs are models for network structure. Often researchers are not interested in the structure *per se* but rather how that structure might affect actor attributes: in particular, social influence processes. One method to examine influence is the *network effects model* (e.g., Friedkin, 1998), whereby actor attributes are entered into an autoregressive model. These methods are similar in approach to certain models in spatial statistics.

If you are studying influence, you will want to check out the work of Tom Valente who has examined network diffusion for innovations and health behaviors (Valente, 1995, 2005, 2010). There is also an ERGM version of an influence model known as the *autologistic actor attribute model* (Daraganova and Robins, 2013). Network-based diffusion has also been studied extensively in economics, where influence processes are often referred to as *peer effects* (e.g., An, 2011). There is new interest in – and some controversy about – peer effects in public health (Christakis and Fowler, 2007). I shall return to this issue in Chapter 10.

Research examples: There is a lot of interest in influence effects transmitted electronically including through social media. For an example on peer effects and contagion, see Aral and Walker's (2011) description of an experiment on viral marketing. For a different take on influence, where contagion is examined using retweets in Twitter feed, see Harrigan et al. (2012). Check out Bond et al.'s (2012) massive experiment on social influence and political mobilization through Facebook.

Stochastic actor-oriented models: Co-evolution of structure and attributes across time

Stochastic actor-oriented models (SAOMs) can be used to model network change across time, but have now become particularly popular in modelling the co-evolution of network structure and actor attributes when you have longitudinal data. The attributes are assumed to affect the structure (selection) at the same time as the network structure affects the attributes (influence), and because these effects are parameterized separately it is possible to parse out whether you have selection or influence, or both, in your data. Snijders (2011a) provides a helpful summary on the details of SAOMs.

The models are used with panel network data, with the network measured at discrete time-points. The models can include structural evolution effects in line with network theory, including popularity, closure and other effects. These can be represented as configurations, akin to an ERGM, but here the model examines the change across time-points whereby some configurations come into and out of existence. Possible selection-based attribute effects include homophily, whereby actors create ties due to shared attributes; influence-based effects include contagion where an actor changes an attribute value through the influence of direct network partners.

The idea behind the models (and hence the term 'actor-oriented') is as follows. Between the time-points when the data is measured, actors are assumed to make decisions to change ties or change attributes. So there is a latent (unseen) series of changes based on actor decisions. The decisions are based on preferences for being in certain network positions (e.g., being in closed structures) or preferring attribute values related to network partners; these preferences are captured by the parameters of the model. The models are estimated by simulations of sequences of small changes between time-points with parameters adjusted until the simulations can reasonably reproduce the data (i.e., when the estimation converges). The parameter estimates (and direction – the signs of the parameters) permit inferences about the processes that drive the network change.

SAOMs are increasingly popular in social network research and are now the preferred method to model the evolution of network structure, and the co-evolution of structure and individual behaviors. As with ERGMs, SAOMs are computationally intensive in estimation, so they are not readily applicable to very large networks.

Research examples: Check out recent special issues of *Social Networks* on these important network models (Snijders and Doreian, 2010, 2012; Snijders et al., 2010). The availability of these methods has led to a marked increase in the collection of longitudinal datasets and innovative investigations into network co-evolution. For instance, a recent issue of the *Journal of Research on Adolescence* is entirely focused on network-behavior dynamics using these models (Veenstra et al., 2013).

Relational event models

Sometimes, of course, longitudinal data is not in the panel form but in the form of time-stamped dyadic transactions between actors, such as emails or other communications. It is not unusual for researchers to aggregate these into panel data by picking out a small number of time-windows and making decisions about how many transactions constitute a tie between actors. Then an SAOM might be applied.

Of course, this is a rather ad hoc approach that involves decisions about how best to aggregate. In fact, the data constitutes a time-ordered sequence of observed events that may be modelled in its own right without aggregation. Butts (2008a) introduced the *relational event model*, derived from event history analysis, but using relational configurations such as those applicable to ERGMs and SAOMs. For instance, a relational event model for email might include a parameter for reciprocity, where the chances of an email from actor i to actor j in part depend on the previous occurrences of an email from j to i. Closure, degree and attribute effects may also be included in a model. Possible transactions at a given time-point are assumed to be independent of one another conditional on the past history of transactions. The model essentially predicts the next transaction in a logistic regression-type framework (there are different possibilities, such as Cox regression, a form of multinomial conditional logistic regression). As a result, the model can be fitted using standard statistical software: Butts has also written R code for fitting relational event models (Box 9.1).

These are among the most exciting in recent network methods and we will undoubtedly see further rapid development in the next few years (for other recent work, see Brandes et al., 2009; de Nooy, 2010; Stadtfeld and Geyer-Schulz, 2011; DuBois et al., 2013; Lerner et al., 2013a, 2013b). A novel combination of transaction sequencing and relational algebras was proposed by Kontoleon et al. (2013).

Research examples: Quintane et al. (2013) used a relational event model in an organizational email study to show that there were at least two time-frames for work activity – long-term and short-term – with different structural dynamics that they argued related to organizational performance. For an example from the physics literature of a comparative analysis of aggregated and disaggregated interaction event data, see Barrat et al. (2013).

Egonet, snowball and respondent-driven sampling

With these important network statistical models introduced, I now turn to analytic methods that apply when a whole network study does not have complete data: sampled data, uncertain node set size, and missing network data.

I begin with sampling. What should you do if you only have partial network data through a sampling procedure? Is there some way to determine what the complete network might be like?

Egonet sampling

Smith (2012) proposed a novel simulation method for inferring global network properties from a sample of egonets, using ERGMs. Given its recent development, this approach has not been used much to date, but it has the advantage that it can be relatively cost-effective to obtain a sample of egonets, compared to the more complex difficulties of undertaking a snowball. However, Smith noted important limitations, including difficulties if the network is disconnected or if the degree distribution is highly skewed. With a skewed degree distribution, high-degree nodes are not likely to be sampled and so properties of the degree distribution and more generally of connectivity may not be well captured by the egonet sample. A snowball sample is more likely to sample high-degree nodes appropriately.

Snowball sampling

As might be expected, network analysis with snowball sampled data and with respondent-driven sampling is not simple. If you have data of this nature, then you will need to master the right analytical techniques. Let me point you in a few directions.

Illenberger and Flotterod (2012) showed how some important network properties can be estimated from snowball sampled data. Good estimates for mean degree and the clustering coefficient can be obtained, at least when the degree distribution is not too skewed. They provided a useful summary of different types of snowball sampling designs.

Pattison et al. (2013) showed how to estimate an ERGM from snowball sampled data, even when the number of nodes in the network is not known. (This differs from earlier approaches – Handcock and Gile, 2010 – which required knowledge of n.) Such methods open up snowball sampling as a means to infer network structure for large, poorly defined communities, or perhaps from populations that generally prefer to remain 'hidden' or are 'hard to reach' (e.g., drug users; see Rolls et al., 2013b).

Snowball sampled ERGM estimation opens a new possibility for big network data collected electronically. Normally ERGM estimation is simply too computationally demanding to be applied to a very large dataset. However, a number of relatively small snowball samples can be extracted from the large dataset, estimates obtained for each, and then combined in a post hoc procedure (e.g., see the section on multiple networks below). This can be done in parallelized computations permitting speedier estimation. Xu et al. (2013) demonstrated an early version of this procedure, but further refinements are necessary for good inference (Stivala et al., 2014).

Respondent-driven sampling

According to Gile (2011), the key to estimation of actor attribute variables with RDS is that through many waves of sampling, the dependence of the final sample on the initial sample is reduced, allowing more confident probability statements and better statistical inference when the seed set is a convenience sample. Gile and Handcock (2010) argued that estimators proposed in earlier literature required quite strict conditions before they could be considered reliable. New methods for better estimation are becoming available (Gile, 2011), but methodological work continues in this area, so expect to see further developments in the future.

If you are going to use RDS, then you need to be familiar with the work of the Hard-to-Reach Population Methods Research Group (http://wiki.stat.ucla.edu/hpmrg/index.php/Hard-to-Reach_Population_Methods_Research_Group). The website offers software, manuals, videos and more. For the most up-to-date approach, use their methods and do not rely on earlier techniques.

Research examples: Daraganova et al. (2012) used a snowball sampled network approach to investigate different sources of unemployment within a depressed suburban area. Dombrowski et al. (2013) used RDS to study the characteristics of a Canadian aboriginal community.

Estimating node set size

Social networks can be used to estimate the size of hard-to-reach populations by various methods. The most widely used has been the *network scale-up method* (NSUM) which has the advantage of being an egonet technique. Bernard et al. (2010) provide a succinct summary. The basic assumption is that the prevalence of hard-to-reach persons in the population will be mirrored in the proportion of such people known (on average) in egonets. An estimate of the overall population (e.g., from a census) is required. Then egonet data is collected: respondents are asked how many people from the hard-to-reach population are known to them, and similarly about a known subpopulation. The latter is used to estimate the total number of alters in the egonet, so that the proportion of the hard-to-reach population can be estimated for each ego.

Total network size can also be estimated from snowball sampling methods. Frank and Snijders (1994) used simple random graph models for this, but more recent work has used ERGMs (Rolls et al., 2013b).

Missing network data

In earlier chapters, I mentioned the desirability of minimizing the missing data in whole network studies, both network tie and actor attribute data. In Chapter 5, I noted that available case analysis (ignoring actors with missing data) can lead to bias in conclusions, although – a little reassuringly – Huisman (2009) showed that for low proportions of missing data, the bias in the descriptive statistics was not too large. So, if you have a small proportion of missingness, then perhaps you can manage by ignoring missing actors. In effect, what you are doing then is redefining the network boundary to exclude those actors who did not respond.

But what to do if either you want to be, commendably, more rigorous, or you have somewhat more missingness than 'a small proportion'? An old technique of *reconstruction*, essentially imputing the missing ties using reciprocity, was proposed by Stork and Richards (1992), but this can over-estimate the presence of ties (Koskinen et al., 2013). More recent imputation methods, often termed *link prediction*, essentially predict edges based on structural features in the observed network data (Hasan and Zaki, 2011).

Link prediction methods can be sophisticated but nevertheless sometimes have an ad hoc flavor given the lack of an underlying model for the network structure. Koskinen et al. (2013) argued for a model-based approach and followed Handcock and Gile (2010) in using an ERGM. In short, if we assume that the missing data is similar to the observed data – *ignorable* missingness, akin to *missingness at random* in standard statistical analysis (Handcock and Gile) – then once we have a good model for the observed part of the network, we can apply it to infer the missing part. (Handcock and Gile also showed a methodological link between ignorable missingness and snowball sampling: in other words, the method is not particular to missing data but to various forms of partial observation.) Handcock and Gile and Koskinen et al. both presented different methods for imputing missing network data using this general idea. Simulations from the estimated ERGM parameters can also inform about structural features of the network, despite the missingness.

These are sophisticated approaches to missingness, and quite new, so not commonly used to date. For many practical purposes, researchers with small amounts of missing data will prefer to stay simple and attempt available case analysis. But when the missingness is rather larger than you want, or your reviewers will tolerate, check out whether these new methods can help you. In particular, follow the advice in Chapter 5 from Žnidaršič et al. (2012) in reporting the extent of missingness more fully.

As I said in Chapter 5, the story of how to conceptualize and handle missing social network data is just beginning.

Research examples: Koskinen et al. (2013) showed that for a collaboration network in a government organization, a plausible model could be obtained with up to 74% of tie variables missing.

Bipartite network analyses

The methods above essentially apply to whole unipartite network studies. Let me now turn to some other network data types, beginning with two-mode or bipartite network analysis.

One commonly used method for analyzing bipartite network data is to collapse the original data into two unipartite networks and then to analyze these separately, using the unipartite methods described in this chapter. It is a convenient way to avoid the complexities of bipartite data and to revert to more familiar techniques. Usually, it is simply bad practice. First, let me describe precisely how it is done; and then I will explain why you should think carefully before doing it.

The idea is simple. Suppose the bipartite data is of interlocking directorships, where directors are linked to the companies on which they are board members. Then a unipartite tie is defined to exist between two directors if they sit on the same board, producing the director–director network; and, similarly, a tie is defined to exist between two companies if they share a director, producing the company–company network. The unipartite networks are often termed *projections* of the bipartite network.

For readers familiar with matrix algebra, these two networks can be easily calculated by matrix multiplication of the adjacency matrix x with its transpose. Calculate x^Tx and xx^T and then binarize the cells by setting to 1 any non-zero cell entry.

What is wrong with this? For a start, the binarization removes substantial information from the original bipartite data. You could use the weighted matrices from the matrix multiplication without dichotomizing the cells, but then the advantage of applying familiar techniques is lost with weighted, not binary, network data. Furthermore, an artefact of the projection method is that high-degree nodes in the bipartite network automatically produce a lot of triangulation in the projected unipartite networks, so the amount of unipartite closure is exaggerated. And of course, to analyze both unipartite networks separately is to ignore how they interrelate (Latapy et al., 2008; Wang et al., 2009). Everett and Borgatti (2013) have shown that, as long as you analyze the two unipartite networks together (*dual projection*) and use weighted data, then sound conclusions can be drawn, at least on some measures (see also Piepenbrink and Gaur, 2013); but in that case, the simple 'fix' of bipartite projection into binary data and the subsequent application of standard unipartite techniques is lost.

If you decide not to go down the track of the Everett and Borgatti dual-projection approach, then you need to analyze the original bipartite structure without transformation. Latapy et al. (2008) and Piepenbrink and Gaur (2013) summarize some basic ideas. Further guidance can be obtained from Borgatti et al. (2013) and Borgatti and Halgin (2011). Many of the analytic ideas relevant to unipartite networks can be extended to bipartite networks but often with distinctive twists, some of which I note in Box 9.3.

BOX 9.3

Bipartite network analysis

Bipartite network analysis is often an extension of unipartite techniques, but the nature of bipartite data means that the regular methods often need adaptation.

- Bipartite networks have two *degree distributions,* one for each type of node. The presence of two types of nodes also affects notions of centrality: centralities should not be compared across node types.

- It is impossible to have a triangle in a bipartite network, so *bipartite closure* is different. The simplest closed structure in a bipartite graph is a 4-cycle. Various bipartite clustering coefficients have been proposed, often based on closed 4-cycles (e.g., Latapy et al., 2008; Opsahl, 2013; Robins and Alexander, 2004).

- Borgatti and Everett (1997) described bipartite extensions of *cohesive subsets* of nodes.

- *Structural equivalence* in bipartite network is simply defined: two nodes of the same type are structurally equivalent if they have connections to the same nodes of the other type. This definition implies separate groupings on the two types of nodes. Blockmodelling of bipartite data using equivalence was described by Everett and Borgatti (1992).

- *Bipartite community detection,* on the other hand, permits different types of nodes to be in the one community (akin to what is called *biclustering* – groupings across the two modes – often used in biological networks, but not that common in social network analysis). See, for instance, Barber (2007) and Melamed et al. (2013).

- *Statistical approaches*: Robins and Alexander (2004) used a bipartite conditional uniform graph distribution. Wang et al. (2009) described an ERGM for bipartite data. Snijders et al. (2013) used an SAOM to examine the co-evolution of bipartite and unipartite networks.

Research examples: Check out the recent special issue on bipartite network analysis in *Social Networks* for examples of up-to-date methods and research illustrations (Agneessens and Everett, 2013). Bruce Kogut's (2012) edited book on corporate governance will be of interest to researchers interested in director interlocks, and to those more generally interested in empirical bipartite network analysis.

Multiple networks

Multiple network studies are often conducted by deriving certain network statistics from each network (e.g., density) and then using that as a variable in a regression across the networks, with other unit-level variables. Standard multilevel modelling predicting individual outcomes within networks, with the units as a macro level, is sometimes used but of course the network means that the usual assumption of independence among individuals does not hold.

After fitting an ERGM or SAOM to the individual networks, it is possible to combine the parameter estimates across networks with a post hoc technique derived from multilevel modelling. Basically, this is a weighted average of the estimates with the weights determined by the standard error of the estimate. Snijders and Baerveldt (2003) described how to do this (see also Lubbers and Snijders, 2007).

Multilevel networks

Earlier studies of multilevel networks (Lazega et al., 2008) relied on a variety of centrality and descriptive techniques. It is only recently that statistical methods have been introduced, including ERGMs (Wang et al., 2013) and SAOMs (Snijders et al., 2013) for multilevel networks. These models can be fitted to data using MPNet and Siena, respectively (Box 9.1).

If you wish to analyze meta-matrices as proposed by Kathleen Carley, then you will want to check out the ORA software and other details on the ORA website (Box 9.1).

Research examples: Lazega et al. (2008) gave a strong theoretical basis for understanding multilevel networks, studying the structure of cancer researchers affiliated with different research laboratories. Wang et al. (2013) applied an ERGM to the Lazega dataset. Bodin and Tengö (2012) used multilevel network configurations to study social ecological systems, but used versions of conditional uniform graph distributions for analysis. A special issue of the journal *Social Networks* on multilevel networks is scheduled to appear in the near future, so check it out for the latest empirical and methodological work in this fast growing area.

Valued and categorical network data

As will be apparent from this survey to date, most network analytic techniques are principally or originally defined for binary data. Extensions to valued data, however, are often limited, so there are not always good or well-established techniques when ties are weighted, or even when they are only categorized into (say) strong and weak ties.

As I have said elsewhere in this book, depending on the research context there may be more mileage in studying a number of different types of binary tie in a multiplex way, rather than one type of tie with a fine-grained measurement of tie strength. You can investigate how the multiplex relational ties associate in your data by using a QAP, ERGM or SAOM. For some research questions, however, weighted ties make the most sense (e.g., financial or trade data between countries) and indeed may be the form of the data in archival databases. In other cases, categories of the one type of tie, such as strong and weak, may be most relevant to the research question.

If you are working with strong and weak ties, then it may be helpful to do the analysis twice, with a network of only strong ties, and then with all ties (i.e., both strong and weak – or perhaps weak only), comparing the results to infer the effects of tie strength. This approach may be a bit clunky but it could be sufficient to address the research question. Multiplex techniques can also be used, although the constraint that a strong tie cannot be weak (and vice versa) needs to be applied, and this may require some adaptation of the standard software.

With weighted network data, a common approach is to dichotomize each tie, setting a particular tie strength as a criterion. Only if the weight is above the criterion is the tie assumed to be present in the dichotomized network. Analysis suitable for binary networks can then be used. The difficulty is to decide on a sensible criterion. Look at the distribution of tie values: if you are lucky it may be bimodal, in which case a cut-point between the modes makes sense. Or there may be theoretical reasons to choose a particular value. In any case, when you come to publish your research, reviewers are very likely to ask about the impact of the criterion on the results, so have a good argument ready. Undertake sensitivity analyses using different cut-points in order to reassure that conclusions are not substantially affected by your choice.

Nevertheless, there is new attention to working with the original weighted network data without resort to binarization, with novel techniques being developed such as those described in the following research examples.

Research examples: If you intend to work with valued network data without dichotomization, check out Opsahl and Panzarasa (2009) where clustering in weighted networks is discussed (see also Phan et al., 2013), and see Opsahl et al.'s (2010) approach to valued centrality, degree and geodesics.

Egocentric network data

I will not say much about egonet data analysis, because often specialized network methods are not required.

- The structure of egonet data was described in Chapter 4. Readers familiar with standard hierarchical linear models will recognize that the ego and alter files in Figure 4.13 have the hierarchical structure of alters nested within egos. If you are not interested in, or do not have data on, the internal egonet structure (the alter–alter file in Figure 4.13), then you can use hierarchical linear models to predict an alter variable (i.e. the dependent variable). Of course, this assumes that alter–alter structure can be ignored and that alters are independent conditional on being nested within ego.

- If your interest lies more in using an ego variable as outcome, then you can aggregate the alter variables and structural features of the alter–alter file (e.g., density) into the ego file as in Figure 4.15. Then you can predict your outcome variable with standard regression.
- Of course, these structural features of the egonet can also be included in the hierarchical linear model analysis above.
- A more obviously network analysis – but perhaps more time-consuming, depending on how many egonets you have – is to note that the alter–alter file in Figure 4.13 has the form of a binary unipartite network, with the alter file providing node attributes. So each egonet can be analyzed using the standard network techniques described in this chapter, and the results for each then associated with the ego-level variables from the ego file. In short, egos can be treated as units in a multiple network study.

Research examples: Cannella and McFadyen (in press) examined knowledge workers' ego networks, using a regression approach by aggregating to the ego-level file, including average tie strength to egos and egonet density as structural variables.

Digital data and big data

I do not have the scope in this book to give a proper review of all the methodological developments to analyze web-based, social media and other forms of big data collected digitally. So let me make a few comments and suggest some directions for those who wish to follow up.

As long as a digital dataset is not too large, then the techniques described in this chapter can be applied. Of course, there are also many other methods for the analysis of social media data: this is a hot field of research and new methods are being developed continually. Sometimes researchers collapse social media data into static networks, or into longitudinal panels; but as this data often involves time-stamped exchanges and transactions, methods such as relational event models are attractive alternatives that better respect the sequencing that we see in social media.

What to do if you have a very large network dataset, perhaps containing thousands or even millions of nodes? Some methods are quite tractable for large networks: for instance, the calculation of density and degree distributions, and hence of inferences about scale-free networks and the like. Even so, some analyses are impractical within a reasonable time period, including ERGMs and SAOMs which require intensive simulation to estimate parameters (although note the new possibilities for parallelized estimation of ERGMs for large data above). Borgatti et al. (2013) offered some advice about 'thinning' the network data down to a more manageable size.

However, it is not always possible or desirable to trim your data down to a tractable dataset. Social network data mining of large datasets is now a research field in its own right, with advances occurring regularly. These developments often take place within computer science or statistics. If you have very large data that you need to analyze, then you may wish to delve into these areas. Many of the underlying ideas about networks that are described in this book remain highly relevant, but additional data analytic techniques may be required to cope with the large data.

Of the software listed in Box 9.1, Pajek is perhaps best placed to handle really large network data. Other software that could be tried for very large graphs includes *Webgraph* (http://webgraph.di.unimi.it); *GraphChi* (http://graphlab.org/graphchi); and *Pegasus* (http://www.cs.cmu.edu/~pegasus). Doreian et al. (2014) used Pajek and *R* to analyze large temporal and spatial networks. Batagelj (2011) described some approaches to large-scale network analysis that can be applied with Pajek.

Research examples: Ackland (2013) and Hansen et al. (2010) are good starting points for social science researchers wishing to conduct social media network analysis. Lusher and Ackland (2011) used an ERGM to analyse a hyperlink network. Harrigan et al. (2012) used a triad census to analyse Twitter data. If you want to investigate big data methods and data mining further, check out the new journal dedicated to large network data mining, *Social Network Analysis and Mining*, or texts such as Aggarwal (2011) and Doreian et al. (2014).

Qualitative network data

Let me conclude with some further comments on qualitative network data.

The analysis and interpretation of general qualitative data is a field in its own right (e.g., Silverman, 2011), involving a range of possible methods that can also be applied to relational information collected in qualitative interviews (Hollstein, 2011). Such information can be used to construct a network representation of the interviewee's responses with regard to their social environment. In that case, the range of techniques discussed in this chapter becomes available, enabling a mixed methods approach. Bellotti (2008) provided a good example, where she used name generators in interviews with younger single adults in Milan, obtaining egonet data for each interviewee. She then studied structural features of the egonets and compared them with themes emerging from in-depth interviews on the meaning of friendship. Understanding about meaning and motivation, including possibly insights into causality, are among the rich interpretations that are available from good qualitative network data.

Bidart and Cacciuttolo (2013) explicitly sought to integrate qualitative, quantitative and structural dimensions in their longitudinal analysis of the transitions to adulthood by young people. I gave some details of their data collection in

Chapter 6. The analysis cycled through qualitative, quantitative and structural phases, with each informing the others, to produce results that are rich in terms of explanatory potential.

In reviewing qualitative network studies, Hollstein (2011) noted a number of different qualitative methods that have been used in network studies, including grounded theory, frame analysis, conversation analysis, interaction analysis and narrative analysis. She also pointed to quantitative methods suitable for qualitative data such as quantitative content analysis, semantic network analysis, and Galois lattices. If you intend to focus on qualitative methods in your network study, her review is a good place to start. See also the section on new methodological approaches for mixed methods designs in Dominguez and Hollstein (2014).

Research examples: Brian Uzzi is well known for research on the embeddness of network ties of exchanges among firms. Uzzi (1996) described a mixed methods network study, drawing on ethnographic fieldwork on exchange ties to provide input into a logit analysis. In a later article, Uzzi (1997) described a qualitative network study identifying features of exchange relationships and their relation to firm performance, thereby developing a number of theoretical propositions about embeddedness of ties.

In conclusion: The key point

There are many network methods, some more sophisticated than others. If you are going to be a creditable network analyst, you have to be broadly familiar with them all and expert in some. The choice of method for a particular dataset is not always easy and careful decisions often need to be made during the analysis. These must be justifiable.

Fancy, novel network methods are great and continue to become available all the time. But, as I said earlier, sophisticated analysis will not rescue poorly conceptualized research and bad data collection.

BOX 9.4

Pulling back the curtain: What goes on in real network studies

We analyzed the sporting team networks using exponential random graph models. Because we were interested in cultural issues, we wanted to see how our attitudinal surveys related to social structure. So we examined social selection effects while controlling for structural effects (e.g., degree effects akin to preferential attachment, network closure). We found that some attitudes were associated with network ties, once endogenous effects were controlled. Athletes tended to choose social partners partly based on certain attitudes.

As I noted in Chapter 8, we conducted a blockmodel analysis of the environmental governance data, using a number of methods including CONCOR. Unfortunately, the blockmodels did not fit the data very well, and were not very insightful. As a result, in our report to the commissioning organization, we concentrated on centrality and connectivity in the network.

Hot topics and further reading

Is social network research just social network analysis (SNA)? Brandes et al. (2013b) argued in *Network Science* that it was not. I think we should stop using the acronym SNA to apply to networks research more generally. Theory, network data collection, and network-based research design do not count as 'analysis'. A scientific field – and that is what Brandes et al. argue network science is – has to have all of these elements. It is not just a method, or a suite of methods, that are applied to particular data structures.

Brandes, U., Robins, G., McCranie, A. and Wasserman, S. (2013b) What is network science? *Network Science*, 1, 1–15.

Further reading

Here are some texts and articles that may be helpful. This is not an exclusive list, and new texts appear regularly, so scout around for other options. Nevertheless, if you want to become a serious social network expert, you will look at several or most of these. If your ambitions are more modest, then the entry point depends on your level of existing expertise and the topic you are researching. If you are a newcomer to networks, without a strong mathematical or statistical background, start from the introductory books (point 3 below). I suggest all readers dip into Wasserman and Faust (1) and Scott and Carrington (2). Those with a particular disciplinary interest might select from the texts in points 4–6. For article-length reviews of network methods, select from point 7. Point 8 includes some important readings on longitudinal network analysis.

1. The now classic text on social network analysis is Wasserman and Faust (1994):

   o Wasserman, S. and Faust, K. (1994) *Social network analysis: Methods and applications*. Cambridge: Cambridge University Press.

2. The two Carrington and Scott texts update many topics covered by Wasserman and Faust:

   o Carrington, P., Scott, J. and Wasserman, S. (eds) (2005) *Models and Methods in Social Network Analysis*. Cambridge: Cambridge University Press.

o Scott, J. and Carrington, P. (eds) (2011) *The SAGE Handbook of Social Network Analysis.* London: Sage.

3. A number of introductory books provide good summaries of important methods and are helpful for those coming to SNA for the first time:

o Borgatti, S., Everett, M., and Johnson, J. (2013) *Analyzing Social Networks.* Los Angeles: Sage. (This also helps as a UCINET guide.)
o Prell, C. (2012) *Social Network Analysis: History, Theory and Methodology.* Los Angeles: Sage.
o Scott, J. (2013) *Social Network Analysis.* Los Angeles: Sage. (This is the third edition of a very popular introductory text.)

4. A number of texts go beyond SNA to a more general network science perspective, among them the book by Mark Newman, a physicist and one of the leading practitioners of network science.

o Newman, M. (2010) *Networks: An Introduction.* Oxford: Oxford University Press.

5. Some texts have a particular disciplinary focus, such as the text by Matthew Jackson, a major figure in economic networks:

o Jackson, M. (2010) *Social and Economic Networks.* Princeton, NJ: Princeton University Press.

6. For those with a strong statistical background, Eric Kolaczyk is the author for you:

o Kolaczyk, E. (2009) *Statistical Analysis of Network Data: Methods and Models.* New York: Springer.

7. Here are a number of recent review articles (including some of my own) that summarize various aspects of SNA methodology:

o Snijders, T. (2011b) Statistical models for social networks. *Annual Review of Sociology*, 37, 131–153.
o Butts, C. (2008c) Social network analysis: A methodological introduction. *Asian Journal of Social Psychology*, 11, 13–41.
o Wasserman, S. and Robins, G. (2012) Social network research: The foundation of network science. In H. Cooper et al. (eds), *APA Handbook of Research Methods in Psychology, Volume 3. Data Analysis and Research Publication* (pp. 451–469). Washington, DC: American Psychological Association.
o Robins, G. (2013) A tutorial on methods for the modeling and analysis of social network data. *Journal of Mathematical Psychology*, 57, 261–274.
o Robins, G., Lewis, J. and Wang, P. (2012) Statistical network analysis for analyzing policy networks. *Policy Studies Journal*, 40, 375–401.

8. Finally, some additional readings on longitudinal network analysis. Skye Bender-deMoll and Dan McFarland (2006) discuss the important issues of aggregating across time, the use of discrete and continuous time, and concepts of time, events and networks. They also show how these play out in the temporal visualizations produced by *Sonia* (see Chapter 8). In an important article, Jim Moody (2002) points out the relevance of the temporal sequence of network relationships to network diffusion outcomes. For examples of methods developed in the physics literature for network dynamics, see the recent special issue of the *European Physical Journal.*

o Bender-deMoll, S. and McFarland, D. (2006) The art and science of dynamic network visualization. *Journal of Social Structure*, 7, 2.
o Moody, J. (2002) The importance of relationship timing for diffusion. *Social Forces*, 81, 25–56.
o Sloot, P., Kampis, G. and Gulyas, L. (2013) Advances in dynamic temporal networks: Understanding the temporal dynamics of complex adaptive networks. *European Physical Journal Special Topics*, 222, 1287–1293.

TEN

Drawing conclusions: Inference, generalization, causality and other weighty matters

If you followed the sequence of this book, you began your social network study with a theoretical research question that suggested a particular study design and measurement. You then proceeded to analyze the data with a method appropriate to the structure of the data and the demands of the design, one that suitably addressed the research question.

I begin this chapter with some comments about the type of conclusions you can draw from this analysis. I go on to discuss more complicated, often disputed, issues of interpretation and inference: generalization in network research, causality in network effects, the use of simulation to extend conclusions further, and the role of network interventions. I end the book with a discussion on the contrast between Big and little (or 'Thick') data, and on computational social science generally.

Linking conclusions to research questions through data and analysis

As in all social science research, a social network study is a package deal, an integrated whole. The research question and structure of the data constrain the effects to be examined and the analysis to be done; and hence the conclusions that can be drawn. Conclusions need to be consonant with the design, data and analysis.

In Chapter 3, I listed some classes of research questions that are commonly seen in social network studies. My goal now is to illustrate the type of conclusions that may follow from these questions, depending on the design, data and analysis. Features of the design include whether the study is of a whole network or of egonets, and whether the data is cross-sectional or longitudinal.

1. Influence or diffusion hypotheses

How does the social environment affect individual outcomes? How do network partners affect individuals? What flows through the network from one individual to another?

If this was your study, you treated the network as a fixed explanatory factor, and focused on an actor attribute as an outcome. You studied the distribution of attributes across the network, checking whether network partners have similar attributes.

You may have collected cross-sectional whole network data, in which case you used one of the current social influence or diffusion models for analysis. If you collected egonet data, you may have used a hierarchical linear model. Apart from the outcome variable, you are likely to have other attribute data. You may have examined whether your outcome was explained by the other attributes alone, whether the network diffusion alone was an adequate explanation, or whether both individual and social processes were occurring together.

With cross-sectional data, your analysis revealed an association between the outcome and the network ties. You could argue that influence is plausible; but usually you cannot entirely exclude social selection as an explanation, so temper your conclusions accordingly.

On the other hand, you may have collected longitudinal panel data. You could use this data to investigate your influence hypothesis in a more fine-grained, longitudinal way. But the longitudinal data may enable you to go further than just a diffusion approach and to study influence effects in a co-evolution framework (point 5 below).

2. Generalized influence hypotheses

How do individuals in certain network positions differ in their individual outcomes? If this was your study, again you focused on attributes but examined them against network position.

If you collected cross-sectional whole network data, perhaps you were interested in structural holes and used measures of constraint or betweenness centrality. Perhaps you used degree centrality as a measure of popularity or network activity. Maybe you correlated the attribute variable with the centrality or constraint score. For a whole network, it is not a perfect analysis because of the dependencies, but people do it. Maybe you conducted a community or structural equivalence analysis, and checked whether nodes in the different communities or equivalence positions tended to have different attribute values.

If your cross-sectional results showed an association between network position and an individual outcome, you concluded that people who occupy certain positions tend to have more of the attribute (whatever it is): for instance, people bridging structural holes in an organization get more promotions. Again, depending on context, you need to be cautious about the direction of effect: perhaps being in the network position leads to the outcome, or perhaps the attribute encourages people to seek particular network positions.

If you collected egonet data, then you might have calculated egonet indices (e.g., alter–alter density), aggregated features of the network structure to the ego level, and regressed these against the individual attribute of interest. You may have concluded that egonet structure relates to the attribute in various ways.

But if you collected longitudinal data, you could study these associations between network position and attributes across time. And longitudinal whole network panel data permits a co-evolutionary analysis to draw firmer inferences about possible causal directions.

3. Selection hypotheses, including generalized selection

How do individuals affect network structure? On what basis do individuals choose network partners, or network positions?

For influence hypotheses (1 and 2), the network is taken as an explanatory factor for the attributes. For selection hypotheses, on the other hand, the attributes are theorized to have effect on network structure.

If this was your study, now you focused on network tie variables, using attributes as predictors. With cross-sectional whole network data, perhaps you concentrated on homophily effects, examining the proportion of homophilous to non-homophilous dyads. Maybe you fitted an ERGM with social selection effects, including homophily. Maybe, as with structural influence studies (2 above), you conducted a structural equivalence analysis to see whether your attribute was associated with network position.

So, given that similar analyses might be conducted for both 2 and 3, how do you know that it is selection here? You do not! Or, rather, your theoretical position may be that selection is the process; and perhaps your data is consistent with that, once it is shown in the analysis. Sometimes, this theoretical argument is compelling: flu is transmitted by contagion, and is not a basis on which people create friendships; sex (male/female) may be a basis for friendship formation, but it is certainly not subject to network diffusion. But when the argument is not so obvious, admit it. In that case, if you want a definite conclusion about causal direction you probably need longitudinal data, and the sensible longitudinal approach is a co-evolutionary framework.

4. Structural hypotheses

How does network structure come into being? What are the self-organizing processes involved? How can we best describe or simplify the network?

If this was your study, you concentrated on network ties, with attributes at best an additional and possibly minor explanatory factor. You looked for reciprocity, closure, preferential attachment and other self-organizing processes. Perhaps you conducted a triad census, and compared it against a conditional uniform graph distribution. You would have examined the degree distribution. Maybe you fitted an ERGM for whole network cross-sectional data, or an SAOM for longitudinal network evolution. Perhaps you examined whether your network has small-world properties.

If you wanted to simplify the network structure, perhaps you identified communities or structural equivalence positions and the relationships between them expressed as blockmodels.

With these results, you can draw inferences about the endogenous network processes that could lead to tie formation. Your conclusions are about how human social relationships structure themselves within your particular research context.

5. Co-evolution hypotheses

How do individual outcomes and/or network structure co-evolve over time?

If this was your study, you have longitudinal panel data on both network ties and actor attributes. You want to distinguish between selection and influence. Your interest may be either in network structure or individual outcomes (or both), but you study the co-evolution of both to observe the processes in your focus (individual or structural) while controlling for the other. In this case you have applied an SAOM.

Your conclusions are focused on network dynamics. You are studying the processes of change in your data, both ties and attributes. You draw inferences about endogenous network dynamics as well as how network ties affect attributes and how attributes (separately) affect network ties.

6. Global network outcomes

What are the global outcomes for a particular network structure? What makes a networked social system effective or responsive?

If this was your study, your focus was on structure as represented by the patterning of network ties. Perhaps you had a case study, or a multiple network study. Perhaps for a case study you sought to understand how the observed structure differed from or was similar to other networks (either other empirical networks, or idealized network structure, e.g., in the form of a scale-free network). Alternatively, in a multiple network study, you identified the major structural effects across all networks.

You could draw on the endogenous network processes studied in question (4) above, but now the emphasis is on the global network patterns as distinct from tie formation processes. Very likely, you included attributes in understanding the network structure. You may have fitted ERGMs or SAOMs, or identified the main structural features of your data in other ways, perhaps through a structural equivalence or community structure analysis. Essentially, you sought an optimal way to describe or model the whole network.

One of the most difficult research issues in social network science is whether an observed network is effective or responsive, whatever those terms mean in your research context. In Chapter 6, I wrote about these issues in the context of network governance. An outcome measure at the network level is not always easy to define, so in your study you would have given this considerable thought even before collecting any data. Is it possible to identify features of the global network structure that relate to this system outcome?

I discuss this issue further below when I write about network interventions. But, to reach firm conclusions, you obviously need to be able to generalize across networks.

Generalization

In standard social science, *generalization* usually refers to making inferences and drawing conclusions from a sample that can be applied to a population. In social network studies, as I have mentioned in earlier chapters, the notion of a population is often ambiguous or poorly defined, so generalization is not straightforward.

As always, much depends on the research design. If you have an egonet study, with participants randomly sampled from a given population, then you can argue that inferences can be made to that population. If you have a multiple network study with units sampled from a population of units (e.g., networks within schools randomly sampled from a school system) then you can again argue that your results generalize to that school system.

Yet so much of social network research involves case studies. In some instances this is inevitable: there is only one internet, so a study of the internet cannot by definition be generalized to other instances. But studies of the internet are frequently not so much about the system as a whole but of processes within the internet. If we study processes within a given social system, then our 'population' may be construed as the set of all nodes – or even of all ties – in the network. We seek to understand the structural 'rules' of social behavior within this system. If we draw sound conclusions, we can be confident that they do indeed apply to this network. Just as we have different levels of analysis in a whole network study, we can have different levels of generalization, and generalizing about behaviors of nodes or the structuring of ties *within* the system is entirely appropriate.

Yet so often we want more, to go beyond the system we study. We want to argue that our case study of a network generalizes to other similar networks. But let's face it: the argument is tenuous and we need to be cautious about our claims. There may be so many particularities about a complex social system that it could be risky to generalize beyond the data we observe. Peer networks within multiple schools located in the same city, or even multiple grades or classrooms within the same school, might be considered as segments of an overall social system with common underlying social processes. But individual school environment and culture are also very likely to affect the network dynamics.

It is easy to say that we should just collect more data on different networks. Yes, of course, it is better to have data on even a small number of networks, rather than just one. Nevertheless, we need to recognize that social network data collection is often difficult and expensive. Suppose you study network governance of environmental resources. There may be a year or more of work in collecting data from a mere handful of the type of systems you are interested in. We need to do more complex data collection, but it often takes time to build up a corpus of data.

So, in the light of data collection issues, I am not arguing that we give up network case studies. What we need are persuasive theoretical arguments that suggest the results could generalize to other similar systems. Then, the results become hypotheses that can be taken into further studies with different data. The conclusions from our case study make us think about other possibilities, other new ideas, for ongoing work.

It is a *program* of research, possibly across many research teams, that will give us confidence that we have generalizable conclusions. Do not believe in the One True Study. In research on complex network-based social systems, I have seen many innovative, thought-provoking single studies. But they never reveal all; at their very best, they lead to a program of work that is taken up by many scholars.

It is from the research program that we more confidently generalize, not the individual study. This is a notable feature in the history of social network research, but rarely explicitly stated. Situate your own research strongly within the context of previous research – even when you intend to debunk that research. Be aware of the cross-currents of network research in other disciplines that are applicable to your study. Devise further empirical studies that advance your previous work. Try to solidify your theoretical base as much as possible.

Social network *analysis* is not sufficient for generalization. We need theory, good argument, careful thinking and further well-designed empirical studies. This is at the heart of drawing sound and ultimately compelling conclusions, including those difficult but much-desired inferences about causal effects.

Causality

How can we make causal claims in social network research? Some argue that as we are studying a social system, with dependencies and feedback effects typical of complex systems, the whole idea of causality is outmoded. We need to keep this argument in mind.

Nevertheless, throughout this book, I have emphasized the distinction between selection and influence (between research questions 1, 2 and 3 above). A selection process entails that actor attributes result in network ties; whereas for an influence process, the patterning of the network ties results in changes to actor attributes. Both processes lead to an association between ties and attributes. If we prefer one process over the other as our explanation, we are inferring a direction of effect, and so we are close to drawing a causal conclusion.

In many cases (but not necessarily all), we do want to understand such directions of effect. Viral marketing requires a social influence process. If positive information about a product spreads across a social network, perhaps face-to-face or perhaps through social media, and enhances purchasing behavior, you have social influence. If, on the other hand, social selection is at play – whereby people who buy the same product form social ties (perhaps through online discussion sites about the product) – then you have tendencies to market segmentation. If you want to sell more product, you need influence, not selection.

Such issues can be sharp for public health interventions. If a health issue is due to individual factors, with no social influence effects, then individual medical treatment may be the obvious response. If contagion (influence) is present, however, then additional interventions may be necessary. With contagious diseases, we know this well. Infectious children, while being treated, may be required to stay home from school to prevent the disease from spreading: there is both a medical and a social intervention.

Of course, in any research on an actual social system, there may be contextual effects common to all actors in the system. Such external influences may relate to both network and attributes, to create a spurious association between the two. For instance, we might see an association between a type of cancer and friendship ties. Are we able to infer that this type of cancer is contagious in some way? Not if the cancer is the result of a dangerous chemical contamination in a specific geographical location, where the location affects the likelihood of both the presence of disease and the presence of friendship.

In public health studies more generally, an individual attribute such as socio-economic status can relate to the health status of an individual as well as affect friendships. Homophily may occur on the basis of socio-economic status, and different socio-economic groups may have different norms of health behavior. If we ignore socio-economic status, we may inadvertently infer that the health status is transmitted by friendship.

The Christakis and Fowler studies

Famously, Christakis and Fowler (2007) argued that social influence processes could result in obesity being diffused across friendship networks. They extracted social network data from the Framingham Heart Study, a research program involving some 12,000 people over 32 years. The network data had some important limitations, including that each participant could nominate only one friend. Such constraints are to be expected given that the original research was not conceived as a network study. So, while this situation is not perfect, I think Christakis and Fowler are to be congratulated for re-analyzing the Framingham data to see what might be concluded from the limited network information available.

In a clever analysis Christakis and Fowler essentially regressed current obesity status on predictors including friend's previous obesity status, and concluded that network influence was present. They argued that their model specification controlled for homophily and contextual effects. In further work (see Christakis and Fowler, 2013, for a summary of the whole research program), they showed that smoking and other attributes were also subject to influence, and that contagion could traverse network paths of length 3 before petering out: *three degrees of influence*.

The result about obesity contagion was immediately contentious. Arguments about the data limitations have to a degree been countered by consistent results from other datasets with better network measurement (Christakis and Fowler, 2013). The analytic method, however, has faced ongoing criticism, including claims that homophily and influence are inevitably confounded (Shalizi and Thomas, 2011). The argument goes back to a long-standing concern in the econometric literature about problems with causal conclusions when endogenous social effects are present (Manski, 1993). Some claimed that the Christakis and Fowler methods were even 'flawed', with precise parameter estimates and confidence intervals invalid (Lyons, 2011). Cohen-Cole and Fletcher (2009) applied the methods to Add Health data (see Box 6.2) to show that even acne, headaches and height were subject to network influence among adolescents. They argued that it was simply implausible that these three conditions could be subject to network effects: the method had to be wrong.

But whether network diffusion is implausible or not depends on what is diffused. As Christakis and Fowler (2013) subsequently argued, behavioral norms can indeed be diffused, and these may include whether an adolescent worries about and reports acne and headaches. In any event, the acne, headache and height results have been placed in doubt by a sensitivity analysis by VanderWeele (2011), who found more robust results for the central obesity and smoking diffusion claims. In the face of the strong criticism by Lyons (2011) about incorrect estimates and confidence intervals, VanderWeele et al. (2012) suggested a weaker conclusion: the Christakis and Fowler approach at least might still have validity in drawing statistical inference, even if the precise estimates were biassed.

Let me return to the Shalizi and Thomas (2011) critique which is, I think, quite important. They showed that latent variables that affected network ties via homophily, as well as other observed actor attributes, could result in the attributes seemingly subject to social influence. In other words, latent homophily can masquerade as observed influence. (Noel and Nyhan (2011) showed how another causal process could undermine diffusion claims: when homophily affected not the creation but the dissolution of ties.)

By definition, latent variables are not measured in a study and so are necessarily unobservable in the analysis. Latent homophily may then occur when an unmeasured attribute variable, not observed or analyzed, creates ties through homophilous processes. To pick up the earlier examples, perhaps we saw evidence for diffusion of cancer across friendship ties but forgot to record location and the chemical contamination; and the location thereby gives rise to latent homophily (people located close to one another are more likely to be friends) as well as affects cancer. Or perhaps we see health status apparently affected by friendship but forgot to take into account socio-economic status, which in turn gives rise to both latent homophily and health status.

So unmeasured variables may drive the effects and yet we know nothing of them. This issue is not just one for the Christakis and Fowler methods but for other models that attempt to distinguish selection from influence including SAOMs.

The Shalizi and Thomas (2011) argument should not be surprising to social scientists more generally. Sewall Wright (1921) developed path analysis leading both to structural equation modelling methods that will be familiar to many social scientists, and to graphical modelling, used by statisticians to determine causal structures. (At the heart of the Shalizi and Thomas paper is a straightforward graphical modelling argument.) Wright (1921) discussed causality and correlation, and through his examples illustrated that causality might be a consistent interpretation of data when there was a temporal ordering of correlated variables, as long as there were controls on all common causal factors (i.e., factors that influence two other variables and thereby induce a correlation). When we have an unmeasured variable that influences both latent homophily and other attributes, then obviously not all common causal factors are controlled. Seemingly, the Shalizi and Thomas critique is powerful because it appears impossible to study all possible sources of latent homophily. This is particularly so in a large-scale social system, where there are so many possible variables that could be studied. We simply cannot measure everything.

Should we give up on social influence studies and network causality?

Whatever our position on these methodological criticisms, it is still clear that they are no excuse to return to earlier and simpler conceptualizations. Pandora's network diffusion box has been opened and cannot be shut. Even if the Christakis and Fowler statistical models are improperly specified as the critics claim, it also follows that statistical models ignoring possible network diffusion may be even more poorly constructed. The critiques here may be a two-edged sword for some: there is no consolation for researchers who wish to debunk Christakis and Fowler in order to return to individualized regressions. The point is not just to go back to a comfortable individualism, but to go forward with further thought and research to try to resolve these issues.

In commenting on the Christakis and Fowler controversy, Stanley Wasserman (2013) stated that it was impossible to directly observe causal effects with an observational study. Randomization and good experimental design were at the heart of making solid causal claims. When experimentation was not possible, as is the case for most network studies, causality can only be inferred, never exactly known.

That position is actually not far removed from that of Sewall Wright (1921) in developing path analysis. In those early articles, he was very careful to argue that a path analysis examined only whether a particular causal hypothesis was consistent with given data – and no more than that. Wright himself faced severe criticism about causal arguments. In a rather biting rejoinder to one of his critics, he said that if a path analysis 'can be shown to agree with independently obtained results it contributes to the demonstration of the truth of the hypothesis in the only sense which can be ascribed to the truth of a natural law' (Wright, 1923: 241). Here he was arguing that our understanding of the laws of nature and concepts of causation are ultimately 'based merely on experience' (p. 241). Perhaps this step is a little too far: for the purposes of network research, we obviously need more than simple experience. I think Wright's point scientifically was that causality is an inference that we draw from many scientific 'experiences'.

So, let us consider how we can best make *scientific* inference in this area (not merely a *statistical* inference). First, it is obviously difficult to be sure of the direction of network effect without longitudinal data. With the right longitudinal data, SAOMs can successfully pick apart selection and influence, but only assuming no latent and no contextual effects. SAOMs remain vulnerable to the latent variable threat. Still, if we are confident that we have the relevant variables in our study, they can do the job for us. So, we have the method: the issue is whether we can measure and observe adequately, given that we cannot measure everything.

Metaphor and theory

Unmeasured variables and contextual effects re-emphasize the value of a research program. When there are many studies involving a variety of methods and data, criticisms against one particular type of analysis or one particular dataset lose force. The development of work across the Christakis and Fowler program and the use of different methods by VanderWeele et al. (2012), strengthen the claims.

But when I spoke of research programs above, I mentioned the need to solidify the theoretical base. Consider obesity diffusion. No one believes that obesity is a contagious disease that spreads like the transfer of viruses. As Wasserman (2013) noted, it is silly to think that we will get fat by sitting next to large people on a bus. Yet, we network researchers are sometimes a little too quick to accept cross-disciplinary metaphors without thinking through the actual mechanisms that might be involved. The standard metaphor for network diffusion and influence is disease: and very often it is simply wrong (e.g., Hodas and Lerman, 2014). Simulation studies have shown that *complex contagion* (where diffusion requires more than a single dyadic tie; Centola and Macy, 2007) has distinctive properties, to the point that we cannot rely on simple intuitions and metaphors.

This is not an uncommon error. Network researchers tend to construe information diffusion (for instance) as akin to disease transmission, even though it has been known by social psychologists – at least as far back as Bartlett (1932) with his method of serial reproduction – that information is seldom passed from individual to individual without modification (see Kashima, 2000), unlike the standard modelling of contagious diseases. In Chapter 6, I wrote of a gap between social network and social psychological research: this is a case where we network researchers have fallen into the wrong metaphor by not thinking through the social psychological processes. Sometimes we do not even realize we are relying on a metaphor, rather than an empirical fact.

So, in developing our theoretical base, we need to think through possible *mechanisms* down to the level of specific social behaviors. If obesity is not to be treated as a metaphorical virus, then what might be plausible alternatives? Obvious candidates are health behaviors and attitudes, which we know can indeed be transmitted from person to person through direct influence or a process of copying close others. Look at the work of Kayla de la Haye (2010, 2011, 2013), who has studied behaviors and attitudes relating to eating and physical activity in peer networks within schools. These are small-scale whole network case studies that show, in these schools, how similar eating and exercise practices may diffuse across the peer network. Assuming that obesity can be related to these practices, such studies provide mechanisms for the possibility of 'obesity contagion'. Of course, none of this proves that obesity diffuses across larger networks. But we must then ask: if such processes happen in these classrooms, why should they not happen elsewhere? If they do happen more generally, what are the implications in terms of obesity diffusion? What further studies do we need to do to confirm these implications?

Additionally, there is a wealth of well-designed experimental research showing that social influence shapes many youth and adult health behaviors, including eating and physical activity, as well as weight norms (see Salvy et al., 2012, for a review). This research outlines a number of different social mechanisms that give rise to social influence. Network studies can build on this strong evidence of diffusion in controlled conditions to examine how these processes play out when the person is situated in a much larger and more complex social system.

The Shalizi and Thomas (2011) critique about latent variables seems so potent at first glance because it will always be impossible to measure everything. We are confronted seemingly by an infinite universe of possible latent effects that cannot all be studied. But Sewall Wright, way back in the 1920s, again has guidance for us. He distinguished between *total causes* 'relative to the whole universe of things', and the situation where 'we can satisfactorily isolate a portion of the universe and deal with causation relative to this limited system' (Wright, 1923: 250). In the 'limited system', we have a more limited universe of possible latent variables.

I think this becomes clearer once we move from the abstract to real concrete research contexts where considering plausible latent effects does not seem so impossible. Think about student behaviors in schools. Starting from results such as those of de la Haye and other researchers, it does not seem so difficult to consider other plausible effects that have not been studied in previous work. To respond to the Shalizi and Thomas concern, these effects must influence both network ties and obesity, constraining the range of possibilities further. Within the school context, it does not seem so impossible to consider and study the main sources of homophily, some of which may have been latent in previous studies. To use Wright's words, there is no 'whole universe of things' to worry about here, and we can make sensible choices. In this way, we can develop a theoretical position from which to build the causal inference, study by study. Gradually, over a program of research, we may eliminate plausible effects that we find are not actually relevant. Then we are in a much better position to draw sound inferences that are not confounded. This is especially the case when the research program also involves well-designed experimental studies.

Notice here how small-scale studies within specific contexts to investigate the detail of social processes complement and inform the larger-scale Christakis and Fowler studies that show effects across a whole community. Again, to borrow from Wright, we may need to isolate a portion of the universe and study these smaller systems in order to handle network causation. I shall return to this connection between the large- and the small-scale in network studies below.

So my position is that, as with generalization, causality is seldom firmly established by a single study. Solid causal inferences can come from a program of research, with studies of different types and different data. There is nothing new here: this is familiar social science practice and there is no reason why network research should be different. It is fallacious to search for the One Study or the One True Method that will do it all for us. Rather, it is through a series of complementary studies that we begin to understand the direction of effects, and – even more fundamentally – what 'causal' can mean within a complex social system.

The issue then becomes a matter of careful theoretical thought and good research design, accompanied by good methods, not a matter of SNA alone. The real 'inference' we want is a scientific inference across a body of work, not a statistical inference pertaining to one study. Let me record here the wise words of prominent network statistician, Tom Snijders, who commented on these matters in 2011 on the Social Networks Discussion Forum list (socnet@lists.ufl.edu):

The assumption that all relevant variables are observed is always questionable, but statistical inference very often is done under such assumptions. We must strive after observational designs where this is, to the best of our knowledge, a reasonable approximation; and we can make progress on this front by what we always do as social scientists: try to find out better what drives these processes, come closer to determining the type of network ties and the individual variables that 'really' matter and how they affect one another. As the great statistician R.A. Fisher said when asked how to make observational studies more likely to yield causal answers (cited by Cox and Wermuth, 2004): 'Make your theories elaborate'. Instead of 'true' causality, we can obtain results about time ordering: are individuals similar first, and then become tied (~homophily) or are they tied first, and become similar later (~influence)? Such results, for richer and more and more relevant variables, can give important scientific advances about selection and influence, based on observational studies combining rich data collection, insightful theorizing, and good modelling.

Simulation

This book is about empirical social network research, not about the many excellent simulation studies that include social network elements. Of course, many modern SNA methods require simulation procedures to obtain results: for instance, estimation of both ERGMs and SAOMs uses simulations, as noted in Chapter 9. These are simulations that occur in the background and can be treated as implicit as far as the research outcomes are concerned. However, in the right circumstances empirical research can be enhanced by effective and explicit use of simulation methods to extend and understand outcomes. This is especially so within the broader scope of a research program.

Why bother to produce simulations if we already have observed data and have reached empirical conclusions? When we have a network-based complex social system, the implications of the conclusions are not always fully apparent. If we have several processes occurring simultaneously in our system, with feedback effects likely, it can be very difficult to surmise the likely overall system outcomes just from a list of the processes that we have inferred. A simulation may help us to understand how these processes operate together. If we have a case study, what we observe is only one instantiation of many possibilities. With one dataset we do not understand the full range of possibilities consistent with that data: simulations let us appreciate the range of plausible outcomes. If we wish to draw conclusions about what might happen with a change to the system (perhaps from some form of policy intervention), then we may be able to adjust a simulation to mimic such a change and study the simulated outcomes.

So, we can think of a simulation based on our empirical study as a 'thought experiment' that helps us understand the implications of our results, or make conjectures of what might be if the world were slightly different (e.g., if we could intervene in certain ways.)

First we need to think about what is to be simulated. Our research question, the design of our study and our empirical conclusions will guide us. If our interest is in network structure, we might simulate networks. If we are interested in processes on networks, we might simulate actor actions on the empirical network structure. In either case, we need a model from which to simulate. We might have estimated a network statistical model and use that to simulate networks, or an agent-based model for actor action on a network.

A good example is provided by Schaefer et al. (2013) where the researchers studied adolescent smoking and friendship networks by applying an SAOM to one of the Add Health schools (see Chapter 6). They noted, however, that to draw conclusions about intervention strategies required more. They then used a simulation-based approach to manipulate the strength of various effects to examine how potential interventions might play out.

The Schaefer et al. article shows how simulations can sharpen ideas about intervention in a single study. Let me briefly describe how simulation studies enhanced a more extensive research program in which I was involved. The research studied the spread of hepatitis C on a network of people who inject drugs, where the network tie was a measure of recent shared injecting, and the data collected used a snowball sample of street drug users (Aitken et al., 2008, 2009). We also developed a simulation model specific to the known process of hepatitis C transmission across a dyad, enabling us to simulate transmission across a network (Rolls et al., 2012). We then performed many simulations of disease transmission across the observed network to understand outcomes such as average time to first infection, comparing these to a complete network (equivalent to random mixing). By doing many simulations, we were able to establish confidence intervals around our estimated outcomes, and so begin to understand the effect of the network structure. In a separate analysis, we used the QAP (Chapter 9) to show that the empirical network structure was associated with actual disease status, so that these network effects could not be ignored (Sacks-Davis et al., 2012).

Having established this much as a first part of our research program, we then needed to take into account that the network data was collected as a snowball sample. We used conditional estimation of an ERGM, suitable for snowball samples (Chapter 9), to develop a statistical model for network structure (Rolls et al., 2013b). Of course, we had little definite evidence about the total number of street-based drug users in our area of data collection. So we developed a simulation approach to estimate the number of actors in this hidden population. Finally, using this estimated number, we simulated a sample of 100 networks from the ERGM, and on each of these graphs we performed 3000 disease simulations (Rolls et al., 2013a). This gave us a range of plausible outcomes about the disease transmission.

We also adjusted our simulations to mimic nine treatment strategies, such as treating infected people at random, treating high-degree users and so on. From our simulations the most effective treatment was a 'bring your friends' strategy, where an infected user and infected network partners were treated together. This is an interesting result in its own right. Often it is assumed, based on preferential attachment arguments, that treating high-degree nodes is the most effective strategy for disease reduction. With hepatitis C, however, treatment does not mean vaccination: there is a possibility of reinfection after treatment. High-degree nodes are the most likely to be reinfected, in which case the treatment is wasted. 'Insulating' infected users from reinfection by also treating partners seems the best method – at least according to the simulations – for preventing disease spread. Again, here we have an instance of the need to think through the actual mechanism of diffusion, rather than relying on 'off-the-shelf' results from other areas.

Of course, while the simulation results are intriguing, they are not sufficient. At the time of writing, a further clinical study is being planned to test a 'bring your friends' treatment strategy among people who inject drugs. We can see here how simulation and empirical work are strongly intertwined in this program such that both are enhanced – where the empirical results inform simulations which then feed back to inform the design of ongoing empirical studies.

Treatment strategies for disease prevention in this case constitute what can be called network interventions, where we take into account or even alter the structure of a network in order to influence outcomes, either for individuals or the system as a whole.

Network interventions

Tom Valente (2012: 49) described *network interventions* as 'purposeful efforts to use social networks or social network data to generate social influence, accelerate behavior change, improve performance, and/or achieve desirable outcomes among individuals, communities, organizations, or populations'.

Some network interventions are more straightforward than others. Valente described the most basic intervention as identifying individuals in the network to act as champions to promote (say) behavior change. Opinion leaders or network brokers can be identified using centrality measures and then recruited to encourage change. (How in turn you get opinion leaders to agree to become network change agents is an oft-neglected issue.) Another approach, *segmentation*, identifies groups of people, rather than individuals. *Induction* interventions aim to create dyadic diffusion across the network (e.g., word-of-mouth marketing campaigns). It is now possible to conduct very large-scale network experiments to test the efficacy of such interventions (e.g., Bond et al., 2012).

These types of intervention are about processes of change occurring over the network. The more interesting and challenging interventions are about changing the network structure to permit more efficient system performance. To some degree, this is the goal of all organizational restructuring, although a shift in formal organizational structures may not always lead to change in practice.

If we are going to change organizations, communities and governance systems, we need to have a much better understanding of what counts as an effective networked system. I have touched on these issues in earlier chapters. Sometimes, system effectiveness is fairly obvious: for instance, if the goal of a commercial entity is to sell more product, then you have a clear outcome measure. But all too often, the outcome is vague. In environmental governance systems, it is easy to use terms such as *resilience* or *sustainability* but it is not always obvious how to measure them precisely. In reality, of course, human social systems typically have multiple goals. In managing an urban waterway, how do you balance sustainability against development against amenity? In short, what counts as an effective network is serious research in its own right.

Even if we can define a good measure of effectiveness for our networked system or systems, it is not always evident how or why the network structure should relate to effectiveness. We can easily appreciate how a poorly structured system might not function well: for instance, in a network governance system, when organizations refused to collaborate at all; or in a military command system, when the troops refused to obey any orders from above. But the converse does not imply effectiveness: more and more collaboration does not mean that an environmental resource is well managed; and blind obedience is not enough to win battles.

These are difficult matters, at the cutting edge of social network science. How best do we change network structure to create better system outcomes? It is not enough to have data and clever methods here: what is required is careful theoretical thought leading into strong empirical research that can reinforce conclusions. Beware those who blithely claim to redesign social networks for guaranteed better results. Too little is known.

Yet, in the end, this has to be one of the bold promises of our network science. At the moment, we cannot really live up to it.

Computational social science: Big data and little data

Lazer et al. (2009: 721) heralded the arrival of *computational social science* and *Big Data*:

> We live life in the network. When we wake up in the morning, we check our e-mail, make a quick phone call, walk outside (our movements captured by a high definition video camera), get on the bus (swiping our RFID mass transit cards) or drive (using a transponder to zip through the tolls). We arrive at the airport, making sure to purchase a sandwich with a credit card before boarding the plane ... We post blog entries confiding to the world our thoughts and feelings, or maintain personal social network profiles revealing our friendships and our tastes. Each of these transactions leaves digital breadcrumbs which, when pulled together, offer increasingly comprehensive pictures of both individuals and groups, with the potential of transforming our understanding of our lives, organizations, and societies in a fashion that was barely conceivable just a few years ago.

> The capacity to collect and analyze massive amounts of data has unambiguously transformed such fields as biology and physics. The emergence of such a data-driven 'computational social science' has been much slower, largely spearheaded by a few intrepid computer scientists, physicists, and social scientists.

Computational social science, according to this account, seems to be 'computational' because it involves the empirical examination of 'Big Data' requiring plenty of computational grunt, a common viewpoint (e.g., Giles, 2012). But there are variations: Conte et al. (2012), while acknowledging big data, has rather more of an agent-based modelling perspective, so that 'computational' also carries the intent of simulation studies. In both cases, the emphasis is on digital data.

Big data is enjoying a wave of popularity. It is beguiling: to think that I can have masses of data at my fingertips, data that is available digitally and automatically, so I do not have to bother with traditional data collection. Instead of standard testing of hypotheses in small-scale studies, I can run sophisticated exploratory algorithms to mine the data and find associations among a myriad of variables. I can use one part of the data to build a model or a prediction algorithm and validate it on another part. Moreover, I can peruse digital networks that encompass the globe, the entire human social system. Isn't that the social system that in the end we really want to study?

Maybe. We can certainly do things with big data that were impossible previously. We can study the fine-grained detail of email exchanges in organizations, students' interactions with MOOC subjects, the emergence of new topics on Twitter. These may give us new insights into organizational communication, student performance, and the precursors of societal change.

But think back to my discussion of network effectiveness in the previous section: for instance, systems of network governance of environmental resources. To shed light on this issue, big data alone will not be enough. Big data or little data: what we need is good data. What counts as good data? It is data that is sharply directed to our research question, well collected, with high levels of reliability and validity.

Of course, to study a large-scale social system, some form of big data is inevitable. But the larger the scale of a social system the more likely that heterogeneities will be present: different cultures, different economic conditions, different historical backgrounds and so on. Unless variables pertaining to these heterogeneities are known beforehand and available as part of the data, data mining in effect has to average across these differences. To what extent can we treat that as an adequate account of the worldwide human social system? Recalling the Shalizi and Thomas (2011) argument about latent variables, with big data there are many more possibilities for latent variables to affect results in ways we do not understand.

I do not really see why computational social science has to be subsumed into big data or even agent-based models. Small data may also require computations to estimate complex statistical effects (e.g., ERGMs and SAOMs). The point of 'computational' to me is to emphasize a computational and quantitative imperative. When we are dealing with networked social systems, it may be necessary to quantify our analysis if we are to understand feedback effects and other complex system behaviors. We may need models with precise parameters that will permit simulation so we can understand these behaviors and conduct thought experiments about interventions.

I believe the real challenge for computational social science is to move from small to big: in other words, to cross levels of explanation to understand how small-scale systems aggregate to large-scale outcomes. It may be possible to do this without computation in selected cases, but for complex social systems some form of computation is likely to be invaluable. Moreover, it is in the small scale that we can investigate the detail of social processes that may be necessary to understand to be more confident about larger-scale inferences, just as the de la Haye work complements the Christakis and Fowler results. But at the same time, we need to take results from smaller studies into the large-scale, to see whether they hold up at the different scale or are washed away by other effects.

Effective intervention requires some understanding of causality. Researchers dealing with large systems are not always convinced that they need to understand micro-processes to intervene successfully. For instance, to estimate influenza transmission in a large city the parameters of mathematically based disease models do not need to incorporate individual micro-behaviors. Yet, to intervene successfully with disease, we have to understand the most basic micro-behavior here: that disease is contagious and transmitted dyadically. In short, the micro-level causality is crucial, large-scale mathematical models implicitly rely on that understanding, and successful interventions require that knowledge. Disease transmission seems so obvious (of course, it was not obvious until modern medicine!) that we sometimes forget that we do understand the micro process of disease transmission, and understand it very deeply. How much more difficult to intervene at the macro level when the causal argument implicates micro-social and cultural behaviors that are not well understood!

It is in the small scale that qualitative research can come into play, providing a rich understanding of human social action and its motivations. It is in the smaller scale that we can 'isolate a portion' of the Big (to adapt Wright's words) to study causality in detail – and it may only be at that scale that we can do it effectively. But from that basis, we can begin to understand how best to aggregate across the small scale to reach the large. To echo a theme from Chapter 1, the best of network research reaches down to the individual at the same time as it reaches up to the whole.

Big data has its critics (e.g., see Marcus and Davis, 2014). Having welcomed the advent of computational social science and big data, David Lazer also has some cautionary words, arguing against what he calls *big data hubris*. According to Lazer et al. (2014: 1205), it is not just about the size of the data:

> There is a tendency for big data research and more traditional applied statistics to live in two different realms – aware of each other's existence but generally not very trusting of each other. Big data offer enormous possibilities for understanding human interactions at a societal scale, with rich spatial and temporal dynamics, and for detecting complex interactions and nonlinearities among variables. We contend that these are the most exciting frontiers in studying human behavior. However, traditional 'small data' often offer information that is not contained (or containable) in big data, and the very factors that have enabled big data are enabling more traditional data collection. The Internet has opened the way for improving standard surveys, experiments, and health reporting... Instead of focusing on a 'big data revolution,' perhaps it is time we were focused on an 'all data revolution,' where we recognize that the critical change in the world has been innovative analytics, using data from all traditional and new sources, and providing a deeper, clearer understanding of our world.

I agree entirely with this quote – except to add that it is not big data alone that opens the most exciting frontier in human behavior, but rather the combination of the big and the little. Or rather than 'little data', perhaps we should be talking of 'thick data' (Wang, 2013). *Thick data* is an idea drawing on the famous notion of a *thick description* by anthropologist Clifford Geertz (1973), where the description of behavior incorporates its context and meaning. In that sense, thick data can bring us a richer understanding of causality and purpose. Through the microscope of the small we see the fine detail that can inform a proper interpretation of what we see through the macroscope of the large. But because of Lazer's 'two different realms', there are too few researchers devising research programs that can encompass both scales.

From this point, whither?

Thirty years ago, social network research was something of a cottage industry hidden away in a few social science departments in some universities around the world. Ten years ago, in contrast, social network research had come sufficiently to the fore for some commentators to think it an academic fad that would inevitably fade. But in a connected, globalized world, with the rise of social media, and with events in one part of the globe having rapid impact in another, it seems so natural to think 'network'. There is no sign of fading: just the opposite.

There have been remarkable advances, especially in terms of methodology and the availability of truly large-scale data. Computational methods have enabled our research to deal with complex networked social systems in persuasive ways. But we need to base our new science solidly, grounded not just in cunning analysis but in fine measurement and telling research that convinces, rather than just promises. We are not entirely there yet. I spoke above of a quantitative imperative, combined with a rich qualitative understanding. We have an empirical imperative as well. We need sound programs of empirical study that are strongly grounded in their own particular research contexts. We need to avoid simple preconceptions and metaphors and resist the temptation to have single explanations across the whole field. We need much more theoretical thought, within specific research contexts but also across network science more generally, and a much deeper commitment to investigating such theory in compelling empirical ways. We need, most particularly, strong research design and good network measurement. It is not enough to be seduced by analysis at the cost of limited observation.

Then, we will indeed have a social network science.

References

Ackland, R. (2013) *Web Social Science: Concepts, Data and Tools for Social Scientists in the Digital Age.* London: Sage.

adams, j., Faust, K. and Lovasi, G. (2012) Capturing context: Integrating spatial and social network analysis. *Social Networks*, 34, 1–5.

Aggarwal, C. (ed.) (2011) *Social Network Data Analytics.* New York: Springer.

Agneessens, F. and Everett, M. (2013) Introduction to the special issue on advances in two-mode networks. *Social Networks*, 35, 145–147.

Airoldi, E., Blei, D., Feinberg, S. and Xing, E. (2008) Mixed membership stochastic blockmodels. *Journal of Machine Learning Research*, 9, 1981–2014.

Aitken, C., Lewis, J., Tracy, S., et al. (2008) High incidence of hepatitis C virus reinfection in a cohort of injecting drug users. *Hepatology*, 48, 1746–1752.

Aitken, C., Lewis, J., Hocking, J., Bowden, D. and Hellard, M. (2009) Does information about IDUs' injecting networks predict exposure to the hepatitis C virus? *Hepatitis Monthly*, 9, 17–23.

Albert, R. and Barabási, A. L. (2002) Statistical mechanics of complex networks. *Reviews of Modern Physics*, 74, 47.

An, W. (2011) Models and methods to identify peer effects. In J. Scott and P. Carrington (eds), *The SAGE Handbook of Social Network Analysis* (pp. 514–532). London: Sage.

Aral, S. and Walker, D. (2011) Creating social contagion through viral product design: A randomized trial of peer influence in networks. *Management Science*, 57, 1623–1639.

Ball, B. and Newman, M. (2013) Friendship networks and social status. *Network Science*, 1, 16–30.

Barabási, A. (2012) The network takeover. *Nature Physics*, 8, 14–16.

Barabási, A.L. and Albert, R. (1999) Emergence of scaling in random networks. *Science*, 286, 509–512.

Barber, M. (2007) Modularity and community detection in bipartite networks. *Physical Review E*, 76, 066102.

Barnes, J. (1954) Class and committees in a Norwegian island parish. *Human Relations*, 7, 39–58.

Barrat, A., Cattuto, C., Colizza, V., et al. (2013) Empirical temporal networks of face-to-face human interactions. *European Physical Journal Special Topics*, 222, 1295–1309.

Bartlett, F. (1932) *Remembering: A Study in Experimental and Social Psychology*. Cambridge: Cambridge University Press.

Batagelj, V. (2009) Visualization of complex networks. In R.A. Meyers (ed.), *Encyclopedia of Complexity and Systems Science*. New York: Springer.

Batagelj, V. (2011) Large-scale network analysis. In J. Scott and P. Carrington (eds), *The SAGE Handbook of Social Network Analysis* (pp. 550–557). London: Sage.

Bearman, P. (1997) Generalized exchange. *American Journal of Sociology*, 102, 1383–1415.

Bellotti, E. (2008) What are friends for? Elective communities of single people. *Social Networks*, 30, 318–329.

Bellotti, E. (2015) *Qualitative networks: Mixed methods in sociological research*. New York: Routledge.

Bender-deMoll, S. and McFarland, D. (2006) The art and science of dynamic network visualization. *Journal of Social Structure*, 7, 2.

Berardo, R. and Scholz, J. (2010) Self-organizing policy networks: Risk, partner selection, and cooperation in estuaries. *American Journal of Political Science*, 54, 632–649.

Bernard, H. and Killworth, P. (1977) Informant accuracy in social network data, II. *Human Communication Research*, 4, 3–18.

Bernard, H., Killworth, P. and Sailer, L. (1980) Informant accuracy in social network data, IV. A comparison of clique-level structure in behavioral and cognitive network data. *Social Networks*, 2, 191–218.

Bernard, H., Killworth, P. and Sailer, L. (1982) Informant accuracy in social network data, V: An experimental attempt to predict actual communication from recall data. *Social Science Research*, 11, 30–66.

Bernard, H., Killworth, P., Kronenfeld, D. and Sailer, L. (1984) The problem of informant accuracy: The validity of retrospective data. *Annual Review of Anthropology*, 13, 495–517.

Bernard, H., Hallett, T., Iovita, A., et al. (2010) Counting hard-to-count populations: the network scale-up method for public health. *Sexually Transmitted Infections*, 86 (Suppl 2), ii11–ii15.

Bian, Y. (1997) Bringing strong ties back in: Indirect ties, network bridges, and job searches in China. *American Sociological Review*, 62, 366–385.

Bian, Y. and Huang, X. (2009) Network resources and job mobility in China's transitional economy. *Research in the Sociology of Work*, 19, 255–282.

Bidart, C. and Cacciuttolo, P. (2013) Combining qualitative, quantitative and structural dimensions in a longitudinal perspective: The case of network influence. *Quality & Quantity*, 47, 2495–2515.

Bidart, C. and Charbonneau, J. (2011) How to generate personal networks: Issues and tools for a sociological perspective. *Field Methods*, 23, 266–286.

Blair, J., Czaja, R. and Blair, E. (2014) *Designing Surveys: A Guide to Decisions and Procedures*. Los Angeles: Sage.

Bodin, Ö. and Prell, C. (2011) *Social Networks and Natural Resource Management: Uncovering the Social Fabric of Environmental Governance*. Cambridge: Cambridge University Press.

Bodin, Ö. and Tengö, M. (2012) Disentangling intangible social–ecological systems. *Global Environmental Change*, 22, 430–439.

Bolton, K., McCaw, J., Forbes, K., et al. (2012) Influence of contact definition in assessment of the relative importance of social settings in disease transmission risk. *PLoS One*, 7, e30893.

Bond, R., Fariss, C., Jones, J., Kramer, A., Marlow, C., Settle, J. and Fowler, J. (2012) A 61-million-person experiment in social influence and political mobilization. *Nature*, 489, 295–298.

Boorman, S. and White, H. (1976) Social structure from multiple networks. II. Role structures. *American Journal of Sociology*, 81, 1384–1446.

Borgatti, S. (1997) Structural holes: Unpacking Burt's redundancy measures. *Connections*, 20, 35–38.

Borgatti, S. and Everett, M. (1997) Network analysis of 2-mode data. *Social Networks*, 19, 243–269.

Borgatti, S. and Everett, M. (2000) Models of core/periphery structures. *Social Networks*, 21, 375–395.

Borgatti, S. and Foster, P. (2003) The network paradigm in organizational research: A review and typology. *Journal of Management*, 29, 991–1013.

Borgatti, S. and Halgin, D. (2011) Analyzing affection networks. In J. Scott and P. Carrington (eds), *The SAGE Handbook of Social Network Analysis* (pp. 417-433). London: Sage.

Borgatti, S. and Lopez-Kidwell, V. (2011) Network theory. In J. Scott and P. Carrington (eds), *The SAGE Handbook of Social Network Analysis* (pp. 40–54). London: Sage.

Borgatti, S. and Molina, J. (2005) Toward ethical guidelines for network research in organizations. *Social Networks*, 27, 107–117.

Borgatti, S., Jones, C. and Everett, M. (1998) Network measures of social capital. *Connections*, 21, 27–36.

Borgatti, S., Everett, M. and Johnson, J. (2013) *Analyzing Social Networks*. Los Angeles: Sage.

Boyd, J. (1969) The algebra of group kinship. *Journal of Mathematical Psychology*, 6, 139–167.

Boyland, N., James, R., Mlynski, D., Madden, J. R. and Croft, D. (2013) Spatial proximity loggers for recording animal social networks: Consequences of inter-logger variation in performance. *Behavioral Ecology and Sociobiology*, 67, 1877–1890.

Brandes, U., Lerner, J. and Snijders, T. (2009) Networks evolving step by step: Statistical analysis of dyadic event data. In *Proceedings, 2009 International Conference on Advances in Social Network Analysis and Mining* (pp. 200–205). Los Alamitos, CA: IEEE Computer Society.

Brandes, U., Freeman, L. and Wagner, D. (2013a) Social networks. In R. Tamassia (ed.), *Handbook of Graph Drawing and Visualization* (pp. 805–839). Boca Raton, FL: Chapman & Hall/CRC.

Brandes, U., Robins, G., McCranie, A. and Wasserman, S. (2013b) What is network science? *Network Science*, 1, 1–15.

Brass, D., Galaskiewicz, J., Greve, H. and Tsai, W. (2004) Taking stock of networks and organizations: A multilevel perspective. *Academy of Management Journal*, 47, 795–817.

Breiger, R. (1974) The duality of persons and groups. *Social Forces*, 53, 181–190.

Breiger, R. (2005) Introduction to special issue: Ethical dilemmas in social networks research. *Social Networks*, 27, 89–93.

Breiger, R., Boorman, S. and Arabie, P. (1975) An algorithm for clustering relational data with applications to social network analysis and comparison with multidimensional scaling. *Journal of Mathematical Psychology*, 12, 328–383.

Brooks, B., Hogan, B., Ellison, N., Lampe, C. and Vitak, J. (2014) Assessing structural correlates to social capital in Facebook ego networks. *Social Networks*, 38, 1–15.

Burt, R. (1984) Network items and the General Social Survey. *Social Networks*, 6, 293–339.

Burt, R. (1987) Social contagion and innovation: Cohesion and structural equivalence. *American Journal of Sociology*, 92, 1287–1335.

Burt, R. (1992) *Structural Holes: The Social Structure of Competition*. Cambridge, MA: Harvard University Press.

Burt, R. (2004) Structural holes and good ideas. *American Journal of Sociology*, 110, 349–399.

Burt, R. (2005) *Brokerage and Closure: An Introduction to Social Capital*. Oxford: Oxford University Press.

Burt, R. and Merluzzi, J. (2014) Embedded brokerage: Hubs versus locals. *Research in the Sociology of Organizations*, 40, 161–177.

Burt, R., Kilduff, M. and Tasselli, S. (2013) Social network analysis: Foundations and frontiers on advantage. *Annual Review of Psychology*, 64, 527–547.

Butts, C. (2008a) A relational event framework for social action. *Sociological Methodology*, 38, 155–200.

Butts, C. (2008b) Social network analysis with sna. *Journal of Statistical Software*, 24, 6.

Butts, C.T. (2008c) Social network analysis: A methodological introduction. *Asian Journal of Social Psychology*, 11, 13–41.

Butts, C., Acton, R. and Marcum, C. (2012) Interorganizational collaboration in the Hurricane Katrina response. *Journal of Social Structure*, 13, 1.

Byrne, D. (1971) *The Attraction Paradigm*. New York: Academic Press.

Cannella, A. and McFadyen, M. (in press) Changing the exchange: The dynamics of knowledge worker ego networks. *Journal of Management*. doi: 10.1177/0149206313511114

Carley, K. (2003) Dynamic network analysis. In R. Breiger, K. Carley and P. Pattison (eds), *Dynamic Social Network Modeling and Analysis: Workshop Summary and Papers* (pp. 133–145). Washington, DC: National Academies Press.

Carlsson, L. and Sandstrom, A. (2008) Network governance of the commons. *International Journal of the Commons*, 2, 33–54.

Carrington, P. (2011) Crime and social network analysis. In J. Scott and P. Carrington (eds), *The SAGE Handbook of Social Network Analysis* (pp. 236–255). London: Sage.

Carrington, P., Scott, J. and Wasserman, S. (eds) (2005) *Models and Methods in Social Network Analysis*. Cambridge: Cambridge University Press.

Cartwright, D. and Harary, F. (1956) Structural balance: A generalization of Heider's theory. *Psychological Review*, 63, 277–293.

Centola, D. and Macy, M. (2007) Complex contagions and the weakness of long ties. *American Journal of Sociology*, 113, 702–734.

Christakis, N. and Fowler, J. (2007) The spread of obesity in a large social network over 32 years. *New England Journal of Medicine*, 357, 370–379.

Christakis, N. and Fowler, J.H. (2013) Social contagion theory: Examining dynamic social networks and human behavior. *Statistics in Medicine*, 32, 556–577.

Cohen, J. (1988) *Statistical Power Analysis for the Behavioral Sciences*. Hillsdale, NJ: Lawrence Erlbaum Associates.

Cohen-Cole, E. and Fletcher, J. (2009) Detecting implausible social network effects in acne, height, and headaches: Longitudinal analysis. *British Medical Journal*, 338, 28–31.

Coleman, J. (1988) Social capital in the creation of human capital. *American Journal of Sociology*, 94, S95–S120.

Conte, R., Gilbert, N., Bonelli, G., et al. (2012) Manifesto of computational social science. *European Physical Journal Special Topics*, 214, 325–346.

Cook, K. and Emerson, R. (1978) Power, equity and commitment in exchange networks. *American Sociological Review*, 43, 721–739.

Cook, K., Cheshire, C., Rice, E. and Nakagawa, S. (2013) Social exchange theory. In J. DeLamater and A. Ward (eds), *Handbook of Social Psychology*, 2nd edn (pp. 61–88). Dordrecht: Springer.

Cox, D. and Wermuth, N. (2004) Causality: A statistical view. *International Statistical Review*, 72, 285–305.

Croft, D., Madden, J., Franks, D. and James, R. (2011) Hypothesis testing in animal social networks. *Trends in Ecology and Evolution*, 26, 502–507.

Daraganova, G. and Robins, G. (2013) Autologistic actor attribute models. In D. Lusher, J. Koskinen and G. Robins (eds), *Exponential Random Graph Models for Social Networks: Theory, Methods and Applications* (pp.102–114). Cambridge: Cambridge University Press.

Daraganova, G., Pattison, P., Koskinen, J., Mitchell, B., Bill, A., Watts, M. and Baum, S. (2012) Networks and geography: Modelling community network structures as the outcome of both spatial and network processes. *Social Networks*, 34, 6–17.

Davis, J. (1970) Clustering and hierarchy in interpersonal relations: Testing two graph theoretical models on 742 sociomatrices. *American Sociological Review*, 35, 843–851.

Dekker, D., Krackhardt, D. and Snijders, T. (2007) Sensitivity of MRQAP tests to collinearity and autocorrelation conditions. *Psychometrika*, 72, 563–581.

de la Haye, K. Robins, G., Mohr, P. and Wilson, C. (2010) Obesity-related behaviors in adolescent friendship networks. *Social Networks*, 32, 161–167.

de la Haye, K., Robins, G., Mohr, P. and Wilson, C. (2011) How physical activity shapes, and is shaped by, adolescent friendships. *Social Science and Medicine*, 73, 719–728.

de la Haye, K., Robins, G., Mohr, P. and Wilson, C. (2013) Adolescents' intake of junk food: Processes and mechanisms driving consumption similarities among friends. *Journal of Research on Adolescence*, 23, 524–536.

deLeon, P. and Varda, D. (2009) Toward a theory of collaborative policy networks: Identifying structural tendencies. *Policy Studies Journal*, 37, 59–74.

de Nooy, W. (2010) Networks for action and events over time. A multilevel discrete-time event history of longitudinal network data. *Social Networks*, 33, 31–40.

de Nooy, W., Mrvar, A. and Batagelj, V. (2011) *Exploratory Social Network Analysis with Pajek*. Cambridge: Cambridge University Press.

Denzin, N. and Lincoln, Y. (eds) (2011) *The SAGE Handbook of Qualitative Research*. Thousand Oaks, CA: Sage.

Diani, M. (2011) Social movements and collective action. In J. Scott and P. Carrington (eds), *The SAGE Handbook of Social Network Analysis* (pp. 223–235). London: Sage.

Dombrowski, K., Khan, B., Moses, J., Channell, E. and Misshula, E. (2013) Assessing respondent driven sampling for network studies in ethnographic contexts. *Advances in Anthropology*, 3, 1–9.

Dominguez, S., and Hollstein, B. (eds) (2014) *Mixed Methods Social Networks Research: Design and Applications*. New York: Cambridge University Press.

Doreian, P. and Krackhardt, D. (2001) Pre-transitive balance mechanisms for signed networks. *Journal of Mathematical Sociology*, 25, 43–67.

Doreian, P., Batagelj, V., and Ferligoj, A.(2005) *Generalized Blockmodeling*. New York: Cambridge University Press.

Doreian, P., Batagelj, V., Ferligoj, A., and Kejzar, N. (2014) *Understanding Large Temporal Networks and Spatial Networks: Exploration, Pattern searching, Visualization and Network Evolution*. Chichester, UK: Wiley.

DuBois, C., Butts, C., McFarland, D. and Smyth, P. (2013) Hierarchical models for relational event sequences. *Journal of Mathematical Psychology*, 57, 297–309.

Eagle, N., Pentland, A. and Lazer, D. (2009) Inferring friendship network structure by using mobile phone data. *Proceedings of the National Academy of Sciences*, 106, 15274–15278.

English, T. and Carstensen, L. (2014) Selective narrowing of social networks across adulthood is associated with improved emotional experience in daily life. *International Journal of Behavioral Development*, 38, 195–202.

Erdős, P. and Rényi, A. (1959) On random graphs. I. *Publicationes Mathematicae (Debrecen)*, 6, 290–297.

Everett, M. and Borgatti, S. (1992) Regular blockmodels of multiway, multimode matrices. *Social Networks*, 14, 91–120.

Everett, M. and Borgatti, S. (2013) The dual-projection approach for two-mode networks. *Social Networks*, 35, 204–210.

Everton, S. (2012) *Disrupting Dark Networks*. New York: Cambridge University Press.

Faris, R. and Ennett, S. (2012) Adolescent aggression: The role of peer group status motives, peer aggression, and group characteristics. *Social Networks*, 34, 371–378.

Faust, K. (2011) Animal social networks. In J. Scott and P. Carrington (eds), *The SAGE Handbook of Social Network Analysis* (pp. 148–166). London: Sage.

Faust, K., Entwisle, B., Rindfuss, R., Walsh, S. and Sawangdee, Y. (1999) Spatial arrangement of social and economic networks among villagers in Nang Rong district, Thailand. *Social Networks*, 21, 311–337.

Ferligoj, A. and Hlebec, V. (1999) Evaluation of social network measurement instruments. *Social Networks*, 21, 111–130.

Ferligoj, A., Doreian, P., & Batagelj, V (2011). Positions and roles. In J. Scott and P. Carrington (eds), *The SAGE Handbook of Social Network Analysis* (pp. 434–446). London: Sage.

Festinger, L. (1949) The analysis of sociograms using matrix algebra. *Human Relations*, 2, 153–158.

Fischer, C. (1982) *To Dwell among Friends*. Chicago: University of Chicago Press.

Fiske, A. (1991) *Structures of Social Life: The Four Elemental Forms of Social Relationship*. New York: Free Press.

Fiske, A. (1992) The four elementary forms of sociality: Framework for a unified theory of social relations. *Psychological Review*, 99, 689–723.

Flynn, F., Reagans, R., Amanatullah, E. and Ames, D. (2006) Helping one's way to the top: Self-monitors achieve status by helping others and knowing who helps whom. *Journal of Personality and Social Psychology*, 91, 1123–1137.

Fowler, J., Heaney, M., Nickerson, D., Padgett, J. and Sinclair, B. (2011) Causality in political networks. *American Politics Research*, 39, 437–480.

Frank, O. (2011) Survey sampling in networks. In J. Scott and P. Carrington (eds), *The SAGE Handbook of Social Network Analysis* (pp. 389–403). London: Sage.

Frank, O. and Nowicki, K. (1993) Exploratory statistical analysis of networks. *Annals of Discrete Mathematics*, 55, 349–365.

Frank, O. and Snijders, T. (1994) Estimating the size of hidden populations using snowball sampling. *Journal of Official Statistics*, 10, 53–67.

Freeman, L. (1979) Centrality in social networks: Conceptual clarification. *Social Networks*, 1, 215–239.

Freeman, L. (2009) Methods of social network visualization. In R.A. Myers (ed.), *Encyclopedia of Complexity and Systems Science*. Berlin: Springer.

Freeman, L. and Romney, A. (1987) Words, deeds and social structure: A preliminary study of the reliability of informants. *Human Organization*, 46, 330–334.

Freeman, L., Romney, A. and Freeman, S. (1987) Cognitive structure and informant accuracy. *American Anthropologist*, 89, 310–325.

Friedkin, N. (1998) *A Structural Theory of Social Influence*. Cambridge: Cambridge University Press.

Friedkin, N. and Johnsen, E. (2011) *Social Influence Network Theory: A Sociological Examination of Group Dynamics*. Cambridge: Cambridge University Press.

Fu, Y. (2007) Contact diaries: Building archives of actual and comprehensive personal networks. *Field Methods*, 19, 194–217.

Gaudeul, A. and Giannetti, C. (2013) The role of reciprocation in social network formation, with an application to LiveJournal. *Social Networks*, 35, 317–330.

Geertz, C. (1973) *The Interpretation of Cultures: Selected Essays*. New York: Basic Books.

Gibson, D. (2005) Taking turns and talking ties: Networks and conversational interaction. *American Journal of Sociology*, 110, 1561–1597.

Gile, K. (2011) Improved inference for respondent-driven sampling data with application to HIV prevalence estimation. *Journal of the American Statistical Association*, 106, 135–146.

Gile, K. and Handcock, M. (2010) Respondent-driven sampling: An assessment of current methodology. *Sociological Methodology*, 40, 285–327.

Giles, J. (2012) Making the links. *Nature*, 488, 448–450.

Girvan, M. and Newman, M. (2002) Community structure in social and biological networks. *Proceedings of the National Academy of Sciences*, 99, 7821–7826.

Gondal, N. and McLean, P. (2013) What makes a network go round? Exploring the structure of a strong component with exponential random graph models. *Social Networks*, 35, 499–513.

González-Bailón, S., Wang, N., Rivero, A., Borge-Holthoefer, J. and Moreno, Y. (2014) Assessing the bias in samples of large online networks. *Social Networks*, 38, 16–27.

Goolsby, R. (2005) Ethics and defense agency funding: Some considerations. *Social Networks*, 27, 95–106.

Gould, R. and Fernandez, R. (1989) Structures of mediation: A formal approach to brokerage in transaction networks. *Sociological Methodology*, 19, 89–126.

Goyal, S. (2011) Social networks in economics. In J. Scott and P. Carrington (eds), *The SAGE Handbook of Social Network Analysis* (pp. 67–79). London: Sage.

Granovetter, M. (1973) The strength of weak ties. *American Journal of Sociology*, 78, 1360–1380.

Granovetter, M. (1985) Economic action and social structure: The problem of embeddedness. *American Journal of Sociology*, 91, 481–510.

Green, H., Tucker, J, Golinelli, D. and Wenzel, S. (2013) Social networks, time homeless, and social support: A study of men on Skid Row. *Network Science*, 1, 305–320.

Gruzd, A. and Haythornthwaite, C. (2011). Networking online: Cybercommunities. In J. Scott and P. Carrington (eds), *The SAGE Handbook of Social Network Analysis* (pp. 167–179). London: Sage.

Handcock, M. and Gile, K. (2010) Modeling social networks from sampled data. *Annals of Applied Statistics*, 4, 5–25.

Handcock, M. and Gile, K. (2011) Comment: On the concept of snowball sampling. *Sociological Methodology*, 41, 367–371.

Handcock, M., Hunter, D., Butts, C., Goodreau, S. and Morris, M. (2008) statnet: Software tools for the representation, visualization, analysis and simulation of network data. *Journal of Statistical Software*, 24, 1–11.

Hansen, D., Schneiderman, B. and Smith, M. (2010) *Analyzing Social Media Networks with NodeXL: Insights from a Connected World*. Burlington, MA: Morgan Kaufmann.

Harrigan, N., Achananuparp, P. and Lim E. (2012) Influentials, novelty, and social contagion: The viral power of average friends, close communities, and old news. *Social Networks*, 34, 470–480.

Hasan, M. and Zaki, M. (2011) A survey of link prediction in social networks. In C. Aggarwal (ed.), *Social Network Data Analytics* (pp. 243–276). New York: Springer.

Haythornthwaite, C. and Andrews, R. (2011) *E-learning Theory and Practice*. Los Angeles: Sage.

Haythornthwaite, C., de Laat, M. and Dawson, S. (2013) Introduction to the special issue on learning analytics. *American Behavioral Scientist*, 57, 1371–1379.

Heaney, M. and McClurg, S. (2009) Social networks and American politics: Introduction to the special issue. *American Politics Research*, 37, 727–741.

Heckathorn, D. (1997) Respondent-driven sampling: A new approach to the study of hidden populations. *Social Problems*, 44, 174–199.

Heckathorn, D. (2011) Comment: Snowball versus respondent-driven sampling. *Sociological Methodology*, 41, 355–366.

Henning, M., Brandes, U., Pfeffer, J. and Mergel, I. (2012) *Studying Social Networks: A Guide to Empirical Research*. Frankfurt am Main: Campus Verlag.

Hite, J. (2003) Patterns of multidimensionality among embedded network ties: A typology of relational embeddedness in emerging entrepreneurial firms. *Strategic Organization*, 1, 9–49.

Hlebec, V. and Ferligoj, A. (2001) Respondent mood and the instability of survey network measurements. *Social Networks*, 23, 125–140.

Hobson, J. (1894) *The Evolution of Modern Capitalism: A Study of Machine Production*. London: Walter Scott.

Hodas, N. and Lerman, K. (2014) The simple rules of social contagion. *Scientific Reports*, 4, 4343.

Hogan, B., Carrasco, J. and Wellman, B. (2007) Visualizing personal networks: Working with participant-aided sociograms. *Field Methods*, 19, 116–144.

Holland, P. and Leinhardt, S. (1970) A method for detecting structure in sociometric data. *American Journal of Sociology*, 76, 492–513.

Holland, P. and Leinhardt, S. (1976) Local structure in social networks. *Sociological Methodology*, 7, 1–45.

Holland, P. and Leinhardt, S. (1981) An exponential family of probability distributions for directed graphs (with discussion). *Journal of the American Statistical Association*, 76, 33–65.

Holland, P., Laskey, K. and Leinhardt, S. (1981) Stochastic blockmodels: First steps. *Social Networks*, 5, 109–137.

Hollstein, B. (2011) Qualitative approaches. In J. Scott and P. Carrington (eds), *The SAGE Handbook of Social Network Analysis* (pp. 404–416). London: Sage.

Hoser, B. and Nitschke, T. (2010) Questions on ethics for research in the virtually connected world. *Social Networks*, 32, 180–186.

Huisman, M. (2009) Imputation of missing network data: Some simple procedures. *Journal of Social Structure*, 10, 1.

Huisman, M. and van Duijn, M. (2011) A reader's guide to SNA software. In J. Scott and P. Carrington (eds), *The SAGE Handbook of Social Network Analysis* (pp. 578–600). London: Sage.

Huitsing, G., van Duijn, M., Snijders, T., Wang, P., Sainio, M., Salmivalli, C. and Veenstra, R. (2012a) Univariate and multivariate models of positive and negative networks: Liking, disliking, and bully–victim relationships. *Social Networks*, 34, 645–657.

Huitsing, G., Veenstra, R., Sainio, M. and Salmivalli, C. (2012b) 'It must be me' or 'It could be them?': The impact of the social network position of bullies and victims on victims' adjustment. *Social Networks*, 34, 379–386.

Ibarra, H. (1992) Structural alignments, individual strategies, and managerial action: Elements towards a network theory of getting things done. In N. Nohria and R. Eccles (eds), *Networks and Organizations: Structure, Form and Action* (pp. 165–188). Boston: Harvard Business School Press.

Illenberger, J. and Flotterod, G. (2012) Estimating network properties from snowball sampled data. *Social Networks*, 34, 701–711.

Israel, M. and Hay, I. (2006) *Research Ethics for Social Scientists*. Thousand Oaks, CA: Sage.

Jackson, M. (2010) *Social and Economic Networks*. Princeton, NJ: Princeton University Press.

Jackson, M. (2011) An overview of social networks and economic applications. In J. Benhabib, A. Bisin and M. Jackson (eds), *Handbook of Social Economics*, Volume 1A (pp. 511–585). Amsterdam: Elsevier.

Johnson, J., Boster, J. and Palinkas, L. (2003) Social roles and the evolution of networks in isolated and extreme environments. *Journal of Mathematical Sociology*, 27, 89–121.

Johnston, R., and Pattie, C. (2011). Social networks, geography and neighbourhood effects. In J. Scott and P. Carrington (eds), *The SAGE Handbook of Social Network Analysis* (pp. 301–310). London: Sage.

Jones, C., Hesterly, W. and Borgatti, S. (1997) A general theory of network governance: Exchange conditions and social mechanisms. *Academy of Management Review*, 22, 911–945.

Jones, J. and Handcock, M. (2003) An assessment of preferential attachment as a mechanism for human sexual network formation. *Proceedings of the Royal Society B*, 270, 1123–1128.

Kadushin, C. (2005) Who benefits from network analysis: Ethics of social network research. *Social Networks, 27*, 139–153.

Kadushin, C. (2012) *Understanding Social Networks: Theories, Concepts and Findings*. New York: Oxford University Press.

Kalish, Y. (2008) Bridging in social networks: Who are the people in structural holes and why are they there? *Asian Journal of Social Psychology*, 11, 53–66.

Kalish, Y. and Robins, G. (2006) Psychological predispositions and network structure: The relationship between individual predispositions, structural holes and network closure. *Social Networks*, 28, 56–84.

Kapferer, B. (1972) *Strategy and Transaction in an African Factory: African Workers and Indian Management in a Zambian Town*. Manchester: Manchester University Press.

Kashima, Y. (2000) Recovering Bartlett's social psychology of cultural dynamics. *European Journal of Social Psychology*, 30, 383–403.

Kashima, Y., Wilson, S., Lusher, D., Pearson, L. and Pearson, C. (2013) The acquisition of perceived descriptive norms as social category learning in social networks. *Social Networks*, 35, 711–719.

Katz, L. and Powell, J. (1957) Probability distributions of random variables associated with a structure of the sample space of sociometric investigations. *Annals of Mathematical Statistics*, 28, 442–448.

Kenis, P. and Provan, K. (2009) Towards an exogenous theory of public network performance. *Public Administration*, 87, 440–456.

Killworth, P. and Bernard, H. (1976) Informant accuracy in social network data. *Human Organization*, 35, 269–286.

Killworth, P. and Bernard, H. (1979/80) Informant accuracy in social network data, III: A comparison of triadic structures in behavioral and cognitive data. *Social Networks*, 2, 19–46.

Klovdahl, A. (1985) Social networks and the spread of infectious diseases: The AIDS example. *Social Science and Medicine*, 21, 1203–1216.

Klovdahl, A. (2005) Social network research and human subjects protection: Towards more effective infectious disease control. *Social Networks*, 27, 119–137.

Klovdahl, A., Potterat, J., Woodhouse, D., Muth, J., Muth, S. and Darrow, W. (1994) Social networks and infectious disease: The Colorado Springs study. *Social Science and Medicine*, 38, 79–88.

Knoke, D. (2011). Policy networks. In J. Scott and P. Carrington (eds), *The SAGE Handbook of Social Network Analysis* (pp. 210–222). London: Sage.

Knoke, D. (2012) *Economic Networks*. Cambridge: Polity Press.

Knoke, D. (2013) 'It takes a network': The rise and fall of social network analysis in U.S. Army counterinsurgency doctrine. *Connections*, 33, 1–10.

Kogovšek, T. and Ferligoj, A. (2005) Effects of reliability and validity of egocentered network measurements. *Social Networks*, 27, 205–229.

Kogovšek, T., Ferligoj, A., Coenders, G. and Saris, W. (2002) Estimating the reliability and validity of personal support measures: Full information ML estimation with planned incomplete data. *Social Networks*, 24, 1–20.

Kogut, B. (ed.) (2012) *The Small Worlds of Corporate Governance*. Cambridge, MA: MIT Press.

Kolaczyk, E. (2009) *Statistical Analysis of Network Data: Methods and Models*. New York: Springer.

Kontoleon, N., Falzon, L. and Pattison, P. (2013) Algebraic structures for dynamic networks. *Journal of Mathematical Psychology*, 57, 310–319.

Koschade, S. (2005) A social network analysis of Aum Shinrikyo: Understanding terrorism in Australia. Paper presented at the Social Change in the 21st Century Conference, Queensland University of Technology.

Koskinen, J., Robins, G., Wang, P. and Pattison, P. (2013) Bayesian analysis for partially observed network data, missing ties, attributes and actors. *Social Networks*, 35, 514–527.

Kossinets, G. (2006) Effects of missing data in social networks. *Social Networks*, 28, 247–268.

Krackhardt, D. (1987a) QAP partialling as a test of spuriousness. *Social Networks*, 9, 171–186.

Krackhardt, D. (1987b) Cognitive social structures. *Social Networks*, 9, 109–134.

Krackhardt, D. (1988) Predicting with networks: Nonparametric regression analysis of dyadic data. *Social Networks*, 10, 359–381.

Krackhardt, D. (1992) The strength of strong ties: The importance of philos in organizations. In N. Nohria and R. Eccles (eds), *Networks and Organizations: Structure, Form and Action* (pp. 216–239). Boston: Harvard Business School Press.

Krebs, V. (2002) Mapping networks of terrorist cells. *Connections*, 24, 43–52.

Krempel, L. (2011). Network visualization. In J. Scott and P. Carrington (eds), *The SAGE Handbook of Social Network Analysis* (pp. 558–577). London: Sage.

Krinsky, J. and Crossley, N. (2014) Social movements and social networks: Introduction. *Social Movement Studies*, 13, 1–21.

Kumar, S., Morstatter, F. and Liu, H. (2014) *Twitter Data Analytics*. New York: Springer.

Labianca, G. and Brass, D. (2006) Exploring the social ledger: Negative relationships and negative asymmetry in social networks in organizations. *Academy of Management Review*, 31, 596–614.

Latapy, M., Magnien, C. and Del Vecchio, N. (2008) Basic notions for the analysis of large two-mode networks. *Social Networks*, 30, 31–48.

Latora, V., Nicosia, V. and Panzarasa, P. (2013) Social cohesion, structural holes, and a tale of two measures. *Journal of Statistical Physics*, 151, 745–764.

Laumann, E. (1966) *Prestige and Association in an Urban Community*. Indianapolis: Bobbs-Merrill.

Laumann, E., Marsden, P. and Prensky, D. (1983) *The boundary specification problem in network analysis*. In R. Burt and M. Minor (eds), *Applied Network Analysis* (pp. 18–34). Beverly Hills, CA: Sage.

Lazega, E., Jourda, M., Mounier, L. and Stofer, R. (2008) Catching up with big fish in the big pond? Multi-level network analysis through linked design.*Social Networks*, 30, 159–176.

Lazer, D., Pentland, A., Adamic, L., et al. (2009) Life in the network; The coming age of computational social science. *Science*, 323, 721–723.

Lazer, D., Kennedy, R., King, G. and Vespignani, A. (2014) The parable of Google Flu: Traps in big data analysis. *Science*, 343, 1203–1205.

Leavitt, H.J. (1951) Some effects of certain communication patterns on group performance. *Journal of Abnormal and Social Psychology*, 46, 38–50.

Lerner, J., Bussmann, M., Snijders, T. and Brandes, U. (2013a) Modeling frequency and type of interaction in event networks. *Corvinus Journal of Sociology and Social Policy*, 4, 3–32.

Lerner, J., Indlekofer, N., Nick, B. and Brandes, U. (2013b) Conditional independence in dynamic networks. *Journal of Mathematical Psychology*, 57, 275–283.

Lewis, J. (2005) *Health Policy and Politics: Networks, Ideas and Power*. Melbourne: IP Communications.

Lewis, J. (2011) The future of network governance research: Strength in diversity and synthesis. *Public Administration*, 89, 1221–1234.

Lewis, K., Kaufman, J., Gonzalez, M., Wimmer, A., and Christakis, N. (2008) Tastes, ties, and time: A new social network dataset using Facebook.com. *Social Networks*, 30, 330–342.

Light, J., Greenan, C., Rusby, J., Nies, K. and Snijders, T. (2013) Onset to first alcohol use in early adolescence: A network diffusion model. *Journal of Research on Adolescence*, 23, 487–499.

Liljeros, F., Edling, C., Amaral, L., Stanley, H., and Åberg, Y. (2001) The web of human sexual contacts. *Nature*, 411, 907–908.

Lin, N. (1999) Building a network theory of social capital. *Connections*, 22, 28–51.

Lin, N. and Dumin, M. (1986) Access to occupations through social ties. *Social Networks*, 8, 365–385.

Little, R. and Rubin, D. (1987) *Statistical Analysis with Missing Data*. New York: Wiley.

Lomi, A. and Pattison, P. (2006) Manufacturing relations: An empirical study of the organization of production across multiple networks. *Organization Science*, 17, 313–332.

Lomi, A., Lusher, D., Pattison, P. and Robins, G. (2014a) The focused organization of advice relations: A study in boundary-crossing. *Organization Science*, 25, 438–457.

Lomi, A., Mascia, D., Vu, D., Pallotti, F., Conaldi, G. and Iwashyna, T. (2014b) Quality of care and interhospital collaboration: A study of patient transfers in Italy. *Medical Care*, 52, 407–414.

Lorrain, F. and White, H.C. (1971) Structural equivalence of individuals in social networks. *Journal of Mathematical Sociology*, 1, 49–80.

Lubbers, M. and Snijders, T. (2007) A comparison of various approaches to the exponential random graph model: A reanalysis of 102 student networks in school classes. *Social Networks*, 29, 489–507.

Lubell, M. (2013) Governing institutional complexity: The ecology of games framework. *Policy Studies Journal*, 41, 537–559.

Lubell, M., Scholz, J., Berardo, R. and Robins, G. (2012) Testing policy theory with statistical models of networks. *Policy Studies Journal*, 40, 351–374.

Luce, D. and Perry, A. (1949) A method of matrix analysis of group structure. *Psychometrika, 14*, 95–116.

Luce, D., Krantz, D., Suppes, P. and Tverksy, A. (1990) *Foundations of Measurement, Volume III: Representation, Axiomatization and Invariance*. San Diego, CA: Academic Press.

Lusher, D. and Ackland, R. (2011) A relational hyperlink analysis of an online social movement. *Journal of Social Structure*, 12, 5.

Lusher, D., Lomi, A., Robins, G. and Pattison, P. (2012) 'Trust me': Differences in expressed and perceived trust in an organization. *Social Networks*, 34, 410–424.

Lusher, D., Koskinen, J. and Robins, G. (2013) *Exponential Random Graph Models for Social Networks: Theory, Methods and Applications*. Cambridge: Cambridge University Press.

Lyons, R. (2011) The spread of evidence-poor medicine via flawed social-network analysis. *Statistics, Politics, and Policy*, 2, Article 2.

Mabry, P., Milstein, B., Abraido-Lanza, A., Livingood, W. and Allegrante, J. (2013) Opening a window on systems science research in health promotion and public health. *Health Education and Behavior*, 40, 5S–8S.

Mali, F., Kronegger, L., Doreian, P. and Ferligoj, A. (2012) Dynamic scientific co-authorship networks. In A. Scharnhorst, K. Börner and P. van den Besselaar (eds), *Models of Science Dynamics: Encounters between Complexity Theory and Information Sciences* (pp. 195–232). Berlin: Springer.

Manski, C. (1993) Identification of endogenous social effects: The reflection problem. *Review of Economic Studies*, 60, 531–542.

Marcus, G. and Davis, E. (2014) Eight (no, nine!) problems with Big Data. *New York Times*, 7 April, p. A23.

Marin, A. and Hampton, K. (2007) Simplifying the personal network name generator: Alternatives to traditional multiple and single name generators. *Field Methods*, 19, 163–193.

Marsden, P. (2005) Recent developments in network measurement. In P. Carrington, J. Scott and S. Wasserman (eds), *Models and Methods in Social Network Analysis* (pp. 8–30). Cambridge: Cambridge University Press.

Marsden, P. (2011) Survey methods for network data. In J. Scott and P. Carrington (eds), *The SAGE Handbook of Social Network Analysis* (pp 370–388). London: Sage.

Mason, W., Conrey, F. and Smith, E. (2007) Situating social influence processes: Dynamic, multidirectional flows of influence in social networks. *Personality and Social Psychology Review*, 11, 279–300.

Mathur, S., Poole, M., Pena-Mora, F., Hasegawa-Johnson, M. and Contractor, N. (2012) Detecting interaction links in a collaborating group using manually annotated data. *Social Networks*, 34, 515–526.

Matous, P., Todo, Y. and Mojo, D. (2013) Boots are made for walking: Interactions across physical and social space in infrastructure-poor regions. *Journal of Transport Geography*, 31, 226–235.

Matzat, U. and Snijders, C. (2010) Does the online collection of ego-centered network data reduce data quality? An experimental comparison. *Social Networks*, 32, 105–111.

McCallister, L. and Fischer, C. (1978) A procedure for surveying personal networks. *Sociological Methods and Research*, 7, 131–48.

McCarty, C., Bernard, H., Killworth, P., Shelley, G. and Johnsen, E. (1997) Eliciting representative samples of personal networks. *Social Networks*, 19, 303–323.

McCarty, C., Killworth, P. and Rennell, J. (2007a) Impact of methods for reducing respondent burden on personal network structural measures. *Social Networks*, 29, 300–315.

McCarty, C., Molina, J., Aguilar, C. and Rota, L. (2007b) A comparison or social network mapping and personal network visualization. *Field Methods*, 19, 145–162.

McCaw, J., Forbes, K., Nathan, P., Pattison, P., Robins, G., Nolan, T. and McVernon, J. (2010) Comparison of three methods for ascertainment of contact information relevant to respiratory pathogen transmission in encounter networks. *BMC Infectious Diseases*, 10, 166.

McClurg, S. and Lazer, D. (2014) Political networks. *Social Networks*, 36, 1–4.

McGrady, G, Marrow, C., Myers, G., Daniels, M., Vera, M., Mueller, C., Liebow, E., Klovdahl, A. and Lovely, R. (1995) A note on implementation of a random-walk design to study adolescent social networks. *Social Networks*, 17, 251–255.

McPherson, M., Smith-Lovin, L. and Cook, J. (2001) Birds of a feather: Homophily in social networks. *Annual Review of Sociology*, 27, 415–444.

McPherson, M., Smith-Lovin, L. and Brashears, M. (2006) Social isolation in America: Changes in core discussion networks over two decades. *American Sociological Review*, 71, 353–375.

Mehl, M. and Conner, T. (eds) (2012) *Handbook of Research Methods for Studying Daily Life*. New York: Guilford Press.

Mehra, A., Kilduff, M. and Brass, D. (2001) The social networks of high and low self-monitors: Implications for workplace performance. *Administrative Science Quarterly*, 46, 121–146.

Melamed, D., Breiger, R. and West, J. (2013) Community structure in multi-mode networks: Applying an eigenspectrum approach. *Connections*, 33, 18–23.

Mercken, L., Steglich, C., Knibbe, R. and Vries, H. D. (2011) Dynamics of friendship networks and alcohol use in early and mid-adolescence. *Journal of Studies on Alcohol and Drugs*, 73, 99.

Merluzzi, J. and Burt, R. (2013) How many names are enough? Identifying network effects with the least set of listed contacts. *Social Networks*, 35, 331–337.

Milgram, S. (1967) The small world problem. *Psychology Today*, 2, 60–67.

Millar, M. and Dillman, D. (2011) Improving response to web and mixed-mode surveys. *Public Opinion Quarterly*, 75, 249–269.

Milo, R., Shen-Orr, S., Itzkovitz, S., Kashtan, N., Chklovskii, D. and Alon, U. (2002) Network motifs: Simple building blocks of complex networks. *Science*, 298, 824–827.

Mische, A. (2008) *Partisan publics: Communication and contention across Brazilian youth activist networks*. Princeton, NJ: Princeton University Press.

Monge, P. and Contractor, N. (2003) *Theories of Communication Networks*. New York: Oxford University Press.

Moody, J. (2002) The importance of relationship timing for diffusion. *Social Forces*, 81, 25–56.

Moody, J. and Mucha, P. (2013) Portrait of political party polarization. *Network Science*, 1, 119–121.

Moody, J. and White, D.(2003) Structural cohesion and embeddedness: A hierarchical concept of social groups. *American Sociological Review*, 68, 103–127.

Moreno, J. and Jennings, H. (1938) Statistics of social configurations. *Sociometry*, 1, 342–374.

Morris, M. (ed.) (2004) *Network Epidemiology: A Handbook for Survey Design and Data Collection*. Oxford: Oxford University Press.

Morselli, C. (2009) *Inside Criminal Networks*. New York: Springer.

Morselli, C. (ed.) (2014) *Crime and Networks*. New York: Routledge.

Newman, M. (2010) *Networks: An Introduction*. Oxford: Oxford University Press.

Newman, M. and Park, J. (2003) Why social networks are different from other types of networks. *Physical Review E*, 68, 036122.

Nissenbaum, H. (2004) Privacy as contextual integrity. *Washington Law Review*, 79, 119–157.

Noel, H. and Nyhan, B. (2011) The 'unfriending' problem: The consequences of homophily in friendship retention for causal estimates of social influence. *Social Networks*, 33, 211–218.

Nowicki, K. and Snijders, T. (2001) Estimation and prediction for stochastic blockstructures. *Journal of the American Statistical Association*, 96, 1077–1087.

Oh, H. and Kilduff, M. (2008) The ripple effect of personality on social structure: Self-monitoring origins of network brokerage. *Journal of Applied Psychology*, 93, 1155–1164.

Opsahl, T. (2013) Triadic closure in two-mode networks: Redefining the global and local clustering coefficients. *Social Networks*, 35, 159–167.

Opsahl, T. and Panzarasa, P (2009) Clustering in weighted networks. *Social Networks*, 31, 155–163.

Opsahl, T., Agneessens, F. and Skvoretz, J. (2010) Node centrality in weighted networks: Generalizing degree and shortest paths. *Social Networks*, 32, 245–251.

Osler, M., Lund, R., Kriegbaum, M., Christensen, U. and Andersen, A. (2006) Cohort profile: The Metropolit 1953 Danish male birth cohort. *International Journal of Epidemiology*, 35, 541–545.

Ostrom, E. (2009) A general framework for analyzing the sustainability of social-ecological systems. *Science*, 325, 419–422.

Ostrom, E., Janssen, M. and Anderies. J. (2007) Going beyond panaceas. *Proceedings of the National Academy of Sciences*, 104, 15176–15178.

Padgett, J. and Ansell, C. (1993) Robust action and the rise of the Medici, 1400–1434. *American Journal of Sociology*, 98, 1259–1319.

Padgett, J. and Powell, W. (2012) *The Emergence of Organizations and Markets*. Princeton, NJ: Princeton University Press.

Patison, K., Swain, D., Bishop-Hurley, G., Robins, G., Pattison, P. and Reid, D. (2010) Changes in temporal and spatial associations between pairs of cattle during familiarization. *Applied Animal Behaviour Science*, 128, 10–17.

Pattison, P. (1993) *Algebraic Models for Social Networks*. New York: Cambridge University Press.

Pattison, P. (1994) Social cognition in context. In S.Wasserman and J. Galaskiewicz (eds), *Advances in Social Network Analysis* (pp. 79–109). Thousand Oaks, CA: Sage.

Pattison, P. (2011) Relation algebras and social networks. In J. Scott and P. Carrington (eds), *The SAGE Handbook of Social Network Analysis* (pp. 447–458). London: Sage.

Pattison, P. and Snijders, T. (2013) Modeling social networks: Next steps. In D. Lusher, J. Koskinen and G. Robins (eds), *Exponential Random Graph Models for Social Networks* (pp. 287–301). Cambridge: Cambridge University Press.

Pattison, P., Robins, G., Snijders, T. and Wang, P. (2013) Conditional estimation of exponential random graph models from snowball and other sampling designs. *Journal of Mathematical Psychology*, 57, 284–296.

Phan, B., Engo-Monsen, K. and Fjeldstad, O. (2013) Considering clustering measures: Third ties, means, and triplets. *Social Networks*, 35, 300–308.

Piepenbrink, A. and Gaur, A. (2013) Methodological advances in the analysis of bipartite networks. An illustration using board interlocks in Indian firms. *Organizational Research Methods*, 16, 474–496.

Powell, W., Packalen, K. and Whittington, K. (2012) Organizational and institutional genesis: The emergence of high-tech clusters in the life sciences. In J. Padgett and W. Powell (eds), *The Emergence of Organizations and Markets* (pp. 434–465). Princeton, NJ: Princeton University Press.

Prell, C. (2012) *Social Network Analysis: History, Theory and Methodology*. Los Angeles: Sage.

Putnam, R. (2000) *Bowling Alone: The Collapse and Revival of American Community*. New York: Simon and Schuster.

Quintane, E. (2013) Comparing networks: Structural correspondence between behavioral and recall networks. In D. Lusher, J. Koskinen and G. Robins (eds), *Exponential Random Graph Models for Social Networks* (pp. 272–283). Cambridge: Cambridge University Press.

Quintane, E., Pattison, P., Robins, G. and Mol, J. (2013) Short- and long-term stability in organizational networks: Temporal structures of project teams. *Social Networks*, 35, 528–540.

Radicchi, F., Fortunato, S. and Vespignani, A. (2012) Citation networks. In A. Scharnhorst, K. Börner and P. van den Besselaar (eds), *Models of Science Dynamics: Encounters between Complexity Theory and Information Sciences* (pp. 233–257). Berlin: Springer.

Rank, O., Robins, G. and Pattison, P. (2010) Structural logic of intraorganizational networks. *Organization Science*, 21, 745–764.

Rapoport, A. (1953) Spread of information through a population with socio-structural bias: 1. Assumption of transitivity. *Bulletin of Mathematical Biophysics*, 15, 523–533.

Reips, U. (2012) Using the internet to collect data. In H. Cooper (ed.), *APA Handbook of Research Methods in Psychology: Volume 2. Research Designs* (pp. 291–310). Washington, DC: American Psychological Association.

Rhodes, R. (2006) Policy network analysis. In M. Moran, M. Rein and R.E. Goodin (eds), *The Oxford Handbook of Public Policy* (pp. 425–447). Oxford: Oxford University Press.

Robins, G. (2013) A tutorial on methods for the modeling and analysis of social network data. *Journal of Mathematical Psychology*, 57, 261–274.

Robins, G. and Alexander, M. (2004) Small worlds among interlocking directors: Network structure and distance in bipartite graphs. *Journal of Computational and Mathematical Organization Theory*, 10, 69–94.

Robins, G. and Kashima, Y. (2008) Social psychology and social networks: Individuals and social systems. *Asian Journal of Social Psychology*, 11, 1–12.

Robins, G. and Pattison, P. (2006) Multiple networks in organisations. Working paper: University of Melbourne.

Robins, G., Pattison, P. and Woolcock, J. (2005) Small and other worlds: Global network structures from local processes. *American Journal of Sociology*, 110, 894–936.

Robins, G., Pattison, P., Lusher, D. and Bates, L. (2010) *Network-based research designs for climate adaptive behaviours within complex social systems*. Report to CSIRO Climate Adaptation Flagship. University of Melbourne.

Robins, G., Bates, L. and Pattison, P. (2011) Network governance and environmental management: Conflict and cooperation. *Public Administration*, 89, 1293–1313.

Robins, G., Lewis, J. and Wang, P. (2012) Statistical network analysis for analyzing policy networks. *Policy Studies Journal*, 40, 375–401.

Roethlisberger, F. and Dickson, W. (1939) *Management and the Worker*. Cambridge, MA: Harvard University Press.

Rohe, K., Chatterjee, S. and Yu, B. (2011) Spectral clustering and the high-dimensional stochastic blockmodel. *Annals of Statistics*, 39, 1878–1915.

Rolls, D., Daraganova, G., Sacks-Davis, R., Hellard, M., Jenkinson, R., McBryde, E., Pattison, P. and Robins, G. (2012) Modelling hepatitis C transmission over a social network of injecting drug users. *Journal of Theoretical Biology*, 297, 73–87.

Rolls, D., Sacks-Davis, R., Jenkinson, R., McBryde, E., Pattison, P., Robins, G. and Hellard, M. (2013a) Hepatitis C transmission and treatment in contact networks of people who inject drugs. *PLoS One*, 8, e78286.

Rolls, D., Wang, P., Jenkinson, R., Pattison, P., Robins, G., Sacks-Davis, R., Daraganova, G., Hellard, M. and McBryde, E. (2013b) Modelling a disease-relevant contact network of people who inject drugs. *Social Networks*, 35, 699–710.

Rubin, D.B. (1976) Inference and missing data. *Biometrika*, 63, 581–592.

Sacks-Davis, R., Daraganova, G., Aitken, C., et al. (2012) Hepatitis C virus phylogenetic clustering is associated with the social injecting network in a cohort of people who inject drugs. *PLoS One*, 7, e47335.

Sageman, M. (2004) *Understanding Terror Networks*. Philadelphia: University of Pennsylvania Press.

Sainio, M., Veenstra, R., Huitsing, G. and Salmivalli, C. (2011) Victims and their defenders: A dyadic approach. *International Journal of Behavioral Development*, 35, 144–151.

Salathe, M., Kazandjieva, M., Lee, J., Levis, P., Feldman, M. and Jones, J. (2010) A high-resolution human contact network for infectious disease transmission. *Proceedings of the National Academy of Sciences*, 107, 22020–22025.

Salvy, S.-J., de la Haye, K., Bowker, J. and Hermans, R. (2012) Influence of peers and friends on children's and adolescents' eating and activity behaviors. *Physiology and Behavior*, 106, 369–378.

Schaefer, D., adams, j. and Haas, S. (2013) Social networks and smoking: Exploring the effects of peer influence and smoker popularity through simulations. *Health Education and Behavior*, 40, 24S–32S.

Schnettler, S. (2009a) A structured overview of 50 years of small-world research. *Social Networks*, 31, 165–178.

Schnettler, S. (2009b) A small world on feet of clay? A comparison of empirical small-world studies against best-practice criteria. *Social Networks*, 31, 179–189.

Schnettler, S. (ed.) (2013) *Small World Research*. Los Angeles: Sage.

Schweinberger, M., Petrescu-Prahova, M. and Vu, D. (2014) Disaster response on September 11, 2001 through the lens of statistical network analysis. *Social Networks*, 37, 42–55.

Schweitzer, F., Fagiolo, G., Sornette, D., Vega-Redondo, F., Vespignani, A. and White, D. (2009) Economic networks: The new challenges. *Science*, 325, 422–425.

Scott, J. (2013) *Social Network Analysis*. Los Angeles: Sage.

Scott, J. and Carrington, P. (eds) (2011) *The SAGE Handbook of Social Network Analysis*. London: Sage.

Selfhout, M., Burk, W., Branje, S., Denissen, J., Van Aken, M. and Meeus, W. (2010) Emerging late adolescent friendship networks and Big Five personality traits: A social network approach. *Journal of Personality*, 78, 509–538.

Shalizi, C. and Thomas, A. (2011) Homophily and contagion are generically confounded in observational social network studies. *Sociological Methods & Research*, 40, 211–239.

Sherif, M., Harvey, O., White, B., Hood, W. and Sherif, C. (1961) *The Robber's Cave Experiment: Intergroup Conflict and Cooperation*. Middletown, CT: Wesleyan University Press.

Shore, J., Chu, C. and Bianchi, M. (2013) Power laws and fragility in flow networks. *Social Networks*, 35, 116–123.

Shum, B., and Ferguson, R. (2012) Social learning analytics. *Educational Technology and Society*, 15, 3–26.

Siciliano, M., Yenigan, D. and Ertan, G. (2012) Estimating network structure via random sampling: Cognitive social structures and the adaptive threshold method. *Social Networks*, 34, 585–600.

Sijtsma, K. (2009) On the use, the misuse, and the very limited usefulness of Cronbach's alpha. *Psychometrika*, 74, 107–120.

Silverman, D. (2011) *Interpreting Qualitative Data*. London: Sage.

Simmel, G. (1908) *Soziologie*. Leipzig: Duncker & Humblot.

Simon, H. (1955) On a class of skew distribution functions. *Biometrika*, 42, 425–440.

Sloot, P., Kampis, G. and Gulyas, L. (2013) Advances in dynamic temporal networks: Understanding the temporal dynamics of complex adaptive networks. *European Physical Journal Special Topics*, 222, 1287–1293.

Smith, J. (2012) Macrostructure from microstructure: Generating whole systems from ego networks. *Sociological Methodology*, 42, 155–205.

Smith, J. and Moody, J. (2013) Structural effects of network sampling coverage I: Nodes missing at random. *Social Networks*, 35, 652–668.

Snijders, T. (2011a) Network dynamics. In J. Scott and P. Carrington (eds), *The SAGE Handbook of Social Network Analysis* (pp. 501–513). London: Sage.

Snijders, T. (2011b) Statistical models for social networks. *Annual Review of Sociology*, 37, 131–153.

Snijders, T. and Baerveldt, C. (2003) A multilevel network study of the effects of delinquent behavior on friendship networks. *Journal of Mathematical Sociology*, 27, 123–151.

Snijders, T. and Bosker, R. (2012) *Multilevel Analysis: An Introduction to Basic and Advanced Multilevel Modeling*. London: Sage.

Snijders, T. and Doreian, P. (2010) Introduction to the special issue on Network Dynamics. *Social Networks*, 32, 1–3.

Snijders, T. and Doreian, P. (2012) Introduction to the special issue on Network Dynamics (Part 2). *Social Networks*, 34, 289–290.

Snijders, T., Pattison, P., Robins, G. and Handcock, M. (2006) New specifications for exponential random graph models. *Sociological Methodology*, 36, 99–153.

Snijders, T., van de Bunt, G.G. and Steglich, C.E.G. (2010) Introduction to stochastic actor-based models for network dynamics. *Social Networks*, 32, 44–60.

Snijders, T., Lomi, A. and Torlo, V. (2013) A model for the multiplex dynamics of two-mode and one-mode networks, with an application to employment preference, friendship, and advice. *Social Networks*, 35, 265–276.

Soltis, S., Agneessens, F., Sasovova, Z. and Labianca, G. (2013) A social network perspective on turnover intentions: The role of distributive justice and social support. *Human Resource Management*, 52, 561–584.

Song, L., Son, J., & Lin, N. (2011). Social support. In J. Scott and P. Carrington (eds), *The SAGE Handbook of Social Network Analysis* (pp. 116-128). London: Sage.

Stadtfeld, C. and Geyer-Schulz, A. (2011) Analyzing event stream dynamics in two-mode networks. An exploratory analysis of private communication in a question and answer community. *Social Networks*, 33, 258–272.

Stevens, S. (1946) On the theory of scales of measurement. *Science*, 103, 677–680.

Stivala, A., Wang, P., Koskinen, J., Robins, G. and Rolls, D. (2014) Estimating parameters of exponential random graph models for very large networks using snowball sampling and parallel computing. Presentation at Sunbelt International Social Networks Conference, Tampa, FL.

Stork, D. and Richards, W. (1992) Nonrespondents in communication network studies: Problems and possibilities. *Group and Organization Management*, 17, 193–202.

Sun, L., Axhausen, K., Lee, D. and Huang, X. (2013) Understanding metropolitan patterns of daily encounters. *Proceedings of the National Academy of Sciences*, 110, 13774–13779.

Szell, M. and Thurner, S. (2010) Measuring social dynamics in a massive multiplayer online game. *Social Networks*, 32, 313–329.

Szolnoki, G. and Hoffmann, D. (2013) Online, face-to-face and telephone surveys: Comparing different sampling methods in wine consumer research. *Wine Economics and Policy*, 2, 57–66.

Tamassia, R. (ed.) (2013) *Handbook of Graph Drawing and Visualization*. Boca Raton, FL: Chapman & Hall/CRC.

Tambayong, L. and Carley, K. (2012) Network text analysis in computer-intensive rapid ethnography retrieval: An example from political networks of Sudan. *Journal of Social Structure*, 13, 2.

Tengö, M., Johansson, K., Rakotondrasoa, F., Lundberg, J., Andriamaherilala, J., Rakotoarisoa, J. and Elmqvist, T. (2007) Taboos and forest governance: Informal protection of hot spot dry forest in southern Madagascar. *Ambio*, 36, 683–691.

Tolsma, J., van Deurzen, I., Stark, T. and Veenstra, R. (2013) Who is bullying whom in ethnically diverse primary schools? Exploring links between bullying, ethnicity, and ethnic diversity in Dutch primary schools. *Social Networks*, 35, 51–61.

Toomet, O., van der Leij, M. and Rolfe, M. (2013) Social networks and labor market inequality between ethnicities and races. *Network Science*, 1, 321–352.

Uddin, S. and Hossain, L. (2013) Dyad and triad census analysis of crisis communication network. *Social Networking*, 2, 32–41.

Uzzi, B. (1996) The sources and consequences of embeddedness for the economic performance of organizations: The network effect. *American Sociological Review*, 61, 674–698.

Uzzi, B. (1997) Social structure and competition in interfirm networks: The paradox of embeddedness. *Administrative Science Quarterly*, 42, 35–67.

Uzzi, B. (1999) Embeddedness in the making of financial markets: How social relations and networks benefit firms seeking financing. *American Sociological Review*, 64, 481–505.

Valente, T. (1995) *Network Models of the Diffusion of Innovations*. Cresskill, NJ: Hampton Press.

Valente, T. (2005) Network models and methods for studying the diffusion of innovations. In P. Carrington, J. Scott and S. Wasserman (eds), *Models and Methods in Social Network Analysis* (pp. 98–116). Cambridge: Cambridge University Press.

Valente, T. (2010) *Social Networks and Health: Models, Methods, and Applications*. Oxford: Oxford University Press.

Valente, T. (2012) Network interventions. *Science*, 337, 49–53.

van der Gaag, M. and Snijders, T. (2005) The resource generator: Social capital quantification with concrete items. *Social Networks*, 27, 1–29.

van der Gaag, M., Snijders, T. and Flap, H. (2008) Position generator measures and their relationship to other social capital measures. In N. Lin and B. Erickson (eds), *Social Capital: An International Research Program* (pp. 27–48). Oxford: Oxford University Press.

van der Hulst, R. (2011) Terrorist networks: The threat of connectivity. In J. Scott and P. Carrington (eds), *The SAGE Handbook of Social Network Analysis* (pp. 256–270). London: Sage.

VanderWeele T. (2011) Sensitivity analysis for contagion effects in social networks. *Sociological Methods and Research*, 40, 240–255.

VanderWeele, T., Ogburn, E., and Tchetgen, E. (2012) Why and when 'flawed' social network analyses still yield valid tests of no contagion. *Statistics, Politics, and Policy*, 3, 1–11.

van Duijn, M., and Huisman, M. (2011) Statistical models for ties and actors. In J. Scott and P. Carrington (eds), *The SAGE Handbook of Social Network Analysis* (pp. 459–483). London: Sage.

van Duijn, M., Snijders, T. and Zijlstra, B. (2004) p2: A random effects model with covariates for directed graphs. *Statistica Neerlandica*, 58, 234–254.

Veenstra, R., Dijkstra, J., Steglich, C. and Van Zalk, M. (2013) Network-behavior dynamics. *Journal of Research on Adolescence*, 23, 399–412.

Wang, P., Sharpe, K., Robins, G. and Pattison, P. (2009) Exponential random graph (p*) models for affiliation networks. *Social Networks*, 31, 12–25.

Wang, P., Robins, G., Pattison, P. and Lazega, E. (2013) Exponential random graph models for multilevel networks. *Social Networks*, 35, 96–115.

Wang, T. (2013) Big Data needs thick data. *Ethnography Matters*, 13 May. Available at: http://ethnographymatters.net/2013/05/13/big-data-needs-thick-data/.

Ward, M., Ahlquist, J. and Rozenas, A. (2013) Gravity's rainbow: A dynamic latent space model for the world trade network. *Network Science*, 1, 95–118.

Wasserman, S. (2013) Comments on 'Social contagion theory: examining dynamic social networks and human behavior' by Nicholas Christakis and James Fowler. *Statistics in Medicine*, 32, 578–580.

Wasserman, S. and Faust, K. (1994) *Social Network Analysis: Methods and Applications*. Cambridge: Cambridge University Press.

Wasserman, S. and Robins, G. (2012) Social network research: The foundation of network science. In H. Cooper et al. (eds), *APA Handbook of Research Methods in Psychology, Volume 3. Data Analysis and Research Publication* (pp. 451–469). Washington, DC: American Psychological Association.

Watts, D. and Strogatz, S. (1998) Collective dynamics of 'small world' networks. *Nature*, 393, 440–442.

Weick, K. and Roberts, K. (1993) Collective mind in organizations: Heedful interrelating on flight decks. *Administrative Science Quarterly*, 38, 357–381.

Wellman, B. (1979) The community question: The intimate networks of East Yorkers. *American Journal of Sociology*, 84, 1201–1231.

Wellman, B. (1993) An egocentric network tale: Comment on Bien et al. (1991). *Social Networks*, 15, 423–436.

White, D. (2012) Kinship, class and community. In J. Scott and P. Carrington (eds), *The SAGE Handbook of Social Network Analysis* (pp. 129–147). London: Sage.

White, H. (1963) *An Anatomy of Kinship*. Englewood Cliffs, NJ: Prentice Hall.

White, H.D. (2011). Scientific and scholarly networks. In J. Scott and P. Carrington (eds), *The SAGE Handbook of Social Network Analysis* (pp. 271–285). London: Sage.

White, H., Boorman, S. and Breiger, R. (1976) Social structure from multiple networks. I. Blockmodels of roles and positions. *American Journal of Sociology*, 81, 730–780.

Williams, D., Contractor, N., Poole, M., Srivastava, J. and Cai, D. (2011) The Virtual Worlds Exploratorium: Using large-scale data and computational techniques for communication research. *Communication Methods and Measures*, 5, 163–180.

Wilkinson, D. and Thelwall, M. (2011) Researching personal information on the public web: Methods and ethics. *Social Science Computer Review*, 29, 387–401.

Wright, S. (1921) Correlation and causation. *Journal of Agricultural Research*, 20, 557–585.

Wright, S. (1923) The theory of path coefficients: A reply to Niles's criticism. *Genetics*, 8, 239–255.

Xu, B., Huang, Y. and Contractor, N. (2013) Exploring Twitter networks in parallel computing environments. *Proceedings of the XSEDE '13 Conference on Extreme Science and Engineering Discovery Environment: Gateway to Discovery*. New York: ACM.

Zagenczyk, T., Purvis, R., Shoss, M., Scott, K. and Cruz, K. (in press) Social influence and leader perceptions: Multiplex social network ties and similarity in leader–member exchange. *Journal of Business and Psychology*. doi: 10.1007/s10869-013-9332-7

Zimmer, M. (2010) 'But the data is already public': On the ethics of research in Facebook. *Ethics of Information Technology*, 12, 313–325.

Žnidaršič, A., Ferligoj, A. and Doreian, P. (2012) Non-response in social networks: The impact of different non-response treatments on the stability of blockmodels. *Social Networks*, 34, 438–450.

Index

activity, network 4, 9, 22–23, 30, 183, 192, 212
actor (see also attributes, actor) 3, 4–7, 9, 18–19, 20–21, 26–27
adjacency list 69
adjacency matrix 20, 65–69, 71–72, 73, 76, 80–81, 84, 91, 186–187, 200
Adolescent Health 53–54, 135, 158
Adolescent Peer Social Network Dynamics and Problem Behavior 135
affiliation network – see bipartite network
aggregation 48, 85, 196
alter 22, 51–52, 53, 82–85, 94–95, 98–101, 103–107, 110–112, 114–115, 125–126, 130, 136–137, 150, 177–178, 184, 185, 199, 203–204, 213
alter-alter tie 51–52, 82–85, 104–107, 110, 136, 178, 184, 185, 204, 213
animal networks 42, 78, 146
anonymity 14, 113, 116, 149–153, 157–158
Antarctic 134
Arab Spring 144
arc 7, 19–20, 23–25
archival records 55, 101, 128, 142, 143, 150, 158, 203
arm's-length ties 35
asymmetric dyad 23, 178
attitudes 14, 37, 52, 60, 78, 79, 207, 221
attributes 8–9, 14, 21, 29, 33–34, 34–35, 41, 47–48, 51–52, 53, 54, 57, 60, 71, 72, 77–80, 86, 91, 102, 116, 118, 133, 168–169, 177–178, 194, 195, 204, 212–214, 216–219
autologistic actor attribute model 194
autocatalysis 30, 36
autoregressive model 195
available case analysis 117–118, 199
average degree 23, 94, 114, 177

behavioral variable 79
Bernoulli graph distribution 192

beta centrality 183
betweenness centrality 26, 32, 37, 117, 131, 182–184, 189, 212
bibliometric 145
big data 2–3, 94–95, 134, 141, 144–146, 204–205, 226–229
binary 20, 46, 64, 66–69, 79–81, 83, 89, 100, 101–102, 113, 168–169, 175, 177, 186, 191, 200, 202–203
bipartite network 21, 23, 43–44, 55, 58, 59, 72–74, 86, 101, 129, 132, 142, 146, 194, 200–202
bipartite projections 200
bird flu 144
BKS studies 110–112
blockmodel 27, 49, 117–118, 139, 171, 172, 186–189, 201, 207, 214
boundary 11, 42–43, 50, 51, 52–53, 54, 55, 56, 58, 59, 60, 65, 70, 76, 86–87, 93, 95–96, 98, 103, 107, 115, 116–117, 118, 135, 152, 199
bridge 8, 28, 32, 117, 184
brokerage 8, 9, 28–29, 32–33, 35, 37, 52, 84, 141, 165, 183, 184, 225
bullying 33, 39–40, 45, 48, 99, 134, 154, 194

case study 54, 59, 143, 214–216, 223
CASOS group 140, 164
categorical 21, 80–81, 168–169, 177, 202–203
causality 2, 10, 49, 53, 58, 205, 213, 216–222, 227–228
centrality 5–6, 9, 22, 26, 32, 37, 86–87, 117, 121, 131, 182–184, 188–189, 201, 202, 203, 207, 212, 225
centralization 9
Children of Immigrants Longitudinal Survey 135
citation networks 145
clique 22, 26–27, 110, 119, 120, 184–185
closeness centrality 183–184

closure 7, 9, 28–29, 30–32, 34, 48–49, 51, 61, 84, 91, 94, 114, 117, 178–181, 182, 185–186, 191, 192, 193, 195, 196, 200–201, 214
clustering algorithm 186–187
clustering, network 30, 178, 185–186, 198–201, 203
co-authorship networks 128, 145
co-evolution 29, 34–35, 37, 41, 102–103, 177, 195–196, 201, 212–214
cognitive data 110, 112
cognitive social structure 54–55, 70, 95, 154
cohesive subgroups, cohesive subset 6, 22, 26–27, 31, 184–185, 201
collaboration network 5–7, 11, 14, 33, 37, 43, 45, 60–61, 70, 86, 99, 109, 120, 132, 133, 134, 142–143, 145, 147, 170, 200, 226
CollegeConnect 144
Colorado Springs study 138
colors of nodes 21, 80, 156, 168
communication network 33, 45, 110, 132, 134, 143, 181
community structure 22, 27, 186, 188–189, 193, 214
complete graph 20, 23, 167
complex contagion 220
complex systems, see complexity
complexity 4, 15, 41–42, 51, 216, 227
component 25, 87, 120, 163
computational social science 226–229
Concor 187, 207
conditional uniform graph distribution 191–192, 201, 202, 214
confidentiality 149–155, 157, 158
configuration 178, 179–181, 192, 193–196, 202
connectivity 12, 14, 22, 25–26, 28, 31, 32, 51–52, 53, 56, 94, 115, 136–137, 138, 153, 184–185, 193, 197, 207
constraint, network 184, 212
contact diary 129, 130, 138
contagion - see social influence
contextual effect 50, 217–220
contextual integrity 157–158
contextual name generator 106
continuous 21, 80, 85, 90, 109, 156, 168–169, 177
coordinator 32
core-periphery 9, 120, 131, 188
covert actors 118
criminal networks – see illicit networks
cyclic triad 24–25, 179
Cytoscape 173

Danish Male Birth Cohort study 135
dark networks – see illicit networks
data collection 15, 47, 49, 50–51, 53, 55, 56, 57–58, 70–71, 87, 89–120, 123–147, 153–155, 159, 206, 207, 216, 222, 224, 226, 228
debriefing 155
defence 75, 140, 160
degree 5, 9, 22–24, 26, 28, 30, 31, 32, 35, 37, 67–69, 73, 87, 94, 97, 114, 117, 156, 177–178, 181–184, 187, 193, 196, 197, 200–201, 203, 204, 206, 212, 214, 224
degree centrality 26, 32, 117, 182–183, 212
degree distribution 5, 22–24, 28, 29, 73, 94, 97, 178, 181–183, 193, 197, 201, 204, 214
degrees of influence 218
de-identified 151–152, 159
demographic 7, 79, 109, 115, 139, 158, 177
density 22–23, 26, 31, 68–69, 71, 73, 76–77, 84, 110, 167–168, 177–178, 182, 184–185, 187–189, 191, 192, 202, 204, 213
dependence 4, 14, 41, 91–92, 182, 190, 192–193, 198, 202
descriptive statistics 22, 79, 117, 177–178, 199
difficult to work with 33, 37, 45, 61, 99
diffusion – see social influence
digital data 50, 96, 124, 129–130, 156–158, 160, 204–205, 226
directed network 7–8, 20, 23, 25, 29, 31, 66–68, 98, 117, 166–167, 178, 183, 192–193
disaster management 132, 143, 144
dislike 33, 45, 99
dominance 146
drop-out 130, 155
duty of care 154
dyad 13, 18, 20, 23–24, 31, 35–36, 48, 49, 59, 89, 91, 95, 98, 104–105, 112, 134, 140–141, 146, 166–167, 178–181, 189, 192–193, 194, 196, 213, 220, 224, 225, 228
dyad census 178–181, 193
dyadic covariate 78, 81–82, 102, 194
dyadwise shared partner 194
dynamics 29, 34–35, 47, 49–50, 58, 103, 134, 135, 143, 189, 196, 208, 214, 215, 228

East York studies 136
economic networks 35, 132, 139, 195, 208

edge 5, 7, 18–21, 23, 25, 30, 64, 66–69, 70, 71, 73, 77, 84, 101, 145, 163, 166–167, 178–179, 189, 191, 199

edge list 64, 66–69, 70, 73, 77, 84, 162, 164

education 35, 92, 145–146

effective size 184

effectiveness 6, 37, 45, 61, 142, 225, 227

efficiency 28, 31, 49, 133

ego, egocentric network, egonet 20, 40, 43, 51–52, 53, 57, 58, 59, 64, 82–85, 89, 92–93, 96–97, 103–107, 108–110, 113, 125, 127, 129–130, 134, 135, 136–138, 143, 144, 150, 151, 177, 178, 184, 185, 197–199, 203–204, 205, 212–213, 215

Egonet software 177

eigenvector centrality 183

electronic data collection 57–58, 101, 130, 133, 134

email 45–47, 58, 96, 101, 112, 114–115, 118, 124, 130, 131, 133, 157, 196, 227

embeddedness 29, 35–36, 139, 206

emergence 6, 29, 36, 186

empty graph 20, 23, 167

endogenous processes 34, 41, 192, 207, 214, 218

environmental governance, see network governance

Erdös-Renyi graphs 192

ethics 99, 135, 149–160

exchange network 134, 139

expansiveness 23

experiment 10, 12–13, 133–134, 154, 195, 219, 221–222, 223, 225, 227–228

exponential random graph model 177, 193–194, 206

Facebook 23, 30, 101, 141, 144, 157–160, 195

face-to-face interview 96–97, 109, 112–114, 125, 126, 136, 217

first name cue method 95, 110

Florence 36, 128, 178

Framingham Heart Study 217

friendship 4, 13, 21, 29, 33, 34, 45, 48, 60, 69, 76, 82, 112, 119, 120, 133, 138, 145, 164, 166, 205, 213, 217–219, 223, 226

Fruchterman-Reingold 164–165

fuzzy actors 118

Gallery of Large Graphs 173

general linear model 10–11

generalization 5, 215–216

generalized exchange 31, 139

generalized influence 33–34, 41, 212

generalized selection 33, 41, 213

geodesic 22, 25, 26, 28, 31, 70, 117, 183, 185, 189, 203

geometrically weighted edgewise shared partner 194

geospatial, geography 3, 50, 79, 81, 137, 139, 194

Gephi 124, 163, 164, 176

global outcome 2, 41, 142, 214, 215, 223, 226

Grand Unified Network Theory 4, 28

graph 5, 18–27

GraphChi 205

graphical modelling 219

group feedback 156

guanxi 32

hard to reach populations – see hidden populations

Hard-to-Reach Population Methods Research Group 198

Hawthorne studies 12–13, 101, 127, 133

health behaviors 34, 79, 134, 138, 194–195, 217, 221

hepatitis C 45, 138, 224

heterogeneity 227

hidden populations 56, 57, 115–116, 198–199, 224

hierarchical closure 179

hierarchical linear modeling 85, 93, 203–204, 212

historical network analysis 36, 128, 143

HIV 43, 45, 57, 138

homophily 29, 33, 48, 79, 81, 82, 194, 195, 213, 217–222

hub 30, 181

Hurricane Katrina 143

hybrid name generator 142

illicit networks 118, 140

image matrix 188

indegree 23–24, 68–69, 117, 187

individual effect 40–41, 78

individualized research design 9–10, 12–13, 19, 39–41, 140, 219

induction 225

inference 10–11, 40, 49, 50, 54, 58, 64, 72, 77, 86, 117–118, 128, 135, 162, 182, 195, 198, 204, 213–222, 227

information networks 1, 22, 25, 32, 45, 61, 120, 132

informant accuracy 110–112

informed consent 149, 153–154, 159
innovation 29, 32, 34, 79, 108, 194
in-star 23–24
interlocking directors 43, 55, 101, 132, 161, 200
internet studies 50, 57, 136, 143–145, 157, 215, 228
inter-organizational 45, 132, 142, 143, 150
intervention 217, 223, 225–226
interview 10, 12, 37, 45–46, 60, 63, 86, 93, 94, 96–97, 99, 100, 104, 107, 109, 111, 112–113, 114–115, 116, 120, 124, 125, 126–127, 132, 136–137, 138, 140, 147, 154, 205–206
intra-organizational 133
Iran 144
isolate 2, 5, 6, 25, 96, 156, 165

Kamada-Kawai 164–165
k-core 185
kinship 30, 139, 161, 189–190
k-plex 185
k-star 24–25, 193
k-triangle 193–194
k-two-path 193

labor market 139
large systems 227
latent variable 218–221, 227
learning analytics 145–146
liaison 32
line 5, 66
link prediction 199
link tracing 56–57
London riots 144
Longitudinal 35, 49–50, 58, 59, 65, 70, 75–77, 102–103, 124, 127, 130–131, 135, 138, 154, 155, 158, 164, 194, 195–197, 204, 205, 207–208, 212–214, 220
loop 19, 23, 187

mail surveys 124, 136
Markov graph model 194
Massively Open Online Courses 145–146
measurement function 90–91
measurement scales 90, 109
Medici 36
meta-matrix 44, 75, 202
metaphor 37, 220–221
missing at random 117
missing data 53, 116–118, 120, 125, 135, 199–200
mixed methods research 64, 126–127, 205–206
mobile data collection 129–130, 144–145
motif 179, 181, 192

multilevel network 21, 43–44, 47, 51, 55, 59, 74–75, 133, 142, 192, 194, 202
multiple networks 53–54, 59, 89, 92–93, 177–178, 190, 202, 204, 214, 215
multiplex network 21, 29, 36, 37, 53, 65, 69–70, 98, 133, 134, 170–171, 172, 178, 187, 190, 194, 203
multitrait multimethod 112, 119
multivariate network – see multiplex network
mutual dyad 24
myPersonality 141

name generator 96–99, 100, 102, 103–104, 106–107, 109, 110–113, 115, 117, 119–120, 126, 127, 132, 135, 137, 142, 150, 152, 154, 205
name interpreter 99–100, 104, 107, 110, 113, 120, 125, 137
NameGenWeb 144
Nang Rong projects 139
National Longitudinal Study of Adolescent Health 53–54, 135, 158
n-clique 185
needle sharing 45, 115, 138
negative tie 18, 20, 28, 33, 37, 45, 59, 60–61, 98–99, 119–120, 154
Netdraw 163, 166, 176
Net-map toolbox 107
network algebra 81, 139, 189–190, 196
network census 52, 93, 95
network doppelgangers 118
network effect 19, 40, 54, 56, 58, 161, 218, 220, 224
network effects model 194
network entrepreneur, see also brokerage 2, 28, 32
network governance (including environmental governance) 14, 49, 61, 120, 132, 139, 142–143, 150, 172, 207, 215–216, 225, 227
network measurement 37, 52, 53, 89–121, 131, 134, 175, 203, 218, 229
network position 6, 33, 41, 48, 49, 149–150, 186–189, 195, 212–213
network scale-up method 198
network science 4–5, 15, 90, 91–92, 143, 181, 207, 208, 215, 226, 229
network structure 3, 7, 9, 11, 13, 14, 22, 26, 29, 34, 35, 37, 41, 47, 48–49, 53, 54, 56–57, 61, 72, 77, 78, 79, 81, 91, 93, 95, 101, 111, 117, 134, 139, 151, 159, 161, 187, 189, 190, 192–194, 195–196, 198, 199, 213–215, 223–224, 225–226
network topology 3, 13
node 5–7, 11, 18–20, 21, 22, 23, 25, 26–27, 30, 31, 42, 43–44, 50–51, 53, 55,

56, 65, 66, 69, 70–72, 73–75, 76–77,
78, 80, 87, 94, 115, 117, 118, 130–131,
132, 142, 145, 147, 152, 156, 162–168,
170–171, 177–178, 179, 181–192, 193,
198–199, 200–201, 204, 212, 215, 224
node list 69
node set 19, 23, 76, 115, 130–131, 198–199
NodeXL 144, 164, 173, 176
non-response 116–118
null dyad 178
null hypothesis significance testing 10,
151, 190

obesity 34, 138, 217–222
observation 13, 40, 47, 89, 90, 96, 101,
111–112, 120, 127–128, 134, 146,
219, 222
Occupy movement 144
online gaming 101, 134
online survey 96, 124–126, 136
ORA 164, 176, 202
outcomes 1–2, 4, 6, 9–10, 13, 28, 34, 41,
42, 47–49, 59–60, 61, 112, 133, 134,
137–138, 142, 149, 171, 182, 202,
204, 208, 212–215, 223–226, 227
out-degree 23, 31, 68–69, 182, 183, 187
out-star 23
Oxford Internet Institute 144

p1 model 192–193
p2 model 192–193
Pajek 124, 163–165, 176, 205
parental consent 135, 153
parsimony 15, 41–42
participant motivation 118–119, 125–126,
135, 155–156
participants 10, 20, 31, 39, 40, 51–52,
70, 79, 91, 95, 98–99, 104–107, 115,
116, 119, 120, 125, 126–127, 128,
129–130, 133–134, 136, 138, 141,
144–145, 149–159, 215
path 22, 25, 26, 28, 30, 31, 33, 38, 81,
178–179, 183, 184, 185, 193–194, 218
path analysis 219–220
path length 22, 28, 31, 38
peer effects 195
Pegasus 205
personal network – see egocentric network
personality 12, 48, 79, 141, 144
physical attributes 79
pilot studies 46, 60, 93, 113, 119,
125–126, 137
Pnet 177, 202
policy networks 56, 61, 142
political networks 141, 144
popularity 5, 9, 22–23, 30, 33, 49, 181,
183, 192, 195, 212

population 9–11, 43, 51–52, 56–57, 89,
92–94, 113, 115–116, 130, 136, 138,
153–154, 198–199, 215, 224, 225
position generator 107–108, 137
power, statistical 103, 151
preferential attachment 28–29, 30, 34,
181, 206, 214, 224
privacy 157–158
probabilistic matching 115
proximity 45, 78, 101, 129, 146
psychology 12, 15, 79, 134, 140–141

quadratic assignment procedure 190–191,
203, 224
qualitative studies 10, 12, 19, 20, 37,
61, 63–64, 89, 120, 126–127, 177,
205–206

R 176–177
random walk sampling 56–57
randomized control study 10
ranked ties 46
reachable 25, 183
recall 95–97, 103, 110–111, 113
receiver 20, 64, 66, 151, 157
reciprocation 7, 9, 22, 23–24, 28–30, 34,
66, 166–167, 178
recognition 95–97, 99, 103, 113, 119
reconstruction 199
regular equivalence 27, 186
relation algebra: see network algebra
relational events 46–47, 58–59, 101–102,
131, 143, 177, 196–197, 204
relationships 4–5, 13, 14, 18, 27, 28–29,
30, 32, 33, 35, 36, 40, 42, 44–47, 48,
51, 58, 59, 83, 95, 96, 99–100, 104–
106, 111–112, 113, 119, 127, 128,
129, 132, 135, 141, 145, 146, 206, 208
reliability 78, 100, 109–110, 112–113,
119, 227
research program 216, 220–229
research questions 7, 10, 39, 41–42, 47–
48, 50, 59–60, 211–215
resilience 225
resource flow 45, 61
resource generator 107–108, 110, 137
respondent driven sampling 57, 59, 72, 93,
116, 136, 138, 198
respondent fatigue 46, 93, 97, 107,
respondent mood 113
respondents, see participants
response rate 53, 93, 117–120, 125, 136–
137, 147, 150

sample 9–11, 20, 43, 50–51, 52, 55–58,
59, 60, 70–72, 79, 82, 86–87, 89–91,
92–95, 107, 108, 110, 114–116, 125,

130, 136–138, 144, 150, 151, 154, 158, 177, 191, 197–199, 215, 224
scale free 30, 181, 204, 214
scale up 23, 51, 94, 198
school networks 30, 34, 39, 45, 48, 50, 53, 54, 76, 92, 99, 129, 134–135, 155, 158, 177, 193, 194, 215, 221, 223
scientometrics 145
segmentation 225
self-monitoring 141
self-organization 29, 34, 37, 48
semipath 25, 179, 183
sender 20, 64, 66, 68, 96, 151, 157
September 11 – see World Trade Center
serial reproduction 220
sexual relations network 45, 138
Siena 177, 202
signed graph 20
simple random graph 192, 199
simulation 31, 57, 171, , 194, 195, 197, 199, 204, 220, 223–225
six degrees of separation 31, 38
small group research 133–134
small world 28, 31, 33, 38, 137, 185, 214
SNA – see social network analysis
snowball sample 43, 56–57, 59, 60, 70–72, 86–87, 93, 114–115, 136–137, 154, 197–198, 199, 224
social capital 29, 35, 101, 107–108, 137–138, 144
social convoy questionnaire 107, 141
social ecological system 44, 55, 78, 139, 142, 192, 202
social influence (including contagion, diffusion) 1, 29, 33–34, 38, 41, 48, 52–53, 95, 129, 134, 136, 138, 140, 144, 183, 194–196, 208, 212–213, 217–222, 225
Social Influence Network Theory 134
social media 143–144, 157–160, 164, 195, 204–205, 217, 229
social movements 141
social network analysis 20, 30, 36, 53, 92, 127, 139, 140, 144, 175–209, 222, 223
Social Network Importer 144
social selection 29, 33, 34, 37, 41, 48, 49, 51, 53, 58, 59, 103, 138, 195–196, 206, 212–214, 216–222
social support 35, 40, 52, 85, 107, 137–138, 152
social system 1–3, 9, 11–14, 18–19, 37, 39–42, 50–51, 60, 63, 77–78, 127,

131, 142, 214, 215–216, 219, 221–222, 223, 225, 227, 229
sociograms 30, 161
sociomatrix, see adjacency matrix
SocioPatterns 124
Sonia 124, 164, 208
spring embedders 164, 166, 170
Stanford large network dataset collection 124
statnet 176–177, 194
status 28, 32, 37, 40, 98, 99, 108, 109, 217
stochastic actor oriented models 103, 131, 177, 195–196
stochastic blockmodel 189
strong tie 28, 32, 38, 94–95, 113, 203
structural balance 33
structural equation modeling 219
structural equivalence 22, 27, 34, 36, 118, 171, 186–189, 193, 201, 212–214
study of daily life 130
subgraph 21, 23, 25, 26, 34, 178–179, 184
survey 45, 52–53, 56, 82, 93, 94, 95–100, 104–105, 106–109, 111–114, 116, 118, 120, 124–127, 132–133, 134–135, 136–137, 146–147, 149–150, 152–154, 158, 206, 228
sustainability 192, 225
system-based research 11–13
system outcome, see global outcome

telephone interview 96, 112–113, 124, 126, 136–137, 147
texts 128
thick data 228
thought experiment 223, 227
tie 5–7, 9, 11, 14, 17, 18
Tastes, Ties and Times data 158–160
top management team 30, 53, 95–100, 133
trade flow 45–46, 128, 139
transaction 46, 58, 77, 111–112, 189, 196, 204
transitive triad 24–25, 31, 179
treatment 10
triad 7, 20, 24–25, 31, 32, 36, 110, 178–181, 191, 193, 205, 214
triad census 178–181, 191, 193, 205, 214
triangle 7, 23–25, 28, 30–31, 33, 165, 178–179, 185, 191, 193–194, 201
triangulation - see closure
tripartite 43, 73
trust 30, 45, 60, 69, 95–96, 119, 133, 190
Tulip 164
Twitter 58, 144, 158, 195, 205, 227
two-mode network – see bipartite network

U|L distribution 191–192
UCI Network Data Repository 124
UCINET 124, 163, 176, 182, 184, 187, 208
undirected 7, 19–20, 23–25, 66–68, 70, 71, 84, 117, 145, 164, 177, 178–179, 185
unipartite network 21
US General Social Survey 103–104, 136

validity 109–113, 117, 119, 120
variance explained 2–3, 12
vector 80–81, 187
Vennmaker 107
vertices, vertex 19
Virtual Worlds Exploratorium 134
Visone 164, 176
Visual Complexity 173

visualization 3, 5–8, 18, 30, 66, 107, 141, 144, 156, 159, 161–173, 176, 178, 208
VOSON 144

weak tie 28, 32–33, 38, 46, 95, 97, 139, 203
Web Hyperlink graph 124
Webgraph 205
Webometric Analyst 144
websites 42, 57, 125, 130, 144, 155, 157
weighted graph 20, 167
whole network study 20, 39, 50, 51, 52–54, 56, 58, 59, 65–70, 75, 82, 86–87, 93, 95–103, 107, 116–117, 124–125, 129–130, 133, 134, 136, 150–154, 177, 184, 185
World Trade Center 143